Bound by a Mighty Vow

Bound by a Mighty Vow

*Sisterhood and Women's
Fraternities, 1870–1920*

Diana B. Turk

NEW YORK UNIVERSITY PRESS
New York and London

NEW YORK UNIVERSITY PRESS
New York and London
www.nyupress.org

Library of Congress Cataloging-in-Publication Data
Turk, Diana B.
Bound by a mighty vow : sisterhood and women's fraternities,
1870–1920 / Diana B. Turk
p. cm.
Includes bibliographical references and index.
ISBN 0–8147–8275–2 (cloth : alk. paper) —
ISBN 0–8147–8282–5 (pbk. : alk. paper)
1. Kappa Alpha Theta—History.
2. Greek letter societies—United States—History.   I. Title.
LJ145.K35T87   2004
378.1'9856'0973—dc22   2004000272

Manufactured in the United States of America

c 10 9 8 7 6 5 4 3 2 1
p 10 9 8 7 6 5 4 3 2

Contents

Preface

In the years spent researching and writing this book, I have learned that people are rarely neutral on the subject of Greek-letter fraternities. Some praise these organizations for their positive influences, while others condemn them as shallow, elitist, and unworthy of scholarly attention.

The purpose of this book is to explore the meaning of sisterhood for those who belonged to women's fraternities between 1870 and 1920. It is not to glorify or damn the female Greek system. Many times throughout this study I have felt pushed and pulled to take a position vis-à-vis fraternities. Supporters at times have wanted me to focus exclusively on the services they provided to members and the community services they performed. Detractors at times have wanted me to write a wholesale condemnation, citing what they see as fraternities' selectivity, anti-intellectualism, and frivolity as the reasons for their position.

I have managed, I hope, to resist both of these pressures. The early history of women's fraternities is too multilayered and interesting for such simplistic approaches. In complicated and at times contradictory ways, women's fraternities both empowered and constrained their many thousands of members. It is my goal in this book to present a fair and accurate picture of their pasts. It is not to lay praise or blame on any person or group.

Acknowledgments

I could not have written this book without the support, guidance, and gentle prodding of many people. My deepest gratitude and indebtedness go to Hasia R. Diner, my adviser, mentor, and friend, who saw the value in this study even before I did and who, through her own example and constant support and guidance, pushed me to stick with the project and bring it to fruition. I am also grateful to the rest of my doctoral committee at the University of Maryland, College Park: Barbara Finkelstein, Gordon Kelly, and John Caughey—all three extraordinary teachers and mentors—and to my outside reader, astute critic Robyn Muncy. Thanks, too, to Eugene Tobin, Vincent Anger, and the late Sydna Weiss, professors at Hamilton College who nurtured my love of learning and encouraged me to enter academia.

I was extremely fortunate to attend graduate school with a group of wonderful, bright, fellow American Studies students: Jenny Thompson, Eric Olson, Deana Whitaker Greenberg, Dave Lott, and David Silver, all of whom offered support and critique as well as timely reminders of when it was time to put away work and meet at the Tick Tock or Bentleys. Special thanks go to Shelby Shapiro, whose intellectual challenges enlivened many a seminar and whose keen insight on early drafts of the dissertation and extensive feedback on final drafts of the book helped sharpen my arguments and clarify my prose.

I am also grateful to colleagues, present and former, in the School of Education at New York University, especially Robby Cohen, whose own careful scholarship coupled with his unfailing support for colleagues provide the best model possible for a junior faculty member to follow; also, Chelsea Bailey, Laura Dull, Kendall King, Cynthia McAllister, Joel Westheimer, and Jon Zimmerman, all of whom provided important feedback on various aspects of this project. Jessica Shiller did crucial research and copyediting for the book, and Emily Klein read and commented on nearly every single line and provided constant support and encouragement, as well as frequent reassurance that I would still be a good person even if I never did finish.

I also owe thanks to those who assisted me in my research: John Straw, former archivist of the Student Life and Culture Archives at the University of Illinois at Urbana-Champaign, who offered early and crucial guidance in shaping this project; Ellen Swain and Chris Sweet, also of the Student Life and Culture Archives, who helped with photograph selection and assisted on numerous additional tasks; archivists and librarians, too many to name individually, at the College of Wooster, DePauw University, Northwestern University, U.C. Berkeley, the University of Vermont, and the University of Wisconsin; and Noraleen Young, Kappa Alpha Theta staff archivist, who helped me locate many hard-to-find documents and assisted with photographs and fact checking. Special thanks go to Judy Alexander, former Fraternity Historian of Kappa Alpha Theta, who shepherded me through the hurdles of gaining access to fraternity archives; Lissa Bradford, former president of Kappa Alpha Theta and chair of the National Panhellenic Congress, who provided not only hours of oral history interviews but also encouragement and invaluable insight into the mechanisms of the fraternity world; Mary Jane Beach, president of Kappa Alpha Theta, who gave her blessing to my research; and Mary Edith Arnold, fraternity archivist of Kappa Alpha Theta, who guided me through the intricacies of nineteenth-century fraternity life, helped me secure documents and materials from other fraternities and sororities and served as my friend and fraternity guide throughout the duration of this project. In many ways, it was the interest of these women to know more about the history of their fraternity that made this project possible. For that and for their support for and trust in me, I extend my deepest appreciation.

I am also grateful to New York University for financial support in the form of a Research Challenge Fund Award and a Goddard Faculty Fellowship Award; Suzie Robinson Hoppe for offering me a home while conducting my research; anonymous readers who critiqued earlier drafts of the manuscript; and Emily Park and Eric Zinner at New York University Press.

More than to anyone, I owe my deepest thanks to my wonderful family: my mother, Barbara Turk, who is my greatest role model; my late father, Bob Turk, whose pride in me still sustains me; my sister, Karen Turk, whose critical eye, wisdom, and goodness I aspire to; my grandmother, Pearl Cohen, a model of "true womanhood" in every way; my mother-in-law Ellen Meisner, a most loving supporter; and most of all, my generous, loving, smart, funny person, Matt Meisner, and our little bundle, Gracie Rebecca.

Introduction

Fraternities' Past and Historians' Present

On May 17, 1875, a student at Asbury College in Greencastle, Indiana, waited alone in a darkened hallway for her initiation ceremony to begin. On the other side of the doorway, the sisters of Kappa Alpha Theta Fraternity prepared for the ritual that would transform the young woman from a "barbarian," or nonfraternity student, into a "Greek sister."[1] Although the waiting student had, weeks before, accepted the "bid" for membership offered to her by the fraternity members, she would have known little of what would transpire inside the initiation room because Kappa Alpha Theta was, and still remains, a secret society.

The young initiate could not have known that once inside the room, she would be asked to pledge her loyalty, "in the name of a nobler womanhood," to Kappa Alpha Theta. She would next be given a Greek name to symbolize her new identity as a sister, and, in a highly ritualized ceremony, would be instructed that henceforth, her words, actions, and behavior would be regarded as reflections not only of her own character, but of the entire fraternity and all of its members.[2]

This ritual of initiation would be enacted over 2,700 times in the last three decades of the nineteenth century and over 8,100 times by 1920, as growing numbers of female collegians pledged themselves to Kappa Alpha Theta.[3] Nearly 80,000 other women would undergo similar initiation processes during this period in their quests to join Kappa Kappa Gamma, Pi Beta Phi, Alpha Phi, Sigma Kappa, and other women's fraternities.[4] Like these other Greek-letter societies for women, Kappa Alpha Theta demanded of its members loyalty and a pledge always to uphold the standards of the society. In exchange, it offered solidarity, support, the overt mark of belongingness in the form of a pin, and, most importantly, membership in and the backing of an organization that sought to take in only those whom its members considered the highest representatives of ideal and noble womanhood.[5]

Founded in 1870 as one of the first Greek-letter fraternities for women, Kappa Alpha Theta postdated several all-male organizations by nearly a century. The first fraternity in the United States, Phi Beta Kappa began in 1776 at William and Mary College in Virginia, when five students came together to form a social club based on the principles of friendship, morality, and learning.[6] Boasting a secret password, an insignia, a handshake, and an initiation ritual, Phi Beta Kappa contained at its inception all of the characteristics that would later come to define collegiate fraternities. In the early 1800s, the Phi Beta Kappa members decided to establish branches of their organization at Yale, Harvard, and Dartmouth Colleges. While this expansion coincided with Phi Beta Kappa's transformation from a secret and social society into an open and honorary one, it also marked the first wave of development of Greek-letter fraternities on American college campuses, constituting the first time a private society had established a branch on more than one college campus.[7] In 1813, a group of male students at Union College in New York petitioned for the right to join Phi Beta Kappa. When the fraternity denied the request, the Union men created a new society, Kappa Alpha. Within eight years, students at nearby schools established four other Greek-letter organizations, each based on principles similar to Phi Beta Kappa's friendship, morality, and learning.

According to historian John Robson, fraternities found their basis in the Greek tradition of wisdom and human struggle for intellectual, physical, and spiritual betterment.[8] Phi Beta Kappa took as its motto the Greek translation of the statement, "Love of wisdom the guide of life," and subsequent fraternities followed suit by adopting Greek statements of inspiration and uplift as their organizations' mottoes.[9] Fearing repression from faculty members—who, despite the high-minded principles espoused by the fraternity men, still distrusted the actions and motives of their students—the early Greek members bound themselves to secrecy.[10] Thus founded along secret lines, the fraternities elected to keep their activities secretive as well, arguing that the true meaning of fraternal bonds would increase in weight and importance if kept for members only. As these organizations expanded to other college campuses and students of different schools founded their own clubs and societies, Greek-letter fraternities became major forces in the social and extracurricular lives of students.[11] By 1870, forty-eight fraternities for collegiate males existed, the bulk of them having branches, or "chapters," on multiple college campuses across the United States.[12]

Despite the proliferation of such societies for men, few clubs for women existed on college campuses in the mid-nineteenth century, a reflection in part of the fact that few women attended college at this time. In 1870, when Kappa Alpha Theta was founded, only 11,000 women were enrolled in institutions of higher education across the United States, a number that paled in comparison to the more than 52,000 men who filled the classrooms of the nation's colleges and universities. Fewer than one-third of American schools allowed women to enroll, and those that did treated their female students very much as second-class citizens. Often ignored in the classroom and ridiculed outside of it, the "pioneering" women who went to college in the early years of coeducation faced fierce opposition from students, faculty, and townspeople, many of whom argued that higher education would "unsex" women and thus upset the "natural" order of society.[13]

Bent on making a place for themselves both academically and socially on campuses hostile to their presence and believing that collective rather than individual action would help them achieve that goal, several of the early female collegians came together in small groups, as had their male predecessors at William and Mary and other colleges years before, and formed organizations of support and friendship to help them navigate collectively the perils of coeducational college life. They conceived of their groups as support networks to help "worthy female students" combat male opposition to their presence on campus. The founders of Kappa Alpha Theta and their fellow female Greek-letter organizations based their societies on ritualized vows of loyalty and used the familial language of "sisterhood" to reflect the potency of their commitments to one another.[14] Using the male Greek societies and social clubs as models, the fraternity women of the 1870s and 1880s crafted elaborate rites and rituals, in which they affirmed and reaffirmed their pledges to support and aid one another.[15] Copying the secrecy of the male clubs, the fraternity women preserved their constitutions, by-laws, rituals, and activities for insiders only, but demonstrated publicly membership in their organizations by sporting large badges affixed to their clothing.[16]

From the start, the sisters of Kappa Alpha Theta considered themselves, in their own words, "bound" together by a "mighty vow," each one of them serving as one "link" in a "mystic chain of sisterhood."[17] In this belief, they were joined by the members of the other women's fraternities, who also saw themselves as integrally connected to the other members of their organizations. With the strength and worth of the entire chain dependent upon the quality of each individual link, the fraternity women regarded themselves as implicated in, and responsible for, each others' performances and behavior, whether in the classroom, the drawing room, the stage or playing field, or in the paid and unpaid workforce. How did these bonds of sisterhood manifest themselves in the lives of the women who shared them? What meanings did the early fraternity sisters assign to their vows, and how did later members use these concepts in their own interpretations of the content, depth, and meaning of their fraternal bonds? In what ways did the vows of sisterhood shared by the women of Kappa Alpha Theta and other women's fraternities shape their collegiate and postcollegiate experiences and, as a result, their identities—as individuals, as members of the middle and upper-middle classes, and as Thetas, Kappas, or Alpha Phis? How, in turn, did the sisters, as "culture-bound" individuals and as members of particular geographic, religious, racial, class, and generational groups, shape and influence the mission and aims of their particular fraternities? This study will address these questions by examining female fraternity life between 1870 and 1920, especially the criteria for and methods of selecting new members; their educational programs for training sisters; fraternities' policies and procedures; and the requirements asked of, as well as rewards granted to, Greek-letter society members.

In addition, this study will also focus on the sometimes-stormy relationship between the early fraternity sisters, the pioneers of women's education, and their second-generation successors.[18] Unlike other female networks such as literary clubs, political committees, and reform-centered groups, women's fraternities recruited their members in their adolescence and maintained ties with them throughout their lives. These organizations thus encompassed at any given time a complex mix of members who represented diverse worldviews and who therefore held differing notions regarding women's higher education, what constituted "woman's sphere," and which kinds of women were worthy enough for fraternity membership.

The first generation of Thetas, Kappas, and Alpha Phis developed their fraternities in direct response to largely male challenges to coeducation and regarded themselves as representatives of womanhood, their ability to succeed on campus a reflection upon their sex as much as upon themselves. Later sisters, their place on campus more assured and competition for "desirable" members stiffer due to the development of rival fraternities, concentrated their efforts on setting themselves apart from and above their female peers, their actions aimed at making their own particular organizations the most prestigious group of collegiate women, their identities shaped more by their specific fraternity membership than by their femaleness.[19] The national scope of organizations like Kappa Alpha Theta and their broad-reaching membership, encompassing different generations as well as social, cultural, and geographic groups, complicated attempts to craft clearly defined aims and values for the fraternities upon which all members could agree. In Kappa Alpha Theta's case, especially as it expanded into a national entity, the fraternity's social as well as geographic base in the small towns of the heartland led to real friction between the Midwesterners and their sisters who came from the more cosmopolitan East or the more sparsely populated West. Differences in approach to issues of class, ethnicity, and religion posed challenges to the fraternity, as members from diverse areas of the country and backgrounds reacted to changes in the campus and societal populations of the early twentieth century with different mindsets and differing concerns.

This inquiry into the past of women's fraternity life in general and Kappa Alpha Theta Fraternity in particular thus offers an examination of an intergenerational, interregional, and intercultural social world. It serves both as an overview of the early history of the women's collegiate Greek system and as a case study of Kappa Alpha Theta. Beginning with the founding of women's fraternities in 1870, the book concludes in 1920, with the departure from campus of the second generation of female collegians. The year 1920 serves as a logical conclusion to this study because it marks the closure of the developmental era of women's fraternities and represents the point at which the women's Greek system essentially reached maturity.[20] Whereas the organizations spent the first fifty years struggling to define and redefine their purposes and missions in response to the differing and changing needs of their members, by 1920 they had jelled into the bodies that they would remain, with only small variation, for decades to come. By this point, too, they had established their positions among the campus and societal elite. This book thus examines the formation and solidification on campus and in American society of women's fraternities. It offers a close look at the mechanisms of development of one of the oldest, largest, and most powerful female networks in America during a fifty-year time period when few other such collectives existed.[21]

In 1870, when the sisters of Kappa Alpha Theta founded their fraternity, they represented four of only a handful of collegiate females to belong to a private society. By 1920, nearly 77,800 other women had joined them in the collegiate Greek system. More than twenty other national fraternities for college women populated the nation's college campuses, and the majority of these organizations boasted between twenty and sixty chapters.[22] Between 1870 and 1920, roughly 30 percent of the female student population belonged to a Greek-letter society. On more than a few campuses, the proportion of affiliated women topped 50 percent, and the prominent role the women's fraternity and sorority members played on campus exceeded in feel what their actual number might suggest.[23]

Despite the popularity of these organizations among the early generations of female collegians, however, historians of women's education have largely ignored Greek-letter societies in their examinations of American college life in the late nineteenth and early twentieth centuries. Of the most widely acclaimed and, in other respects, most thorough studies of the early years of women's higher education, few have granted women's fraternities or sororities more than passing notice. Even more striking, those scholars who have addressed them have seemed to focus mainly on issues of exclusion—who was *not* taken as a member—rather than exploring who *was* included and what these women may have sought and gotten from their Greek-letter affiliations.

Barbara Solomon's pioneering history of women's higher education, for example, touched only briefly on female fraternities, noting that they brought "mixed results" to campus. While conceding that these organizations served as "institutional support group[s] for young women," Solomon spent little time exploring this function and quickly moved away from the experiences of those inside the Greek system to focus on those excluded from its circle.[24] In a similar manner, historian Lynn Gordon, in an otherwise illuminating and detailed account of women's collegiate experiences between 1870 and 1920, offered little discussion of the women's Greek system, noting mainly that on certain campuses, the appearance of women's fraternities in the 1890s "exacerbated social class distinctions by shutting out those whose social status or ethnicity did not qualify them for membership."[25] Likewise, in *Campus Life: Undergraduate Cultures from the End of the Eighteenth Century to the Present*, a rich depiction of student life across the centuries, Helen Lefkowitz Horowitz adopted a rather vague yet biting tone when addressing the history of women's fraternities and sororities. Referring to Greek-letter organizations as "discriminatory [and] intent on retaining archaic social distinctions that warp the personal and intellectual growth of [their] members," Horowitz neither offered a discussion of the missions of the women's societies, nor did she examine in any real sense who belonged to them, other than to assume, not entirely accurately, that "affluence" and "elitism" served as the historical bases of their founding. Asserting that affiliated women "gained a moment of glory when their beauty or popularity singled them out for social honors," Horowitz essentially dismissed the women's Greek system, choosing to minimize the important role that these organizations played in the history of women's education and in the development of women's networks.[26]

Of the most prominent historians of women's higher education, only one has taken the role of the women's Greek system seriously: Paula Giddings, who traced the development of historically black Delta Sigma Theta Sorority's development from its founding in 1913 through the mid-1980s. A study that located the basis for Delta Sigma Theta's formation specifically in racially grounded debates over African American women's roles on college campuses and within the black American community, Giddings's *In Search of Sisterhood: Delta Sigma Theta and the Challenge of the Black Sorority Movement* explored the ways that a female Greek society helped its members build community both among themselves and with those around them. While her concern rested mainly with the mechanisms of the African American sorority movement—a very different entity than the historically white Greek system—Giddings's book provides an example of how a historian might tackle the complex and sometimes contradictory aspects of a secret, selective organization.[27] Despite her model, no historian of women's education has yet undertaken a similar study of a historically white Greek society, and thus the history of this movement remains very much unknown.[28]

One underlying cause of this silence may be that many of the scholars who pioneered the history of women's higher education potentially had certain social and political objectives for their studies; they may have feared dilution by paying attention to what some consider "frivolous" organizations. Like scholars who focus on other previously marginalized groups, women's historians at times have seemed to shy away from exploring "conventional" or "conservative" topics, preferring instead to focus their attention on those in the past who pushed against gender barriers, such as organized female workers or medical students, or those who adopted explicitly activist or what came to be known as feminist stances, such as the suffragists and the proponents of women's health and safety. To many, fraternities and sororities simply smack of elitism. Therefore, it seems likely that certain scholars have declined to explore this history because they could not identify with, and therefore did not really consider, the experiences of those who joined elite (and, to many, elitist) white, middle- and upper-middle-class organizations.[29]

But this is not reason enough for us to rest with glossed accounts of the history of the women's collegiate Greek system. Between the 1870s, when women's fraternities first formed, through the end of the second decade of the twentieth century, nearly 80,000 women pledged themselves to a Greek-letter organization. Given the high number of women who chose fraternity membership, it is crucial for historians to ask themselves what meanings these organizations held for those who belonged to them. It is important for scholars to look for more multidimensional ways of examining the female Greek system, rather than focusing simply on the question of exclusion.

The present study is an attempt to address this need. It represents a quest to understand why, in the first fifty years of coeducation, more than a third of American female college students pledged themselves to a Greek-letter organization and what role these organizations played in shaping the collegiate and postcollegiate experiences of so many thousands of women. It seeks to nestle women's fraternity life within the cultural worlds of late nineteenth- and early twentieth-century coeducational college life and within white, middle- and upper-middle-class society, to read the concerns and actions of their members within the contexts of their environs.[30] Looking deeply rather than broadly, it seeks to understand fraternity culture, in particular that of Kappa Alpha Theta Fraternity, not just from the perspective of an outside critic, but also as an insider might, by making sense of the internal mechanisms, concerns, and values that drove its membership.

A major impediment to scholarly understanding of women's fraternities lies, of course, in the secrecy with which these organizations did and do shroud themselves. Secret societies have remained secretive for so long in large measure because they have limited outsiders from knowing much of their business. Most fraternities and sororities have kept close guard on their records and have preserved their documents for the eyes of members only. Knowing this, when I began this study in the spring of 1995, I was fully aware that it would be very difficult to research the history of organizations defined in many ways by their secrecy.[31] I thus approached this project with caution as well as with an underlying fear that I, as a non-Greek, might be unable to gain access to enough material to support a project of this size.

My first visit to Kappa Alpha Theta's headquarters in Indianapolis only compounded my concern. Fraternity archivist Mary Edith Arnold, while excited about my project, appeared tentative about sharing private fraternity documents. Understandably, she remained somewhat suspicious of what an outsider's motives might be in wanting to study her fraternity: Why did I want to know about Kappa Alpha Theta? And what was I going to do when and if I found "bad things" about the fraternity? Was I going to focus only on what I might consider negative events of the past, such as accounts of anti-Semitism or elitism within the fraternity, or was I going to approach my study in a balanced way, evaluating both the "bad" and the "good" as I saw fit?

As she and I came to know each other over hours of discussing women's education and the fraternity's role in its development, Mary Edith Arnold soon came to recognize that I was not interested in ferreting out only the "negative" aspects of the fraternity's history. I was and remain dedicated to performing as fair and accurate a study of early fraternity life as possible. In order to do so, I needed access to all of Kappa Alpha Theta's historical documents, including those that were written for private consumption and those whose authors assumed would never be seen by a nonmember. I needed to know both what the fraternity wanted known about its past as well as what it might, in the context of the late 1990s and early 2000s, consider its "skeletons in the closet." Convinced of my need for access and trusting that I would aim for accuracy and balance and would shy away from sensationalism, Arnold convinced the other members of the Kappa Alpha Theta leadership to open the archives to me. Complete entrée soon followed, as did official support and encouragement from the fraternity's officers, especially as they came to see the benefits that might result from broader understanding of their organization's past among the nonfraternity public. While at times certain leaders have questioned me about particular findings, at no point has anyone within Kappa Alpha Theta or any other of the women's fraternities attempted to shape or in any way alter the history I have written.

My findings are thus based on close analysis of nearly all of the documents pertaining to Kappa Alpha Theta's early history housed in the fraternity archives and in other collections. I have examined all the existing minutes of the Alpha (Asbury College, later DePauw University), Beta (Indiana University), Epsilon (College of Wooster), Delta (University of Illinois), Sigma (University of Toronto), Tau (Northwestern University), and Alpha Beta (Swarthmore College) collegiate chapters as well as occasional entries recorded in other collegiate and alumnae chapters' minutes; all official reports sent by the individual chapters to the Grand Council of the fraternity as well as those sent by the Grand Council to the chapters and to alumnae; Kappa Alpha Theta's bimonthly newsletters; all issues of the fraternity quarterly, the *Kappa Alpha Theta*; private and fraternity correspondence; and assorted reminiscences, private journals, and oral histories written by Thetas during or concerning the period in question.[32] In addition, I have looked closely at documents related to the founding and development of the National Panhellenic Congress (NPC), the umbrella organization for the women's fraternities to which Theta did and does belong, as well as at a broad range of materials pertaining to Kappa Kappa Gamma, Alpha Phi, Sigma Kappa, Pi Beta Phi, Kappa Delta, and assorted other Greek-letter societies, to gain an understanding of the typicality of the Theta sisters' experiences. Finally, I have drawn from numerous campuses' yearbooks, catalogs, scrapbooks, and other archival collections to gain as complete a picture as possible of female fraternity life and to situate my findings within the larger context of women's higher education.

Throughout this study, I have sought to respect the boundaries of secrecy in Kappa Alpha Theta and its fellow Greek-letter organizations. Thus, I do not dwell in any length on the central tenets of initiations, passwords, or Greek mottoes. In my analysis of what sisterhood meant to the early generations of fraternity women, what is important is the meanings that members attached to their rites and rituals and not the specific contents of these particular practices.

I am well aware that the topic of Greek-letter societies is a highly charged one, and some readers may be inclined to read this study through the lens of their own position vis-à-vis fraternities. Certainly, since the nineteenth century, women's fraternities have been the focus of much popular (if not scholarly) attention, both positive and negative. In ways that I will explore, these organizations played both supportive and constraining roles for their members. While helping women succeed in classroom environments previously closed to them and easing their paths in social settings and in securing paid and unpaid vocations, women's fraternities also presented very specific and somewhat narrow models of womanhood to which members had to subscribe to remain in good standing. It is my hope that this book will help facilitate scholarly understanding of the women's Greek system and that more open and substantive discussion will ensue about the relative merits of fraternity membership—both for women in the past and for women in the present.

1

Of Serious Mind and Purpose
The First Generation of Fraternity Women

On January 27, 1870, four women at Asbury College in Greencastle, Indiana, gathered together in a darkened room and initiated themselves into a secret society. Pledging lifelong vows of loyalty to one another and swearing to uphold a set of carefully outlined ideals, these four students conceived of and established Kappa Alpha Theta, the first Greek letter women's fraternity.[1]

In creating Kappa Alpha Theta and establishing "chapters" of their organization on other newly coeducational campuses across the United States, the four women acted in response to opposition they faced from male students, faculty, and other critics of coeducation. Isolated and denigrated by those who both doubted their intellect and challenged their femininity, the founders of Kappa Alpha Theta recognized that if they bonded together and provided mutual aid to one another, their efforts might quell the hostility surrounding coeducation and carve a more permanent place for women within institutions of higher education.

Such a feat entailed not only handling college work and thereby quieting the critics who claimed that women lacked the brains to learn at a high level, but also dampening fears that high-level learning would render women "unsexed." Considering themselves and their fraternity sisters the most "worthy" female collegians, the founders and early members of Kappa Alpha Theta saw themselves as best suited among their peers to help assure women's place on campus. Testing the elasticity of, but not breaking their allegiance to, Victorian notions of the "feminine ideal," the early sisters of Kappa Alpha Theta strove to prove themselves the intellectual equals of men while at the same time continuing to fulfill the tenets of "true" and "noble womanhood." How did they do so and to what ends?

In their efforts to establish a place for themselves on campus, the first generation of Theta sisters encountered challenges from all sides. How did the sisters of the 1870s and 1880s conceptualize their mission for Kappa Alpha Theta, and how did their aims evolve over these two decades? What beliefs did they draw from and react to, in shaping their identities as fraternity members, as collegians, and as women? To what extent did the founders of other female Greek-letter organizations share their experiences and their concerns? And how successful were the early fraternity women at performing the delicate balancing act required of them, as they strove to broaden but not dilute the tenets of "true womanhood"?[2]

In 1870, only 11,000 women of the roughly 3,075,650 females between the ages of eighteen and twenty-one in America attended college. Male students outnumbered women by a ratio of nearly five to one. Despite the fact that Oberlin College had broken the barrier between the sexes thirty-three years earlier by opening its doors to both male and female students, an overwhelming majority of American colleges and universities still refused to admit women.[3] The first female collegians to enroll in schools in the early years of coeducation thus constituted a tiny minority. Most often the daughters of college professors and other members of the educated elite, these "pioneering women" hailed mainly from middle-class families who could afford to pay the tuition and forgo the labor of their offspring.[4]

The passage of the Morrill Act of 1862, providing federal funds to states for the development of what came to be called Land Grant Colleges, helped pave the way for coeducation at both state-supported and private schools. By neither explicitly demanding nor prohibiting coeducation at the new schools, the act unintentionally invited debate over coeducation and opened up a forum in which could be heard the demands of tax-paying state residents who wanted their daughters educated.[5] The states responded slowly, however, so that by 1867, only two state universities, Iowa and Wisconsin, had opened their doors to women. Three years later, when the four women of Asbury College founded Kappa Alpha Theta, fewer than one-third of the nation's 582 colleges permitted women to matriculate.[6]

The promise of fuller classrooms and increased tuition dollars proved appealing to many colleges of the late nineteenth century, however, and the number of schools allowing women to enroll thus increased dramatically. While in 1870, only eight state universities admitted women, this number rose dramatically in the next two decades, as schools sought to boost enrollment numbers that had lagged in the wake of the Civil War.[7] By 1890, 40,000 women attended institutions of higher education, 70.1 percent of them at coeducational schools. Though still outnumbered by male students at a rate of almost three to one, the proportion of 18–21-year-old women attending school rose vis-à-vis the rate for men, as 2.2 percent of women compared to 4.4 percent of men enrolled in higher education.[8] Whereas college attendance had been a rare occurrence for women in the nineteenth century, female collegians by 1900 were no longer regarded as "social rebels" by white, middle-class America.[9] As historian of women's education Patricia Palmieri asserted, "The pioneer band of college women had been so successful in weathering the dangerous experiment that in the twentieth century college attendance for women was not a sacerdotal or strange experience, but a socially sanctioned endeavor."[10] By 1920, the number of women attending colleges jumped to 283,000, 81.3 percent of whom attended coeducational institutions. This group comprised 47.3 percent of the collegiate population in the United States.[11]

In spite of their growth in numbers, however, the women seeking a college education in the nineteenth and early twentieth centuries faced constant obstacles whose natures and sources varied. Whereas critics and commentators of the 1820s through the 1850s had largely denied the need for women to receive a collegiate education and used as their justification the accepted social distinctions between males and females, by the mid and later decades of the nineteenth century, scientists and doctors joined the debate, providing "scientific evidence" that females were physiologically unsuited for academic training.[12] Influential books such as Dr. Edward Clarke's *Sex in Education: Or, a Fair Chance for the Girls*, published in 1873, provoked attention with the argument that higher education damaged a woman's health by inhibiting her reproductive system.[13] Clarke's book went through seventeen printings and attracted the serious attention of both detractors and promoters of women's education. For those inclined to agree with him, Clarke's findings "put the stamp of scientific truth on the ancient suspicion that the female brain and body could not survive book learning." Even strong advocates of women's education such as Julia Ward Howe took the threat of his work, if not his justifications, seriously.[14] For those reared with the Victorian belief that separate spheres for men and women represented the natural state of society, coeducation posed a challenge to the very core of American middle-class life.[15]

Detractors of coeducation had less to fear than they supposed, however. Despite the increase in women attending coeducational colleges between 1870 and 1920, female higher education did not in many ways challenge the traditional spheres separating the sexes. On most coeducational campuses, segregation and inequality characterized the relationship between male and female students. Both in the classroom and in the extracurricular arena, women and men operated in very different spheres, and their opportunities for mixing were few indeed.[16] Campus rules as well as social mores prevented the two sexes from close interaction. Some male students resorted to violence to keep others of their sex from interacting with women, while other students simply ignored the newcomers and carried on as though their schools had never admitted women. As historian Rosalind Rosenberg noted, "Whether women's presence was generally accepted or not [on any particular campus] they remained a group apart. As pictures of lecture halls reveal, a fairly strict pattern of segregation prevailed, with women seated on one side of the room, men seated on the other."[17]

At Asbury College, a small and prestigious liberal arts school that changed its name in 1884 to DePauw University, coeducation trod a particularly thorny path. A Board of Trustees' decision on June 26, 1867, "to receive (on a trial basis) Female students into the regular classes of the University," alarmed Asbury's students and faculty alike, both having on previous occasions stated their opposition to coeducation.[18] Yet with classrooms only partially filled in the wake of the Civil War and the school in desperate need of the funds that a boost in student enrollment would bring, the Board of Trustees decided to try coeducation.[19] Reluctant to embrace the new measure full-scale, however, they voted to phase in coeducation gradually by confining female enrollment to college courses only, thereby prohibiting women from enrolling in the "preparatory classes," or precollegiate program, that most students of the time took prior to admittance into the college proper.[20] With this restriction in place, few women bothered to apply to Asbury in its first year of coeducation. Only Bettie Locke, Laura Beswick, and Alice Allen from nearby Greencastle, and Mary Simmons from Missouri, possessed the required training and desire to enroll.[21]

Having left for summer vacation with their school single-sex, the men of Asbury returned in the fall of 1867 to find four "foreigners" among their ranks. Responding to what they called the Board of Trustees' "back-handed actions," the male students immediately launched a newspaper campaign against the new arrivals. In the October 2, 1867, issue of the *Asbury Review,* the student newspaper, the editors declared their strong skepticism toward having women on their campus: "It *may* have been wise to have opened Asbury's halls to both sexes. It is to be hoped it will be proven so in the end; but—then—well, 'time sets all things right.'"[22] Labeling coeducation a "hazardous undertaking," other writers complained that "the young ladies of this city are the only ones benefited by this experiment,—this beautiful arrangement." One student, noting that neither Yale nor Harvard nor any other "first class institution in the country" had succumbed to pressure to coeducate, argued that the presence of women would soil Asbury's reputation and endanger its national stature: "Mixed schools have never attained great celebrity. . . . What good argument can be advanced in favor of making a *mixed school* of Indiana Asbury University, which points with pride to a long list of graduates, prominent for wisdom and piety, and which, till now, has had a first-class reputation among the colleges of the West?"[23]

In another complaint against coeducation published in the *Asbury Review* in the fall of 1867, one writer rallied his fellow students,

> [L]et us present an almost unanimous petition to the Board of Trustees for a change of affairs. . . . Let us ask the faculty, which is always so willing to rectify our wrongs, to second us in our efforts. Confident that our cause is just, we wait impatiently, yet hopefully, for this action of the Board to be repealed. If it is not, there are other halls of learning which have not yet experienced the withering touch of this erroneous and demoralizing system.[24]

The article bore only a single byline, yet the editors of the paper took care to note the high level of support for the author's position. "We have admitted into our columns an article reflecting severely upon the *new feature of Asbury*—admittance of females. The writer is most too severe, perhaps, but it so nearly expresses the unanimous view of all the students, that we have no hesitancy in inserting it."[25]

As Asbury's first year of coeducation progressed, the arguments waged against coeducation in the campus newspaper continued, finally reaching a peak in February 1868, when the faculty, who had previously supported efforts to keep the college all male, resolved to put an end to the printed attacks. Commanding the editors to "make a public and full disavowal of any endorsement of the offensive language of said articles," the faculty exacted from the male attackers a statement that read,

> We are *sorry* to learn that certain articles which have appeared in recent numbers of the *Review,* have been construed as personal, by some of the members of the institution. It certainly is not the design of the editors to publish anything that would reflect upon the personal character of anyone, and we are assured that such was not the intention upon the part of our contributors.[26]

The editors' apology marked the end of the debate against coeducation in the *Asbury Review,* as the paper suspended publication that same month, but it did not mark an end to the debate on the campus itself. To the large numbers of male students who liked to compare Asbury with Harvard, Yale, and the nation's other prestigious universities, the women's presence in their classrooms proved a particularly bitter pill to swallow, as it also did for those professors who saw their reputations potentially threatened by Asbury's move to coeducate.[27] From outside the college walls as well as from within, female collegians heard their presence challenged. As DePauw historian George Manhart recounted, "The town gossips also talked of the immodesty of the college girls, perhaps allowing their ankles to be seen as they ascended the stairs of the college building." Derided and criticized from all sides, the women students set themselves the goal of proving their critics wrong. Popular sentiment on campus still maintained "the new plan was experimental. It was up to the first girls to make good."[28] As one of the pioneers and a founder of Kappa Alpha Theta later noted, "Somehow we realized that we were not going to college just for ourselves—but for all the girls who would follow, if we could just win out."[29] Against the backdrop of opposition, resentment, and ridicule, the "pioneers" of women's higher education at Asbury struggled to win acceptance.[30]

To combat collectively the resentment against them, the first women at Asbury turned to each other for sustenance and support. Two years after their admittance to the college, one of the pioneers, Bettie Locke, conceived of the idea of creating a female society along the lines of the fraternities to which many of the male students belonged.[31] With the encouragement and guidance of her father, a professor at Asbury and himself a fraternity man, Locke recruited another student, Alice Allen, to join

The first women admitted to Asbury College (later renamed DePauw University), in 1868, were (left to right) Laura Beswick, Alice Allen, Mary Simmons, and Bettie Locke. Locke and Allen, along with two other Asbury students, Jennie Fitch and Bettie Tipton, founded Kappa Alpha Theta in January 1870. The following September, Mary Simmons became a Theta. Laura Beswick later became a charter member of the Epsilon Chapter of I.C. Sorosis (later renamed Pi Beta Phi) at Asbury College. (Courtesy of Kappa Alpha Theta Fraternity, © 2003.)

in her preparations. The two set themselves to studying parliamentary procedure in anticipation of writing a constitution and conducting formal meetings. They also initiated correspondence with J. Fred Newman, a jeweler in New York City widely used by the male fraternities, and elicited his help in designing and creating an appropriate "badge" for their society.[32] The process of selecting other women to join them from the eighteen then enrolled at Asbury took time, for although they were impressed with a few at first glance, they wanted to wait and see how the women would perform in their studies. When word arrived that Hannah Fitch, a student they had been eyeing, had placed at the top of her class, Locke and Allen decided to ask her to join them. They followed the same course with another student, Bettie Tipton, and when she, too, proved a capable student, they shared their secret with her as well. On January 27, 1870, Locke, Allen, Fitch, and Tipton exchanged vows of loyalty and secrecy in the room where Allen and Fitch boarded. Nearly two months later, the package they were awaiting from the jeweler arrived. Adorned now with the badges they had so painstakingly designed, the newly sworn members of Kappa Alpha Theta marched into chapel, their large, ornate pins signifying to all their membership in a secret fraternity.[33]

The Asbury community was well accustomed to seeing fraternity pins affixed to members' clothing. They were not prepared, however, to see such ornaments adorning the dresses of female students.[34] According to a professor on campus, the male students of Asbury treated the sight of the women sporting fraternity badges in the same manner as they had treated coeducation: with hostility and ridicule. They poked fun at the shape of the pin, which resembled a kite, and predicted derisively that the "kites would soon go up."[35] Yet in spite of—or perhaps because of—the reception they received from the men, the Theta women pushed on in their efforts to build their fraternity. Their goal was to foster a "bond closer than that of common interest and womanhood," to create a vehicle that would enable them to face collectively the rigors and challenges of charting a new path.[36]

The struggles of the Asbury women and the methods they chose for responding to these struggles bore similarities to the experiences of pioneering women on other newly coeducational campuses. At Syracuse University, for example, the women who founded Alpha Phi Fraternity came together to combat ostracism and ridicule. Barraged by challenges such as that issued by a prominent legislator, that "women should refrain from meddling 'in such things as are proper for men who are stronger,'" the sisters of Alpha Phi conceived of their fraternity as "a tie which should unite and a circle of friends who could sympathize." In their efforts, they had much in common with the founders of I.C. Sorosis (later renamed Pi Beta Phi), who united against the critics of "[female] aggression upon men's privileges" by vowing "to be equal in every respect to the strongest men's fraternity."[37]

Sigma Kappa Sorority, too, grew out of the desire of the first female students of Colby College for companionship and support, as they made their pioneering way through the previously all-male institution in 1874. Like their Theta counterparts at Asbury, their Alpha Phi peers at Syracuse, and their I.C. Sorosis sisters at Monmouth College, the first women

Founders of Kappa Alpha Theta designed the
original kite-shaped Kappa Alpha Theta badge.
It was crafted by J. Fred Newman of New York
City and introduced on the Asbury campus in
March 1870. (Courtesy of Kappa Alpha Theta
Fraternity, © 2003.)

who enrolled at Colby found themselves shut out from many of the cur-
ricular and extracurricular activities of the college. "The peculiar isolation of their position among the numerous male students drew [the first
female students] into close comradeship, the more so as they soon learned
that there existed much opposition to their presence in the college, not
only among the students, but among the professors as well." Considering
themselves representatives of their sex and responsible for making a place
for women on campus, the founders of Sigma Kappa devised a Greek-letter society that would enable them to combat collectively the opposition
surrounding them. Their goal, they wrote, was to unite with other female

collegians "in a closer bond of sisterhood" than would be possible without the ties of a secret fraternity.[38]

Adopting different names on different campuses and framing their founding stories in slightly different terms, the first Greek-letter organizations for women thus formed out of similar needs and for similar purposes. With few exceptions, the women who founded and joined female fraternities in the 1870s did so to provide mutual assistance and aid to those struggling to combat opposition to their presence. Their primary goal was to prove themselves capable of handling college work as women. Thus, most of the women's fraternities adopted explicitly academic foci and included in their missions decidedly intellectual concerns.

In Kappa Alpha Theta, for example, the sisters wrote in their constitution: "The object of this society shall be to advance the interests of its members, to afford an opportunity for improvement in composition and debate and elocution, to cultivate those social qualities which become a woman, and to provide for its members associates bound by a common interest."[39] With the primary goal of proving themselves capable of handling college work at the same level as their male peers,[40] the founders and women they subsequently selected to join them spent much of their time together reading and critiquing one another's essays and scholarly performances.[41]

In the 1870s, Asbury College and other institutions of its kind required students to perform weekly recitations in elocution, oratory, composition, and rhetoric. Concerned that each member "credibly acquit [herself] before the larger college audience," the sisters established as a regular part of their fraternity program the practice of reading their pieces aloud in front of one another. In the bylaws of their constitution, they stipulated that performances "consist[ing] of dialogues, debates, [and] the reading of select pieces" should take place in each of their fraternity meetings, followed by "criticisms" of these performances by the members present.[42] The minutes of the early chapters' meetings contain frequent references to one sister "performing her Sophomore speech" or another sister "deliver[ing] her Junior oration."[43] Regularly in the first two decades of the fraternity's existence, and continuing sporadically thereafter for another decade or so, the sisters of Kappa Alpha Theta read speeches, declamations, and essays to one another and listened to responses of both criticism and praise from their fellow Thetas.[44]

For example, at nearly all of their meetings, the sisters of the Asbury, or Alpha, chapter recorded entries such as, "Secretary read her Chaple

[sic] performance, and it was slightly criticized by Sister Jennie Fitch."[45] "Sister 'Virginia' was called upon to deliver [an] oration,—entitled *Individual Culture,* [a] production [that] met with the hearty applause of the society, and the universal exclamation—good!" one group of Thetas noted. Another sister documented in her chapter's minutes that "Sister Pentie gave us her speech on 'Inconsistence' which was greeted with applause."[46] Generally, the fraternity women responded favorably to the performances, with sisters reporting that one member had "delivered her Junior oration in a *very credible* manner" or that another performed and "did honor to the fraternity." On certain occasions, however, Theta members found their performances poorly received by their sisters. At one meeting, for example, after three sisters had practiced their readings and declamations in front of the Alpha chapter, the chapter secretary noted that "several criticisms were offered on the performances."[47]

The Theta sisters of the Alpha chapter continued to perform for one another well into the 1880s, and as they developed other branches of the fraternity on different college campuses across the country, their new sisters adopted the custom as well. In practicing their essays before one another, the sisters sought to ensure that each member's public performances would be well received by the wider campus community.[48] For example, the sisters of the Alpha chapter passed a motion requiring their "girls who [were] to speak at commencement [to] give their essays before the fraternity." When they did so, "all were criticized" by the fraternity.[49] In the Greencastle chapter and in other branches of the fraternity, the Thetas adopted rules to guard against sisters backing out of rehearsing their speeches in front of the fraternity. They imposed fines of ten to twenty five cents on those sisters who "failed to perform."[50]

Like their peers in Kappa Alpha Theta, the early members of Kappa Kappa Gamma also focused on academic achievement. Much of their time together was spent on preparation for class and chapel performances, and like their Theta sisters, they levied fines on those who failed to perform. Most Kappa chapters passed bylaws requiring that "all performances which were to be given in public, in oratorical contests . . . and elsewhere, should be rehearsed previously in chapter meeting," and the written testimonies of early members indicated that such practices took place.[51]

The founders and early members of Sigma Kappa, too, regarded academic concerns as central to their mission.[52] Their main goal was to assist members with support and solidarity as they "reach[ed] out . . . toward a broader culture than the old occupations of home-making and teaching."

Dedicated students who excelled in their studies, all the early Sigma Kappas put intellectual endeavors first. They were firm in their desire that "other girls might not suffer for any shortcomings of theirs."[53]

Like their Theta and Kappa peers, the Sigma Kappa sisters spent much of their time together practicing their literary pieces in front of one another.[54] They were joined in this endeavor by the women of Alpha Phi, who placed intellectual and scholarly endeavors at the top of their priorities and made much of the election of two of their members to Phi Beta Kappa.[55] In all of the histories of the first women's fraternities, concern with intellectual performance and a sense of responsibility to "make good" as female collegians hold primary place. Indeed, the only women's fraternity of this time not to share a central concern with providing support for academic and intellectual ends was Delta Gamma, an organization founded at an all-women's school and therefore removed from the challenges facing the other women's fraternities in coeducational colleges.[56]

In reading and performing for their groups, the first generation of fraternity women provided one another with support and solidarity. Regarding each sister's performance as a reflection not just of her own abilities and initiatives but of those of her fraternity in particular and womanhood in general, the sisters placed enormous pressure upon one another to show both their fraternity and their sex in the best possible light. The tone and content of their meeting minutes and written testimonies reflect deep investment in each other as "links in a chain" of unity. In Kappa Alpha Theta and in the other women's fraternities, the time and care the sisters dedicated to hearing and critiquing one another's essays and performances showed the extent to which they regarded their organization as implicated in the actions of each member.

In Kappa Alpha Theta, the sisters' reactions to their rehearsals suggested a deep interest in the performances of each member. "Artie gave us her speech. We all felt that on the 16 Dec[ember] we should be proud of our representative," one group wrote. Another noted, "Rose [delivered her Junior oration] and did honor to the fraternity." These commentaries show the extent to which the sisters saw themselves as representing not only themselves but also their fraternity in each of their performances.[57] To them, the strength of the whole rested on the actions of each member. In order to ensure that Kappa Alpha Theta as a whole achieved its collective goal of proving women capable of college work, each chapter of the fraternity had to ensure that all of its members "acquitted themselves credibly" in the classroom.[58]

Because of this concern with proving themselves capable as women and as Thetas—or Kappas, Sigma Kappas, or Alpha Phis—of high levels of achievement, the female fraternity members of the 1870s and early 1880s used academic performance, as measured by grades and faculty recommendations, as a key factor in choosing those to whom to issue "propositions" or "bids" for membership. Superior students themselves, the founders and early members of the women's fraternities sought to take in only those whom they considered the "most desirable" of the few females then enrolled in college. In their terms, "desirable" meant, to a large degree, intellectually gifted and academically ambitious.[59]

From the start, the sisters of Kappa Alpha Theta limited membership in their society to women enrolled in college.[60] In their constitution, they stipulated: "No one can become a member of this society unless she has been a student of the university or college for at least six months and during that time sustained a good moral character, evinced a social disposition, and received a high standing in her studies."[61] While concerned that prospective Thetas possess sociability and a moral grounding, they chose academic abilities as the deciding factor when determining whom they should invite to membership.

In selecting new women upon whom to "pin" their badge, the first generation of Thetas took several months to make their decisions, the better to see how their fellow female collegians performed in the classroom. Because they required each member to pass favorable judgment on all potential sisters, each woman of Kappa Alpha Theta needed time to evaluate all facets of a prospect's character.[62] Willing to risk "losing" an otherwise attractive candidate if her grades were not high enough, the Theta sisters chose to wait and see how their prospects performed in their studies during the first six months of enrollment before deciding whether to issue them propositions for membership. The sisters assigned certain members to visit the faculty of particular academic departments, to "find out who were good students and nice girls." When cases arose in which particular students appeared attractive but performed poorly in the classroom, the fraternity women appointed representatives to "go and see them and tell them we are talking of them and only awaiting for them to make some improvement in their studies."[63]

Other women's fraternities followed similar paths, also taking their time to evaluate prospects' intellectual capabilities before determining their desirability as members. Pi Beta Phi, for example, selected new members on the bases of intellectual pursuit, literary merit, and "honor, virtue, and sterling work." Committed to producing "intellectually strong women who [would rise in their] ranks and [stand] out as leaders in thought and reform," the sisters of Pi Beta Phi, unlike their Theta peers, opted to take in members from outside the college ranks, so eager were they to bring teachers and other female thinkers into their fold.[64]

Kappa Kappa Gamma, which, like Theta, restricted membership to collegians, also placed performance in the classroom at the forefront of selection. Considering themselves the "choicest spirits among the girls" and deeply concerned with what they labeled the "quality" of their membership, the early Kappas mirrored the Thetas in the care and caution they exerted before issuing bids for membership. Willing to lose potential members to avoid taking in someone who might prove, after longer acquaintance, unworthy of the Kappa badge, the Kappa Kappa Gamma sisters acted conservatively in expanding their number. Their goal, the founders argued, entailed admitting into their organization only the "very brightest and best of all who came."[65]

In establishing new branches of their organizations on other campuses in a process that mirrored the male fraternities, the sisters of Kappa Alpha Theta and the other women's fraternities maintained the same concern with academics that they practiced on their home campuses. They generally wrote to the deans and registrars of colleges and requested the names of the "smartest girls in college."[66] In Kappa Alpha Theta, as it developed from a single chapter into a "national" society, the early sisters privileged scholarship above all else.

Unable to evaluate personally the women at other colleges who would become their "sisters" once a new chapter of the fraternity was established, the Theta members relied on word-of-mouth from friends and relatives familiar with the campus and on recommendations from professors, registrars, and deans when selecting what they termed "likely names" for membership.[67] For example, when choosing women to form a branch of the fraternity on the Northwestern Christian University campus in Indianapolis, later renamed Butler University, a Beta sister at Indiana University wrote to the Alpha chapter in 1873: "We asked several of the professors to give us the names of the smartest girls in college and the list every time was headed by Mellie Ingals' name, following hers immediately was Nannie Cunningham." Based largely on these faculty recommendations, the Beta sister decided to initiate the two women and issue them a charter for a new chapter of the fraternity.[68]

The members of Alpha Phi also used grades and class standing when selecting women to found new branches of their fraternity. In seeking charter members at Cornell University, for example, the women considered numerous factors but placed excellent scholastic standing at the top of their list of criteria.[69]

For the fraternity women, grades and class standing represented a tangible measure that they could evaluate when selecting members at other colleges. As such, they must have provided comfort to some—*She is an excellent student, so she must be like us*—that otherwise may have been lacking as they brought in sisters from other colleges. Indeed, other than grades and class standing, the sisters had little else besides occasional feedback from family and friends upon which to base their judgments. Thus, they held great sway in selection processes.

The importance of grades and faculty recommendations only increased in situations in which the sisters were unable to meet personally those to whom they were entrusting a charter for a new chapter. With Theta's establishment of the Vermont and Cornell chapters, for example, and Kappa's establishment of several of its early branches, the distance between chapters proved too great for members to travel. In these cases, the fraternity women had to entrust to the mail the secrets of their organizations and place in unknown hands the responsibility of upholding the ideals of their organizations. With so much riding on so little firsthand information, the grades and faculty recommendations on behalf of new prospects must have brought a measure of assurance to an otherwise uncertain move.[70]

Once a woman was chosen and initiated into a fraternity, the other members of her chapter kept close watch on her grades, to make sure she continued to represent the fraternity favorably in the classroom. In Kappa Alpha Theta, when the sisters found one of their number lacking in her studies, other members intervened. At one meeting of the Alpha chapter, for example, the sisters "moved and seconded that sister Eta talk to ___ before her examination and urge the necessity of improvement in her class standing." Another time, the Theta group "[a]ppointed someone to look into the scholarship of ___, since we hear that she is not doing as well as formerly, and if she finds the report true, to talk to her."[71] To ensure that each member kept her grades at the same high level as she had attained upon entering the fraternity, the sisters of the Alpha chapter went

In the late 1880s, women's fraternity chapters spread rapidly from the Midwest to the East, West, North, and South. Members such as these Wisconsin Thetas eagerly exchanged correspondence with sisters at a distance, learning as much as they could of the activities and proclivities of their distant peers. (Courtesy of Kappa Alpha Theta Fraternity, © 2003.)

so far as to write into their bylaws that "it shall be the aim of each member of this chapter not only to continue in the good standing which she had maintained, but to make as good a grade as possible improving on the former."[72]

For the first generation of fraternity women, then, scholarship served as the primary determinant when selecting whom to invite to membership. The early members conceived of and used their sisterhoods as vehicles to help them meet largely academic needs: they sought to help one another perform better in the classroom and form a network of solidarity to help those who were struggling against opposition to coeducation.

By many accounts, this help paid off. According to reports in the *Kappa Alpha Theta* journal, first published in 1885, as well as accounts included in the frequent correspondence exchanged among chapters, the sisters of Kappa Alpha Theta served as valedictorians, senior orators and historians, salutatorians, student newspaper editors, and class officers on a frequent basis.[73] In its first thirty years of existence, Theta had more than ninety of its members inducted into the Phi Beta Kappa Honor Society.[74] At Illinois Wesleyan College, the Delta chapter members boasted to their fellow Thetas that, "with but one or two exceptions, all [nine] sisters expect to complete [all four years of college]," a rare occurrence in early years of coeducation. Fifty-five percent of the first generation Thetas earned college degrees, and an additional 20 percent completed more than one year of higher education. Of the graduates, 15 percent went on to pursue a second degree, and 52 percent entered some kind of profession, many of them as teachers or professors.[75] Hanover's Nu chapter alone boasted ten teachers and four professors among its roll of fewer than fifty sisters.[76]

Members of other women's fraternities also earned success in the classroom. In Sigma Kappa, for example, two of the five founders earned Phi Beta Kappa honors upon completing their studies. All founders ranked among the top scholars in their year cohorts, and one graduated at the very top of her class.[77] All the early Sigma Kappas worked outside the home at some point in their lives, in professions ranging from library science to banking. One earned an advanced degree, and two won honorary doctorates in literature from their alma mater.[78]

In Kappa Kappa Gamma, too, the focus on academics reaped rewards for the members. Its chapter histories are full of commentaries on members' graduating *cum laude* and winning scholarships, oratorical contests, and other academic prizes. In 1883, for example, Kappas won all but one academic prize and every declamation contest offered by Franklin College. Members of the fraternity went on to careers in teaching, business, and community leadership, and Kappa celebrated those who excelled academically in its histories and journals.[79]

In addition to furthering themselves academically, the sisters of Kappa Alpha Theta and their peers in other women's fraternities also strove to advance themselves personally and socially, as individuals, as fraternity members, and as women. The sisters of the 1870s and 1880s struggled to make themselves models not only of educated womanhood but also of "ideal womanhood."[80] As they proved themselves as capable intellectually as their male peers, the women of Kappa Alpha Theta, Kappa Kappa Gamma, Pi Beta Phi, and other Greek-letter organizations found their femininity attacked and their morals questioned by many both within and outside the classroom, simply because of their college attendance. Thus, as well as striving to prove their intellectual worth as women and as students, the first generation of fraternity women also struggled to uphold and evince certain moral and social standards, to show themselves and those around them that college education did not "unsex" them.[81]

While boosting their academic skills and their status on campus as the smartest of the female collegians, the fraternity women sought at the same time to ensure that each member presented herself as an epitome of female propriety and morality. Especially as the classroom performances of the first female collegians essentially nullified critiques of their intellectual capacities, the early members of Kappa Alpha Theta and other fraternities turned much of their energies to negating the popular claims that higher education would render them "unwomanly." For the sisters who attended college in the 1880s particularly, proving themselves feminine and "well-rounded" served as vital concerns.

The early Theta sisters recognized that public opinion often painted collegiate women in an unfavorable light. Thus, they and their successors of the 1870s and 1880s strove to counter these images by presenting themselves in as "proper" a manner as possible.[82] "Everyone was willing to find fault with us for being so immodest as to seek to attend [a] school which was also attended by boys. . . . They said we were rude and unladylike," noted founder Bettie Locke [Hamilton].[83] To refute these critiques, the earliest members prescribed in Article Two of their constitution that in addition to affording "an opportunity for improvement in composition and debate and elocution," the fraternity should also help its members "cultivate those social qualities which become a woman."[84] Next to grades and intellectual capacity, the sisters of Kappa Alpha Theta looked for "sociability" and a "solid moral character" in those whom they selected for membership in their fraternity. While the fairly straightforward category of scholarship proved the deciding factor, if a woman did not "evince a social disposition" or "sustain a good moral character," the somewhat nebulous characteristics that to them epitomized "ideal womanhood," then she would not be considered eligible for Theta.[85]

As with their examination of prospective members' academic abilities, the early sisters of Kappa Alpha Theta took care to evaluate the characters and qualities of each of their fellow female collegians. Dedicating great time and energy—at least a portion of each fraternity chapter meeting—to "lively discussion[s] concerning the respective merits of certain promising Barb[arians]," the Theta women of the 1870s to mid-1880s picked and chose carefully those among their female collegians who might be "worthy to be a Theta."[86] One sister wrote of a fraternity meeting in 1876, "At last came the exciting talk about the new girls. Several committees [were] appointed to look after all the desirable girls."[87] At another meeting, the Theta sisters "proceeded to disect [sic] the 'new girls' in the Freshman and Second prep. classes, to see if there were any who possessed the qualifications of a [Theta]."[88]

As with their academic performances, the fraternity women subjected themselves to constant scrutiny by their sisters even after being initiated into the fraternity, to ensure that each member continued to represent herself, the fraternity, and womanhood in the best possible light. The Pi Beta Phi sisters, for example, proscribed "devotion to the highest ideals of perfect womanhood" as both a criterion for membership and a quality to be striven for by all members. To ensure fulfillment of the ideal, the sisters critiqued one another's conduct and "[made] it a point to correct and advise the 'sisters' in regard to anything respecting manners, morals, or conversation and everything that is at all objectionable."[89]

This commitment to self-improvement also manifested itself in the fraternity sisters' eagerness to take up what they called "the study of literary works." In most middle- and upper-middle-class, white, Victorian-American social worlds of the mid- to late nineteenth century, it was expected that refined, cultured women would be knowledgeable in the fields of literature, drama, and poetry. The college curriculum of the day, however, excluded the study of these fields except as a manner of charting metaphor and meter. Students studied Greek, Latin, mathematics, philosophy, and English grammar, and, especially after the publication and subsequent popularity of Darwin's *The Origin of Species,* science. They did not, however, study literature, drama, or music, since "the dissemination of knowledge and the inculcation of aesthetic appreciation . . . took a distinctly inferior place to the much more crucial task of instilling what

Maclean referred to as 'mental discipline.' The subject of literature . . . was really not a fixture of American universities until [the 1890s]."[90] Because they could not hope to gain from their academic pursuits the literary exposure necessary to make them the well-rounded and refined models of womanhood that they wished to become, the first generation of fraternity sisters, especially after 1880, used much of the time allocated to performances in their chapter meetings as opportunities to take up the study of largely-agreed-upon authors, such as William Shakespeare, Charles Dickens, Henry Wadsworth Longfellow, Nathaniel Hawthorne, and Charles Kingsley, with the often-stated goal of "improving" themselves and their knowledge of the arts.[91]

In 1882, for example, the Beta chapter of Kappa Alpha Theta voted to "take up some author at each meeting and discuss his works, have essays, declamations, and select readings from his productions." At their next several meetings, they addressed, respectively, the works of Longfellow, Dickens, J. G. Holland, and John Greenleaf Whittier. On each occasion, two sisters performed readings of the assigned author's work and another presented his biography. According to their own assessment, the Theta sisters found these performances "both instructive and interesting."[92]

Other chapters followed similar programs. At Cornell University, the Iota chapter of Kappa Alpha Theta discussed literary works in fraternity meetings, prompting one member to report that "the [chapter's] committee on drama gave a report upon Henry Irving's presentation of 'Faust,' while on literature one of the committee gave a sketch of Thomas De Quincy's life and [an]other read extracts from his essays."[93] In the Tau chapter at Northwestern, the sisters recorded that "the question of reading some book continuously through our meetings was considered and the matter was favorably received, the book decided upon being 'Hypatia' by Charles Kingsley."[94] At the Alpha chapter meetings at Asbury, the members decided "to reform and lead better lives and so [they] decided to study [Oliver Wendell] Holmes."[95]

Nearly all enclaves of fraternity sisters followed literary programs, most of them addressing similar authors and works. In Kappa Kappa Gamma, for example, the Beta Gamma chapter of Wooster, Ohio studied Tennyson, Helen Hunt Jackson, Whittier, and Browning in their meetings one semester, then followed in the next with readings from Shakespeare, with various characters' roles read by different sisters. Kappa's Epsilon chapter at Illinois Wesleyan also focused on literary endeavors, holding a regular program that featured both orations and debates. The sisters took these performances seriously, dedicating great time and care to their presentations. As one sister later noted, the discussions took place with "little of the humorous nature which crept in with the passage of years."[96]

In their frequent correspondence with one another, fraternity sisters of different chapters advised one another about what sort of literary program their own groups were following and which authors they and their sisters were studying.[97] As a result of these letters and other methods of communication, Theta chapters as far apart as Vermont and Kansas all dealt with the same groups of authors and topics in their meetings.[98] In their letters to the *Kappa Alpha Theta* quarterly, Thetas of each chapter of the fraternity detailed the contents of their own branch's literary programs. Entries such as an Omicron sister's report, which noted, "At present we are reading the works of Holland and Hawthorne," dominated the chapter letters to the journal. Although nowhere did they specify what factors, other than individual or collective desire, inspired them to make particular selections, nearly all of the works the Theta sisters chose were ones widely celebrated in nonacademic circles. Journals such as the *Atlantic Monthly*, *Scribner's* magazine, and *Harper's* magazine all published excerpts, book reviews, and write-ups on these works and featured their authors in articles and in "Books of the Month" sections.[99] Some chapters of the fraternity mentioned reading these journals, indicating their awareness of the privileged status accorded these authors by journal editors.[100] Others, such as the Beta chapter, so thoroughly mirrored the journals' selections that it is likely the sisters had access to such literary magazines or else received suggestions from others who either read the reviews and "Book of the Month" recommendations or else shared the editors' literary sentiments.[101]

By taking suggestions from one another and sticking mainly to authors already featured in the literary journals of the day, the sisters of Kappa Alpha Theta and other women's fraternities strove, in the words of a Lambda chapter member, "to get a share of what is the best" in literary training.[102] Considering their college curricula deficient in an area they deemed necessary to their full development as individuals and as women, the early fraternity sisters spent their time together examining the well-regarded books of their age and used their chapter meetings to broaden their understanding and appreciation of literary works.

The women of Kappa Alpha Theta and their peers in other women's fraternities were not the only students pursuing literary studies at this time.

Across the country during the mid- and later decades of the nineteenth century, male and female collegians were taking it upon themselves to remedy what many considered to be inadequate college curricula by pursuing examinations of literature on their own. At a time when, according to historian Lawrence Levine, most college faculties considered literature unworthy of study except to chart grammatical constructions and derivations of words, male and female college students joined together in literary societies and intellectually oriented fraternities in which they took up the study of Shakespeare, Longfellow, and other writers, to ensure that they might receive, in the words of the Theta sisters, a "well-rounded education."[103] As historian of higher education Frederick Rudolph argued, "The [nineteenth-century] classroom was in reality far better at molding character and at denying intellect rather than refining it. The literary societies, on the other hand, owed their allegiance to reason, and in their debates, disputations, and literary exercises, they imparted tremendous vitality to the intellectual life of the colleges, creating a remarkable contrast to the ordinary classroom."[104] In the words of University of Wisconsin historians Merle Curti and Vernon Carstensen, "While their elders might talk in generalities about modifying the course of study and the internal organization of the college or university to meet the current educational demands, the students in their literary societies tried to provide what they felt to be important to their education."[105]

In their literary society gatherings and in their fraternity meetings, male and female collegians of the mid to late nineteenth century thus took active roles in defining their own intellectual and academic needs. With rigid curricula limiting their intellectual pursuits and the culture of the classroom geared more toward the preservation of ideas than toward the development of new thoughts, those attending America's colleges and universities added on their own what they found lacking in the classes: the study of literature for literature's sake.[106]

Yet the language the fraternity sisters used to describe their endeavors suggests another, equally driving concern: that of acquiring an appreciation and knowledge of literature, not just to make them well-rounded students, but more, to make them well-rounded women. One Theta sister spelled out this concern in an article entitled "A Word to Our Girls," published in one of the early issues of the *Kappa Alpha Theta*. Expounding upon what she labeled a "serious defect" in the education of college women, a failure to pursue a course of general reading outside of academic pursuits, the author advised her fraternity sisters to develop "an understanding and appreciation for. . . [the] greatest poets and thinkers." "Remember, dear girls," she wrote, "There is a certain education which you acquire in school and from your teachers; but that higher kind of training, that which is worth most to you, comes from yourselves."[107] Warning that too narrow a concern with academics, as defined by the college curriculum, risked limiting a "woman's true education," she advised her fraternity sisters to take up literary studies to assure a well-rounded training.[108]

By supplementing their curriculum with literary pursuits and proving themselves competent in handling college work, the first generation of Kappa Alpha Theta and other Greek-letter sisters strove to make themselves well-rounded women who could collectively refute the charge that higher education rendered its female students "narrowly focused" and "unwomanly."[109] By performing literary work in an attempt to meet their own and societal expectations of what an "educated person" and an "ideal woman" should know—in the words of one Pi Phi sister, to attain "the highest and best that can be made of the lives of each of us"—the fraternity sisters of the 1870s and 1880s strove both to adhere to and to broaden popular social prescriptions of "true womanhood." While defying by their very presence on coeducational campuses a central tenet of the Victorian standard of "true womanhood" that decreed "separate spheres" for men and women, the first generation of Kappa Alpha Theta, Pi Beta Phi, Kappa Kappa Gamma, Sigma Kappa, and Alpha Phi members effectively redefined for themselves the feminine ideal, broadening it to include intellectual capacity along with the more socially accepted traits of morality and social grace. In this manner, they essentially constructed for themselves an ideal of "true womanhood" for which they were uniquely suited to serve as models: the "true" or "ideal" fraternity woman."[110]

Most of the women's fraternities incorporated this ideal of "true womanhood" into their mission statements and initiation ceremonies. In Kappa Alpha Theta's initiation ritual, a minutely scripted ceremony designed to transform outsiders into sisters, the members of the fraternity invoked "a nobler womanhood" as their cause and a loyal stance in pursuit of this ideal as their mission. Only by pledging herself "in the name of a nobler womanhood" to "assist, support and defend the members of this fraternity in all their laudable efforts toward a higher intellectual and moral life" and by promising to "uphold [Theta's] high ideal" could a prospective Theta member win a "place in the mystic circle" of the

fraternity. In exchange for pledging to be "an earnest, faithful, and enthusiastic worker for [the fraternity's] advancement and welfare" and for
agreeing to "enter the fraternal bond" with the sisters of Kappa Alpha
Theta, new initiates were promised that "Theta's influence will be a help
and a strength in growth toward the best." At the same time, they would
also be warned that "only through the noblest, purest womanhood can
we hope to attain truest sisterhood," and thus the responsibility for conducting themselves like "true Thetas" would rest upon their shoulders.[111]

By their own accounts, the early Thetas and their Greek-letter peers
placed great significance in the vows each sister pledged upon her initiation into her fraternity and regarded these vows as infused with meaning
and responsibility. As an example, the Alpha chapter of Kappa Alpha
Theta recorded the following description of the initiation of a new sister:
"At Theta's alter she knelt and took the *solemn* vow. . . . She was placed
within our 'growing Circle.' . . . Confident that she will never prove unworthy of the confidence that we have bestowed in her or recreant to the
trust we have confided in her, we wish her *success*."[112] As this description
indicates, the ritual of initiation involved a "bestowal" of the fraternity's
"confidence" in its new members, in exchange for their "solemn vow" of
loyalty, sisterhood, and willingness to live up to the ideals of the fraternity.

The founders and early members of Theta and other women's fraternities thus constructed for themselves a Greek system with both tangible
and immediate, yet amorphous and idealistic, goals. In a very primary
sense, they sought to aid one another in the struggle to combat opposition to their presence on campus; to help one another achieve at a high
level in the classroom and the performance hall; and to prove to themselves, their peers, and the wider society around them that women could
and would make a place for themselves on coeducational campuses. By
their own accounts, they managed to achieve these ends.

Although as chronicler of Greek life Ida Shaw Martin noted at the turn
of the twentieth century, "Just how much the sorority did for the first generation of college girls in making their position secure and in demonstrating their right to educational privileges equal to those enjoyed by
their brothers is not perhaps to be found in records," records do show
that members found their fraternities a supportive and enabling factor in
their academic and personal struggles on campus.[113] By applauding their
academic successes, improving through suggestion and criticism their
scholarly performances, monitoring one another's grades and results, and

providing timely intervention should those grades slip, the first generation of fraternity sisters ensured that each member approached her studies with the support and backing of the whole sisterhood and that each one performed in a manner that reflected positively upon herself, the entire fraternity, and her sex.

As well as aiding each other in academic and literary matters, the sisters of Kappa Alpha Theta also clearly enjoyed one another's company and reaped great personal and social benefits from their association. Like most of their female peers, both Greek and independent, the majority of the sisters lived with their families in towns surrounding their schools, and the responsibilities of caring for siblings and household chores undoubtedly took much of their time and energy not spent in the classroom. Some had long walks or horseback rides to and from school, which placed additional constraints on them. Others who lived beyond travel distance boarded in local houses or, on occasion, roomed with Thetas who lived nearby. All the sisters, like their non-Theta counterparts and male peers, endured long hours of academic classes, most of them taking courses in English, mathematics, Greek, Latin, modern languages, elocution, and occasionally natural sciences all at once.[114]

Yet despite the pressures of family and classes, and despite the constant burden of traversing almost uncharted territory in pioneering coeducation, the sisters of Kappa Alpha Theta and those of other Greek-letter societies found time to meet together weekly, initially in a room in one of their houses and later in rented halls and manors.[115] According to Kappa Alpha Theta historian Estelle Riddle Dodge, from the start the fraternity "put new life into the girls after their discouraging experiences in a men's world." Citing the testimony of one of the founders, Hannah Fitch [Shaw], Dodge stated of the newly pledged Thetas that "now they were ready to cope with anything. Chapter meetings were the bright spots of college life. Here the girls met and sang together, then joined in the business of the sessions with sparkle and joy. They sat in a circle and planned for the years to come."[116]

Other Greek-letter members wrote in similar terms about their own organizations. Indeed, the testimonies of the early members recount time and again the extent to which their meetings provided outlets otherwise not available to them. As the words of one Alpha Phi founder summed up the feeling: "Alpha Phi supplied a very great and pressing need in the lives of the Original Ten [members]. Our difficulties were greatly lessened and our days made happier by its affectionate, joyous meetings."[117]

The bonds uniting members of the same fraternity extended into many arenas, both academic and social. At the University of Illinois, members of Kappa Alpha Theta's Delta chapter lived and studied together in the same house in the years following the turn of the twentieth century. (Courtesy of Kappa Alpha Theta Fraternity, © 2003.)

While their weekly or biweekly gatherings focused on activities designed to improve themselves and their fraternity, the women of Kappa Alpha Theta and other fraternities also created opportunities to spend time together outside of formal meetings. They held performances in conjunction with members of the male fraternities, hosted socials at the homes of members living nearby, and stayed behind after the business portions of their meetings to sing and waltz together.[118] To mark special occasions, the sisters of the 1870s and 1880s bought apples, popcorn, and molasses, and organized candy-pulls or made cakes and ice cream for themselves or for enjoyment with would-be Thetas.[119] They held "jollifications" at which they played games and ate "sweets." On occasion, they accompanied the "boys" of Beta Theta Pi or Phi Gamma Delta on carriage rides and to banquets.[120] Each Halloween, the chapter parties at which they sought to enjoy themselves "by every manner means that could be devised."[121]

Infrequent though they may have been, these occasions together provided most of the social outlets available to the fraternity women as female collegians of the 1870s and 1880s. Long hours of classes, mandatory chapel, strict course-work requirements, and pressure to achieve academically limited the time students could spend socializing. In addition, many schools during this time period held strong ties to or affiliations with some form of religious organization, and on those campuses, students found themselves under close surveillance and subject to stringent rules regarding social activities.[122] While most fraternity sisters belonged to and took active roles in literary societies and competitions, few other activities provided social or extracurricular outlets for the female collegians of the 1870s and early 1880s.[123] Despite their increased number on campus, most women found the majority of activities closed to them on the basis of their sex.

Indeed, on most campuses, activities offered exclusively to male students outnumbered those allowing female participants by almost eight to one, despite the fact that women accounted for at least one-fourth and often up to one-third of the college student population.[124] At the University of California at Berkeley, for example, despite the fact that women constituted a quarter of student body in 1880, female students held only a minor place in campus affairs. Of the thirteen nonfraternity student clubs, only two literary societies and two glee clubs allowed female members, while the quartette, instrumental, whist, chess, and dance clubs, among others, took in only male students.[125] At Northwestern University, a similar situation existed. Of the thirty-four extracurricular activities available for students, men had sixteen options open exclusively to them, while women found only nine female-only options, five of them literary societies.[126] Likewise, at the University of Wisconsin, male-only clubs outnumbered female-only clubs by fifteen to three in 1885. Twenty-five years later, when women accounted for 39.6 percent of the college student population, this discrepancy had improved only marginally, with organizations open to male members topping those permitting women by a ratio of more than 3.5 to 1.[127] Female students thus had few opportunities for social and extracurricular engagement; membership in Kappa Alpha Theta and other women's fraternities brought thos en belonging to them not only solidarity in their intellectual pursuits also a sense of camaraderie and companionship that they might oth- wise have struggled to find.

In addition to the somewhat tangible goals of ensuring superior academic performance and enhanced social outlets, the fraternity women of the 1870s and, especially, the 1880s also sought to achieve more idealistic ends: to take on the primary role of scholars without sacrificing their identities as women. While challenging social expectations regarding woman's place by their very presence on coeducational campuses, the first generation of Kappa Alpha Theta sisters and their peers in other female societies at the same time strove to conduct themselves in a manner in keeping with social expectations for womanly behavior in late nineteenth century middle-class America. "[The] ideal college woman," one sister wrote, "Is the woman who has been, not only foremost in her class work, but also has maintained strict watch over personal appearance and over social observances."[128] Rather than rejecting social expectations concerning proper feminine behavior, as they perceived other female collegians doing, the first generation of Theta, Pi Phi, and Alpha Phi sisters simply added intellectual performance to society's other standards for womanliness. In doing so, they constructed for themselves a definition of "ideal womanhood" that included traits that they, by virtue of their fraternity membership, were already striving both to develop and to exhibit. As one Theta member argued, "An 'Ideal Theta'[is] neither a purely intellectual, nor a merely social girl, but both in one. . . . [A] perfectly rounded woman, whose intellect all will acknowledge and yet one who charms the hearts of all who meet her, by her gracious presence."[129] Striving for this ideal, the first generation of fraternity sisters created for themselves an identity that combined the seemingly conflicting roles of "scholar" and "woman," in the hopes that their efforts would help assure their place and that of their sex inside the walls of higher education.

Thus, rather than serving as the wholly conservative agents that critics often assume, the early women's fraternities, while espousing the model of "true womanhood," in many ways helped broaden and redefine this notion, adding to its formulations and bending and shaping its contents to suit their members' evolving interests and needs as they negotiated the complex and changing social worlds of America prior to the turn of the twentieth century. In fact, the Theta sisters and their peers in other women's societies of the time actually rejected certain aspects of the "true womanhood" concept—most notably, the "virtue" of submissiveness—

while retaining other elements of the ideal. Their acceptance and promotion of the Victorian standard did not therefore translate ipso facto into conservatism. Rather than serving as the constricting forces that some have taken them to be, fraternities such as Kappa Alpha Theta actually played markedly supportive roles for their members, easing their paths academically, socially, and politically while in college, and socially and economically after graduation, by positing models for behavior that in many ways challenged socially prescribed boundaries around women's roles.

In 1898, Kappa Alpha Thetas from DePauw University enjoyed a group outing in nearby Brookville, Indiana. Among them was Mary Ritter (Beard), pictured in the lower left-hand corner, who later became a well-known historian and activist for woman suffrage. (Courtesy of Kappa Alpha Theta Fraternity, © 2003.)

2

The Most Socially Eligible

"At Home" with the
Second Generation of Fraternity Women

The dire predictions regarding the health of women who attended college proved groundless, and in the 1880s, a larger number of schools opened their doors to female students. According to historian of women's education Mabel Newcomer, whereas roughly 4,600 women had attended coeducational colleges in 1870, by 1890 that number had increased to 39,500 and within ten years had grown still further, to 61,000 women.[1] With their presence on campus more accepted by male peers and social commentators alike, female collegians of the 1890s and early 1900s encountered less pressure to prove themselves and their right to attain a higher education. Freed of the pioneers' burden of forging a path and representing their sex, the second generation of female collegians turned their attentions largely to social and extracurricular concerns.[2] Especially within the chapters of Kappa Alpha Theta, Kappa Kappa Gamma, Pi Beta Phi, and the other women's fraternities, the "gay coed" replaced the "serious scholar" as the identity of choice for those who came of age in the decades immediately surrounding the turn of the twentieth century.

As much shapers of their environments as products of middle- and upper-middle-class American society, the fraternity women of the 1890s through the 1910s adopted a set of customs and concerns that placed a premium on appearance and sociability. Relieved of their predecessors' charge of representing all womanhood in their actions, the second-generation sisters adopted aims for their fraternities that differed dramatically from those of the first generation. No longer struggling and isolated female collegians in need of solidarity and support from others in the same predicament, the sisters of the 1890s and early 1900s deemphasized the intellectual aspect of their fraternities' missions while accentuating the social side of Greek-letter life.

Within Kappa Alpha Theta Fraternity, rather than spending their weekly meetings listening to one another recite papers and declamations, the sisters of the 1890s and early 1900s hosted parties and "at homes" for themselves, prospective members, and their male peers, rating themselves and one another according to the success of the entertainments and festivities they sponsored. To make their parties the most celebrated and popular affairs on campus and themselves the most attractive in a campus culture that placed increasing emphasis on heterosexual socializing,[3] the Thetas of the second generation pledged and initiated women whose appearances and behavior would make a favorable impression upon their guests. Facing stiff competition from the growing number of women's fraternities developing on campuses across the country, the Theta sisters on most campuses issued their bids in a hurry, often within days or even hours of meeting a new prospect, in an almost frenzied eagerness to "pin" the most "taking" students around them. With their peers in Kappa Kappa Gamma, Pi Beta Phi, Alpha Phi, and the other women's fraternities doing likewise, a shift occurred among the women's Greek-letter organizations, as the sisters turned away from intellectual and scholarly pursuits and centered instead on social and what some perceived as largely superficial affairs.

The altered policies, practices, and concerns of the second-generation sisters provoked alarm within the ranks of their alumnae, who shuddered to see their cautious methods and serious concerns cast aside by their younger sisters. Together with the alumnae of several other women's fraternities, which themselves were undergoing the same evolution in focus as Theta, the first generation of Kappa Alpha Theta sisters noted with fear the "haste" and "excess" of their collegiate members. Shocked by the speed with which the latter were pledging new members and the extravagance they displayed in their activities and entertainments, the older sisters worried about the toll these actions would take on their fraternities. They questioned the extent to which the second-generation members understood the meaning and purpose of a Greek-letter fraternity. How could two generations of fraternity women adopt for themselves such radically different concerns and practices and still claim each to be fulfilling the ideals of a "true" member?

Women's fraternities grew steadily in the latter decades of the nineteenth century. From only a handful of organizations with a few small chapters in 1880, by 1898 the female Greek system boasted seven societies, with a membership of almost 1,200 women. Only seven years later, that number had reached seventeen organizations, to which 20,065 members belonged. As one of the oldest and best established of these organizations, Kappa Alpha Theta contributed large numbers to the mass of female Greeks. Twenty years after its founding, it boasted a membership of 1,180 women. Of these, 877 belonged to the alumnae rank, and 303 were active collegiate members in one of Theta's twenty college chapters.[4]

The fraternity sisters of the 1890s entered college at a time when the presence of women on campus provoked less opposition than in the past. Many educators and social thinkers were finally admitting that women, rather than irreparably harming the hallowed halls of higher education, were actually having a positive influence upon the male students.[5] Female enrollments were growing so rapidly that in some institutions, women students outnumbered their male peers.[6] Yet high enrollments did not mean full integration. Although socializing between the sexes became more common in the 1910s, throughout the period between 1890 and 1920, de facto segregation characterized day-to-day life on most coeducational campuses.

Indeed, in most American institutions of higher education, female students lived and studied in worlds largely separated from men. With their own residence halls, meeting rooms and lounges, student government associations, advisers, and, by the early 1900s, deans of women, female students governed and monitored themselves, sponsored and joined their own extracurricular and co-curricular activities, produced their own plays, and ran their own sports teams, all without input or involvement from male students.[7] Inspired and mentored by women's advisers and deans of women, the female students of the late nineteenth and early twentieth centuries created woman-centered social worlds essentially separate from, though not at all equal to, those of the male students.[8]

In the classroom, whether due to institutional restrictions or to free will, most female students pursued different paths than their male peers. Although in the 1870s and 1880s, most students regardless of sex had followed a curriculum set by the faculty at their respective institutions, by the turn of the twentieth century, this was no longer the case. Whether due to choice—this time period marked a general loosening of requirements—or to newly instituted guidelines that, while privileging vocational training, proscribed different courses for men and women, collegians of the early 1900s began to travel academic paths specific to their sex.[9] In 1900, for example, more than 70 percent of the 61,000 women enrolled in coeducational schools throughout the country pursued courses in education and teacher training. That same year, the bulk of their male counterparts selected engineering and agriculture as the foci of their studies.[10] While on some campuses, students continued to study core subjects in mixed-sex classes, at other places such as the University of Chicago and Brown University, the faculty and administrators chose to institutionalize gender separation by creating coordinate colleges for women and removing them entirely from the male classroom as well as the male extracurricular world. Thus, in most American colleges and universities, "[male and female students] were likely to be studying in segregated groups even while occupying the same campus."[11]

Female college students in the United States thus often passed their days largely separated from the male students enrolled at the same institutions. While in the 1910s, loosening restrictions on student behavior and heightened interest in dancing and other forms of heterosexual entertainment helped increase opportunities for male/female socializing, women students for the most part found their day-to-day lives largely populated with members of their own sex.[12] As Barbara Solomon noted,

> Women at all types of institutions identified more with each other than with male students. Opportunities for socializing with men had clear limits. . . . Contrary to popular opinion, the patterns of coeducation in the late nineteenth and early twentieth century did not permit free association of the sexes outside the classroom. Students were always under strict surveillance. . . . Although boys and girls often sat at the same dining tables, they lived in completely segregated dormitories and were heavily chaperoned in their limited social intercourse.[13]

Women's fraternities played important roles in these sex-segregated campus settings of the turn of the twentieth century. As creators as well as products of female-only spaces, they both shaped and reinforced the norm of sex-specific groups. Yet, unlike other clubs and organizations

Foods class at the University of Illinois, ca. 1890, AGR 11-13. (Courtesy of the University of Illinois at Urbana-Champaign Archives.)

that erected boundaries along gender lines, women's fraternities also set women off from women. While their earlier incarnations had entailed helping all women make a place for themselves on campus, fraternities of the 1890s and early 1900s adopted much more member-specific foci.

Whereas the female collegians of the 1870s and 1880s had faced challenges to their presence on campus and had turned to one another for aid in improving their academic and literary abilities, the second-generation students, especially the fraternity members, did not conceive of themselves primarily as scholars, nor did they feel pressure to prove to skeptics their capabilities as women. Unlike their predecessors, who had considered themselves representatives of their sex as much as of their fraternities, the second generation sisters took as their central mission the promotion of themselves and their chapters ahead of all other female collegians and securing for their chapters and themselves a socially exclusive and elite status.

In a shift remarkable for its speed and its encompassing nature, the fraternity women of the second generation jettisoned their academic and literary work in favor of social activities. They built upon their predecessors' concerns with "true womanhood," developing this concept into one that elevated sociability and grace. In Kappa Alpha Theta, a change the sisters made to the preamble of their constitution exemplifies their changed focus: in 1893 they replaced the rather humble mission statement of "hoping to cultivate a feeling of confidence and reliance among our most worthy fellow students" with the bolder assertion, that Kappa Alpha Theta acted "in the name of a nobler womanhood."[14] More confident in their place on campus and less driven to prove their worth to critics, the sisters of the decades surrounding the turn of the twentieth century centered their energies on setting themselves and their fraternity off from, not male taunters as in earlier times, but fellow female collegians whose appearances and social skills, not academic abilities, placed them in a category below "good Theta material." Their primary means of achieving this position of distinction lay in adopting an almost entirely social program for their fraternity.

While certain Theta chapters continued to hold occasional literary exercises in their meetings, the bulk of the fraternity abandoned literary programs in favor of holding "cozies," dances, and other forms of entertainment.[15] Beginning sporadically in the later years of the 1880s in some chapters and strengthening into a fraternitywide practice in the 1890s and early 1900s, the members of each chapter began to hold "spreads" and "at homes" at most of their meetings. A Mu chapter correspondent from Allegheny College explained this trend to her fraternity sisters in a letter to the *Kappa Alpha Theta* journal, in which she stated, "[spring] season was one of the most pleasantest of our existence as a chapter of Kappa Alpha Theta, as we were at that time reveling in 'spreads.'"[16] Like the Mu sisters, the Phi chapter Thetas at Stanford in the 1890s also held frequent spreads during their fraternity meetings. To bolster their social proclivities still further, they decided to alternate business meetings with social affairs and held receptions, picnics, and luncheons on alternate weeks throughout the month. In addition, throughout most of the 1890s, the Stanford Thetas hosted monthly "at homes," to which they invited male friends and faculty members as well as prospective members.[17]

When not hosting banquets, spreads, and cozies, the Theta sisters of the second generation spent much of their time planning these affairs. Entries such as "planned reception" and those recounting details of refreshments and entertainments filled the chapter minutes of this period.[18] As the new century took hold and male-female socializing became more acceptable, men began to feature prominently as guests at these affairs. On more than one occasion, the sisters of the Beta chapter at Indiana, unable

Thetas at Indiana University, like female students at many other schools, delighted in the opportunity to gather informally at nighttime "spreads" with their sisters, sharing the pleasures of food and laughter. (Courtesy of Kappa Alpha Theta Fraternity, © 2003.)

to agree upon which of the men's fraternities to invite to a reception, decided to entertain each of them at parties on successive Saturday nights. For several month-long periods, their meetings centered on issues related to planning, organizing, and hosting these social affairs.[19]

In addition to increasing the frequency of these festive affairs, the sisters of the second generation also changed the type of events they sponsored. Whereas in the 1870s and 1880s, a candy pull or an evening spent dunking for apples served as a treat to mark a special occasion, in the 1890s and early 1900s, the sisters began to hold much more elaborate and expensive celebrations.[20] The Thetas of the Phi chapter, for example, held an elaborate affair in 1896, which they described in their minutes in the following words:

> October 30th was a notable day in our memory because on its evening Phi entertained three score and ten friends. . . . A German [dance], prettily arranged and gracefully led by our own May Queen, furnished the nucleus for the evening's pleasure. The house was ample, the decorations Theta and tasty, the guests congenial, the music enticing, and if we may accept the testimony of eyewitnesses, our sentence would be "A Delightful Evening."[21]

Other chapters held similar events. The Upsilon chapter Thetas at the University of Minnesota recounted an occasion that "the 'boys' declared

A 1912 house party at the University of Michigan. (Courtesy of Kappa Alpha Theta Fraternity, © 2003.)

The 1908 Senior Ball at the University of Illinois. (Courtesy of the University of Illinois Archives, Kappa Kappa Gamma Records, series 41/72/29, Senior Ball, 08.)

was a success. . . . The house was decorated with black and gold ribbons and bows of the same appeared on the napkins, forks, and spoons, while sandwiches were wrapped in black and gold papers. Souvenirs were kite-shaped tied in black and gold. Dancing, conversation, and music by the Mandolin Club, were the amusements."[22] These affairs took great preparation, as exhibited by the Tau sisters, who recorded of one preparty schedule: "During the remainder of the month of April and until the middle of May, the meetings of this society were held regularly seven times a week—often seven times a day. There being a pressure of business preparatory to the approaching reception which was to take place May 15th at the Avenue House." The sisters sorted themselves into committees to deal with hotels, music, refreshments, and favors, the last of which reported a coup in locating souvenirs of the "latest style" which were "the shape of a dainty painted envelope tied with narrow peko edge ribbon and perfumed with sachet powder."[23]

With the high levels of energy, attention, and resources that the second generation Thetas put into the parties they hosted, it is hardly surprising that they chose to describe these occasions in their chapter entries to the fraternity journal. But in addition to detailing their own parties and affairs, the Theta sisters of the 1890s and 1900s also recounted with pride the elaborate social activities sponsored by other organizations on their campus. In a marked shift from the letters written by the first-generation Thetas, which described the literary programs followed by particular branches in fraternity meetings, the chapter correspondents of the 1890s and early 1900s filled their entries to the *Kappa Alpha Theta* with detailed accounts of the "hops," "spreads," fancy-dress parties, and "tally-ho's" that they and their fellow sisters had attended. For example, in her letter to the journal, a Kappa sister at Kansas bragged, "The Phi Gamma Deltas give 'hops' every two weeks. . . . All the boys who attend are splendid dancers; their hall is lovely, especially for dancing, and the evenings spent there are always delightful. The Phi Kappa Psis also have parties every two weeks, sometimes devoted to cards, and others to dancing."[24]

Few if any Theta chapters ever admitted to lacking for invitations from the men's fraternities. Rather, the sisters recorded facing the uncomfortable predicament of finding themselves in too great demand. Of one of their meetings, the Theta sisters of Northwestern University noted, "More or less discussion and discomfiture in regard to approaching fraternity parties as the Thetas found it was impossible to occupy two places at the same time."[25]

The detailed descriptions of social affairs that the Thetas of the 1890s and early 1900s included in their chapter letters to the fraternity journal indicated that they took great pride in the number of social events they both attended and hosted. Evidence of their campus's spiritedness as well as the individual popularity of the sisters, a strong presence at parties and other festivities suggested both to themselves and to their peers that Theta as a fraternity was much sought after on campus. In their quest to make Kappa Alpha Theta the most popular and sociable organization on campus, some chapters even imposed fines on members who were "tardy or late to parties."[26]

The Theta sisters of the 1890s and early 1900s were not alone in their social outlook. All of the leading women's fraternities underwent the same change in focus as Theta. In Alpha Phi, Chi Omega, Delta Delta Delta, and Pi Beta Phi, to name just a few, much discussion took place concerning the whirl of social activities and the elaborateness of entertainments. No longer did sisters discuss sophomore speeches or senior orations. Now, they planned parties and arranged for rush affairs.[27] The striking change in focus from literary works to social events is best exemplified by the history of Kappa Kappa Gamma's Epsilon chapter: from

Interior gym, P.E. class, ca. 1910, PHE 3. (Courtesy of the University of Illinois at Urbana-Champaign Archives.)

an entirely academic and literary focus in its early years, the chapter shifted in the mid-1880s to largely social concerns. Meetings in the first decades had been spent reciting and debating; by 1890, they were all about planning menus and hosting banquets.[28]

While perhaps taking this social focus to greater heights, the fraternity women of this time period were joined by their non-Greek peers in shifting their attention away from academics and onto social endeavors. Indeed, most collegians of the period engaged in a wide variety of non-scholastic activities and spent more time and energy on their social and extracurricular lives than had their predecessors. The growing prominence of college athletics, both in their participatory form and as spectator entertainment, fundamentally altered the form and feel of college extracurricular life. Increasing concern with physical well-being, a movement inspired in part by Theodore Roosevelt and his fellow advocates of the "strenuous life," and the concurrent rise in popularity of intramural and intercollegiate athletics, attracted students by the thousands, both male and female, to take part in sport in the name of their schools. Students who did not participate often attended the major contests, and the men's football, crew, and baseball teams in particular often drew spectators by the thousands. An air of festivity and excitement surrounded most athletic events. Male sports stars became campus heroes, the center of rallies, parties, and other celebrations, and the female athletes, too, found their social prestige augmented by the prowess they showed on the field or court.[29]

Aside from athletics, other extracurricular activities attracted the collegians around the turn of the twentieth century, and according to historian Barbara Solomon, "[c]ollege women became avid joiners." On some campuses, play writing and acting became "the thing to do," with the number of college theatrical groups soaring to meet student demand. In most schools, the roster of newspapers, literary magazines, music and theater groups, student government organizations, and other interest-based organizations, especially the Greek letter societies, swelled in number, and increasingly large groups of students, especially women, chose to take part.[30] Inspired by female professors and administrators who themselves were involved in the social reform movements of the Progressive Era, many collegiate women belonged to the Y.W.C.A. and to other voluntary organizations. Groups of students volunteered together in local settlements and community centers, and the minutes of many fraternity and sorority chapters were filled with cheerful accounts of parties sponsored for local youth groups and other needy populations.[31]

To a large extent, the students who enrolled in college after 1890, especially the women, arrived at school with the intention of "having fun." Many of those who flocked to campus in this period viewed their time in school as an opportunity to find a spouse—a "way station to a proper marriage" or at least a pleasant diversion for a few years before the commitments of adulthood took over. As historian Helen Lefkowitz Horowitz described the relatively affluent, less-studious women who comprised the second generation of female collegians, "Neither they nor their families had sacrificed to send [them] to college. . . . Such women wanted to enjoy their college years and saw them as an extension of the round of parties appropriate to their courting age."[32]

Key players in this increasingly social setting were the men's fraternity members. Especially in the new century, as heterosexual socializing became more common on most college campuses, the large number of men's fraternities took on great allure for the women and became the focus of much discussion as to which "house" was inviting which women to its parties and which popular fraternity men were courting which Greek-letter women.

Men's fraternities had expanded along with their female counterparts in the latter decades of the nineteenth century, and by 1910, almost a quarter of a million men belonged to upwards of twenty-six men's fraternities.[33] Their concerns, like the women's groups, had changed radically in the years surrounding the turn of the century, "from an express emphasis on intellectual development and moral education [in the mid-1800s], to social, recreational, and extracurricular activities [after 1900]."[34] While, like their female counterparts, the men's groups had served as quasi-literary clubs and cultural outlets in the early years of their existence, by the turn of the twentieth century they too had become essentially social forums.[35] Dominating campuses in ways that exceeded their numbers, the men's Greek system controlled many aspects of college life. "With their prestige confirmed by official undergraduate organizations, recognized by the administration, and broadcast in the student newspaper, fraternity men had powerful instruments for ruling the campus. It was they who defined and continued to control the major social events of the college year: the proms, student plays and musicals, elections, freshman hazing. Their activities had strong appeal."[36]

As the most popular men on campus, the men's fraternity members held power over who among the women would be considered "the pick of the coeds." "College dating created and confirmed the system of prestige on campus," Horowitz wrote in her study of campus culture in the early twentieth century.

> Students did not simply choose the most physically desirable members of the opposite sex for parties and fun; they chose in ways that established and strengthened their social position. . . . Fraternities and sororities gave students access to members of the opposite sex. Not only did they provide the settings and the occasions for socializing; the group prestige they lent made the individual a worthy candidate for a potential date.[37]

The men's fraternities thus served as campus trendsetters, and along with their female counterparts provided campuses with both the bulk of their social activities and their standards—or "ranking order," as Horowitz put it—of desirability as dates.

In campus settings that featured a college education not as a means to an end but rather as an end in itself, a pleasant social time, the collegians of the 1890s and early 1900s considered academic achievement secondary to their social pursuits. "Good grades were pleasant to get, but they had no intrinsic relation to future life," Horowitz noted.[38] To complement their decreased interest in academics, more flexible college curricula on most campuses, bolstered by growing numbers of electives and wider choices of programs, allowed many students to pursue less rigorous courses of study and enabled them to branch outside of the traditional liberal arts programs into the fields of education, home economics, and social work.[39] College was now a different place than it had been in the previous generation, and many of those who would have shunned higher education for its rigid focus on scholarship, especially the classics, in previous years now eagerly enrolled for its social advantages.[40]

In the decidedly nonacademic, highly social, and extracurricular-oriented settings that characterized most American college campuses of the 1890s and early 1900s, few pursued as high-paced social schedules or enjoyed the prestige associated with such involvement as the members of women's fraternities.[41] A 1910 survey of thirty-nine colleges, including a representative sampling of differently sized institutions in a variety of settings and locations, found that fraternity women engaged much more actively in social affairs than did their non-Greek counterparts, to a degree that ranged from "slightly more" to three to five times as much. "Not only in amount, but also in kind, does the social life of the fraternity girl differentiate itself from that of the non-fraternity girl," the report's authors stated. "To the former goes more theater-going, more of the formal, elaborate functions; that is more of Society as distinct from sociability."[42] A key cause of this disparity in opportunity, the study concluded, stemmed from the "constant interchange of social courtesies," whereby on a particular campus, the chapters of certain fraternities, both male and female, would entertain one another in series of reciprocal affairs, each one inviting to its functions those societies that had either previously entertained its members or else would soon do so on a comparable occasion.[43]

Most Theta chapters took part in entertaining circles such as this, and as a result, spent much of their time planning and organizing elaborate festivities. Yet the decorations, entertainment, catering, and favors considered necessary at these functions did not come without great expense, and the resulting increases in the financial cost of fraternity membership proved dramatic. From the 1870s and early 1880s, when dues ranged from a dime to twenty-five cents per term, charges increased by the early 1900s to between $1 and $3 per month ($4 to $12 per term) to pay for the bolstered social schedules of fraternity women. At the same time, initiation fees also increased. Unlike in earlier decades, when new members of the fraternity paid little or nothing to enter, most chapters instituted initiation taxes by the late 1880s, and by the turn of the twentieth century the amount ranged from $7 to $15 per initiate. Some of this money went to fund the postinitiation celebrations held on behalf of the new members by their fraternity sisters. Whereas in 1879, when the Alpha chapter welcomed its new members by authorizing its treasurer to "draw enough money from the treasury to purchase some good apples for the occasion," by the 1890s the Theta sisters were holding elaborate spreads costing $10 or more following each initiation.[44]

In order to pay for these functions, the fraternity women found it necessary to supplement the dues and initiation fees that had previously bankrolled their activities. In the 1890s and early 1900s, all chapters levied additional taxes, called assessments. Comments such as "additional tax of $2 due in two weeks to pay for flowers and prize at freshman party" filled the meeting minutes of the different Theta chapters, and the officers of the other women's organizations noted with increasing concern the taxes and assessments that their collegiate members were levying to pay for their entertainments.[45] When even additional assessments failed to pay for desired events, the sisters turned to their alumnae members to support their social affairs.[46] At a time when the fees for rent and board that a collegian paid for an entire year hovered between $25 and $30 per month, the sisters of most chapters of Kappa Alpha Theta—and the other prominent and highly social fraternities—routinely contributed more than that amount to fund the parties sponsored by their fraternity each semester.[47]

Marking a change from 1880, when one Theta branch had decided to postpone holding a banquet "as not all the girls were fully decided as to whether they could afford this added expense or not,"[48] in the 1890s and 1900s little discussion took place in the chapters regarding limiting expenses or curbing costs. With their own popularity as fraternity members and as individuals resting on the frequency and degree of their social endeavors, the sisters of Theta, Kappa, Pi Phi, and other fraternities did not allow expense to get in the way of their activities in the decades surrounding the turn of the twentieth century.[49]

The marked change in focus of the collegians from the early decades to the 1890s and 1900s did not come without notice from fraternity alumnae. Issues of the *Kappa Alpha Theta* from the late 1890s contained numerous treatises commenting on the second-generation sisters' more social outlook. Perhaps still sensitive to the charges leveled against them as "pioneers," that they had pursued their scholarship to the detriment of ir "womanliness," a sizable number of graduated Thetas wrote to the fraternity journal to advise their younger sisters not to neglect their social opportunities. "All the time spent without a serious purpose is not wasted," an editor wrote in the *Kappa Alpha Theta*. "It is not the smallest part of our education that comes to us during the hours when we are off duty as it were and can afford to throw ourselves heart and soul into the pursuit of happiness and the cultivation of the sense of humor that we as women are so often told that we do not possess."[50] Another graduated Theta advised her collegiate sisters in 1901, "The social side at college does more for a girl than the instruction that she receives from the professors. . . . A pleasant personality is much more to be desired and cultivated than the most profound intellect that lacks personality."[51]

These alumnae may have been writing from the heart, perhaps believing that their own collegiate experiences had been too centered on scholarship. Likely, though, they were also responding to a concern increasingly posited by social commentators and critics of the time: that college women were harming the nation by shunning marriage and children in selfish pursuit of their own careers.

In the early 1900s, the issue of "race suicide" became a prominent one in American society, fed by social commentators such as G. Stanley Hall and Charles Eliot and thrust into the spotlight by President Theodore Roosevelt, who delivered an address on the topic to Congress in 1905. White Anglo-Saxons in America were committing "race suicide," they argued, and none were more to blame than the highly educated, white, middle- and upper-middle-class college-educated women who were marrying later and less often than their peers of other classes and races and who were bearing fewer children than their nonwhite, non-Protestant, and foreign-born peers. Unfeminine and self-centered, these women were focusing on their careers and leaving the future leadership of the nation "in the hands of immigrants from Central and Eastern Europe whose fertility was quite high, but whose intellect was deemed inferior."[52]

Oft-cited statistics spoke volumes in support of this argument: while an average of 3.7 children was needed from every married woman able to bear offspring in order to sustain the size of the Anglo-Saxon race, the average number of children born to college-educated mothers fell far below that in the time period, to less than two for some groups of graduates and as low as .84 for other alumnae. College women bore fewer than half as many children as did the general population of women of their age.[53] And prior to the 1910s, college women did indeed marry later and less often than their age peers. Though these differences were less striking between collegians—disproportionately high numbers of whom hailed from the white middle- and upper-middle classes—and other members of the same demographic group than they were between collegians and their age cohorts in the general female population, the fact remained that higher education correlated with lower marriage rates, especially for the first-generation collegians. And even when marriage rates accelerated in the 1910s, the low birthrate for collegians remained; thus the charges of "race suicide" swirled.[54] Sensitive even as collegians about focusing on academics to the detriment of womanliness, the alumnae fraternity women of the first generation likely recoiled from these charges and strove to combat them as best they could. Reminding their younger sisters of the benefits of socializing with peers potentially served this purpose.

In an environment in which social opportunities took precedence over academic or literary training, the traits regarded as desirable in a sister also changed. Whereas the fraternity women of the previous generation had spent their time critiquing one another's academic and literary productions, the Thetas, Kappas, and Pi Phis of the second generation focused on appearances and social bearings when judging one another and providing instruction and correction.

Between the late 1880s and roughly 1910, most collegiate chapters of Kappa Alpha Theta held criticism sessions in their weekly or biweekly meetings as a means of allowing members to voice judgments or air negative comments about fellow sisters.[55] In adopting this practice, the sisters ostensibly strove to create a forum in which each sister's character would be strengthened and improved by the feedback and criticism of her fellow Thetas. Some branches appointed particular members to serve as "critics," a job that entailed writing down and presenting at fraternity meetings various commentaries and criticisms of each woman in the chapter. Some used an anonymous method, whereby an unspecified sister handed her criticisms to the chapter president, who then read them aloud at fraternity meetings. Other groups, opposed to sharing their comments aloud, appointed a member, who, "in a spirit of fraternal love, should meet her sister and offer the criticism privately." Still other branches adopted more public systems that entailed "the name of each one on the roll (of those who were present) being presented and the bearer there is subjected to a critical examination." After an evening spent in this manner of criticism, one fraternity member observed, "It appears that many of us have much room for improvement."[56]

Most recording secretaries, whether intentionally or not, cast their accounts of the criticism sessions in terms laden with earnestness and desire for self-improvement. According to their entries, the Theta sisters found criticisms "highly profitable," especially when, as befitted the socially inclined Thetas of the 1890s and early 1900s, they centered on "personal appearance." Critical judgments by sisters, they noted, gave "the girls an opportunity to see themselves as others see them."[57] While in the secretaries' accounts, most Theta women found "good, straight-forward, and helpful criticisms" useful in making "everyone [feel] an earnest desire to try very hard to overcome their habits, conquer . . . unruly dispositions and develop womanliness so essential to every girl's nature," occasional sisters admitted to finding criticisms a "nightmare" and a "terrible torture chamber method." As one sister put it, sharing personal criticisms at meetings represented an "inquisition" that served as "the bane of my existence when an undergraduate."[58]

Despite the largely personal nature of many of the criticisms, the rather surface topics they addressed, and the potential they bore for hurt feelings among those chastised, the women of Kappa Alpha Theta, according to their meeting minutes, claimed that the practice of exchanging judgments was central to teaching one another how to look, act, and be a "true Theta." "Kind admonitions to fraternity members to remember their vows and uphold them" served to reinforce among sisters the responsibilities they bore for upholding the fraternity's good name.[59] Appointing seniors and chapter officers to determine and present the criticisms added to the weight and seriousness the members accorded their judgments. According to one Theta, "Much of the true spirit of our fraternity was manifested in giving and receiving criticism. We all felt the better for the experience." Whether this was in actuality the case, the sisters went to great lengths to note their satisfaction with this practice in their private meeting minutes.[60]

Many alumnae members of Kappa Alpha Theta applauded their younger sisters' intentions in trying to correct perceived faults in their fellow members. "Not alone faults of character, but disagreeable and inelegant personal traits should be made the subject of criticism. . . . No fault should be too great, no personal negligence too slight to be legitimately considered within the field of fraternity criticism," one alumna editor of the *Kappa Alpha Theta* wrote.[61] Other writers in the fraternity journal concurred. Tying criticism and the willingness to tell offenders of their faults to fraternity loyalty and the responsibilities inherent in Theta membership, one sister declared, "Under the instruction received in the fraternity, imparted through the medium of criticism, all the better parts of our nature are made to stand out more boldly in relief. . . . The desire of self is made subservient to the best interests of others." Indeed, she argued, "Take away the molding influence of fraternity life, and the result is nothing that bears a semblance to sisterhood."[62] Another Theta praised the benefits of criticism, but also warned of its dangers, cautioning, "Criticism is a good thing—a most excellent thing, but, like other good and excellent things, is better taken in small doses and at the right time."[63] Urging them to preserve "that feeling of sisterhood which will allow us to say no slighting word of a friend to a third person," the woman advised the undergraduate Thetas that if they found faults in the characters of their sisters, to tell them to the offenders' faces, rather than whispering behind their backs.[64]

With their attentions and even their criticisms centered more on appearances and social concerns than on academic accomplishments, the fraternity women of the 1890s and early 1900s shifted their criteria for selecting new women upon whom to "pin" their fraternity "colors." No longer primarily concerned, as were their predecessors, with a prospective initiate's grades or faculty recommendations, the second generation of sisters sought instead to pledge the prettiest and most sociable women from among the new crop of female collegians arriving on campus each year. From a primary concern with an individual's ability to perform well in her studies and sustain high grades throughout her collegiate career, the members of the 1890s and 1900s began instead to seek out more social students and ask only that those they picked display "a desire to be an earnest student."[65]

At a fraternity convention in 1881, the Theta sisters had done away with the six-month waiting period before making selections, because the rule at times prevented the fraternity from competing with other women's organizations that did not have such restrictions and so could issue bids for membership immediately. At the same time, however, the Theta women had formally instituted the process of "pledging" used by other women's organizations. Pledging entailed promising oneself to the fraternity at an early date, with the understanding that there would be a waiting period before initiation, so that both pledge and chapter might have the opportunity to get to know one another better.[66]

Selling the merits of their fraternity over other women's Greek-letter societies was not a new practice to the sisters of Kappa Alpha Theta. As early as 1875, Thetas on many campuses had competed actively for prospects with members of other women's societies.[67] Yet the comparatively friendly and playful rivalries of this earlier period paled in comparison to the battles waged by the women's fraternities of the 1890s, when eleven organizations consisting of anywhere from a handful to more than twenty chapters competed for members.[68] The arrival of Kappa Kappa Gamma, Pi Beta Phi, Alpha Phi, Delta Gamma, and other female fraternities onto the same campuses where Theta chapters existed prompted the sisters of these different societies to compete with each other to "rush" and then "pledge" the best new student prospects. With increasing numbers of female collegians choosing to pledge themselves to Greek-letter organizations, rivalries to claim the most promising new students increasingly consumed the energies of the fraternity women.[69]

Indeed, pressure to secure the most desirable new students upon arrival at school or risk losing them to other women's fraternities prompted the fraternity women to woo quickly those whom they found the most "taking."[70] An editor of the *Kappa Alpha Theta* journal described the "rush" process as one where, "in order to have the first opportunity of presenting their respective merits, rival fraternities carry the contest over a new student so far that it assumes the appearance of a Freshman rope-pull."[71] An entry in Theta's Tau chapter minutes from this period demonstrates the competition the Theta sisters felt to win prospects away from other organizations. While gratified at having initiated six "charming new girls" into their chapter, the Tau members were most pleased that by winning these students for Theta, they had gotten "ahead of [their] sister sororities."[72]

On most campuses, Kappa Kappa Gamma served as Theta's main competitor.[73] Founded only one month after Theta and boasting roughly the same number of chapters, the Kappas competed successfully against the Thetas throughout the nineteenth and early twentieth centuries, armed as they were with essentially the same level of tradition, reputation for prestige, and network of supportive alumnae. This competition led the Theta sisters to take extreme measures to secure the pledges of the most desirable new girls. According to an account of the rushing season at the University of Illinois in the late 1890s, "With five sororities rivalry was rife. . . . Rushing and bidding might take place at any time, and usually did. Representatives of several sororities often met a train if it was known when a likely freshman was arriving, and sometimes the most aggressive was able to get a girl's consent to pledge almost before she realized what was happening."[74]

At the University of Kansas, the Theta sisters reported similar intensity:

Just now the news comes of another victory of our sisters over the I.C. [Sororis Society]'s and the K[appa] K[appa] G[amma]'s—Edith Clark has given her pledge to the Thetas. The contest was one of the most heated we have ever had, though our girls did all rushing in the most dignified manner, and entirely outside of the echoing corridors of the University. The young men were quite wrought up and arrayed themselves according to their own individual tastes, and behaved quite as they are said to do on presidential election occasions; yes, shall I say it—they staked money.[75]

The Thetas of the Alpha Xi chapter at the University of Oregon faced similar competition:

Rush week was one of the most strenuous and exciting that has ever been known at Oregon. From the time the girls were met at the train the night of their arrival until the morning of pledge-day, a week later, they were not lost sight of for a minute by the five nationals. Some rushees had their suitcases at one house, trunks at another, and themselves at still another. The days and nights were filled with formal and informal parties, as well as individual rushing stunts. George Fitch's Siwash stories were put to shame in the face of some of the events taking place here on pledge-day; kidnapping even being resorted to by one of the prominent nationals in the case of an attractive freshman.[76]

Letters written in 1897 by a Theta at the University of Nebraska demonstrated the air of high stakes and excitement that surrounded her chapter's "rush" to win a particularly desirable prospect:

October 5: The Greeks are waging the fiercest of battles over Miss [Selma] Wiggenhorn. The Kappas had her up here this summer, but would not let anyone else meet her. We did not rush her much before last week, then we went with a rush and have been the most devoted of lovers all the week. We have carried her off bodily before the Kappas' very eyes. Friday we are to have a glorious moonlight tally-ho ride. Then perhaps we will be ready to issue her an invitation. Today the Kappas have looked like graveyards, and called a special solemn conclave. We are devoured with curiosity to know the wherefore. It is great fun!

Sunday, October 30: We are still rushing Selma. The Kappas saw they could not get her, and so have withdrawn their invitation. We had never considered the Delta Gammas as rivals, but they campaigned so vigorously that we began to get uneasy. Some of our lovely alumnae also got excited on the subject, with the result that Selma is just about to live with us until next Friday when she is going home to get permission to join a fraternity. Friday evening, she was in our rooms at a little fudge party. We had a pretty chafing dish, and the girls had a very cozy time together.

Sunday, November 14: Hurrah! Hurrah! Victory! Selma is ours! We are as happy a crowd of girls as you can find in the U.S. She is so sweet![77]

Like Rho chapter's battle for Selma Wiggenhorn, most branches of Kappa Alpha Theta found themselves in struggles to woo particularly desirable pledges away from other women's societies. To win these competitions, the Theta branches generally staged elaborate "rush parties" and other functions in the hopes that such a display would convince desirable candidates to join Theta. While individual chapters used different methods to attract those they labeled "good Theta material," each branch of the fraternity used parties and other forms of social outings as their primary means of enticing new students.

"Spreads," teas, and receptions served as the most common forms of rush entertainment in the 1890s, while after the turn of the century, card parties, dances, and other, more structured events gained popularity.[78] The number of parties each chapter organized varied by campus and year to year, in accordance with the rules that governed rush at different times and on the different campuses. Some Theta chapters entertained high school students over the summers preceding matriculation at college and then pledged them upon arrival on campus, while others "rushed heavily" in the first few weeks of the fall semester by holding weekly parties for a specific period such as a month and then issued their invitations. Still

T.B.D. (standing for "Truth, Beauty, Development") was a well-established local society at the University of South Dakota when its members petitioned Kappa Alpha Theta for a charter and membership in the national organization. The group was installed as Theta's Alpha Rho chapter in 1912. In this photograph, ca. 1908, the sisters gathered together for tea and treats. (Courtesy of Kappa Alpha Theta Fraternity, © 2003.

other chapters held one function each month and chose their pledges over the course of a full semester.[79]

To outdo the other societies on campus with the grandeur or cleverness of their functions in the hopes of winning the "likeliest" pledges, sisters of the different branches of Kappa Alpha Theta frequently turned to members of other chapters for advice on types of parties, attractive decorations, and other methods of enticing students to pick Kappa Alpha Theta over all the other societies on campus. In the fraternity journal, the sisters wrote descriptions of the affairs their chapters organized and extolled the virtues of the type of function they had chosen. For example, in a 1912 issue of the *Kappa Alpha Theta,* a member of the Alpha Delta chapter at Goucher College claimed the benefits of a walking party, while a sister of the Tau chapter noted that a matinee dance "was informal enough for the freshmen to feel at ease and enjoy themselves . . . [and] for this reason [the chapter] had a better chance to judge and perhaps to be judged." Most of the chapters chose activity-centered functions such as drives, dances, theater trips, and picnics as their chosen form of attracting desirable pledges, though some Thetas strove for novelty, such as the members of the Kappa chapter at Kansas, who organized a "rest party" on the assumption that most rushees would be tired and frazzled from too many social affairs hosted by other organizations on campus. Even at a function at which "everyone was told to entertain herself just as she pleased," however, the Thetas still provided enticements to their would-be members. At the Kansas chapter "rest party," the sisters "dressed in kimonos, and the rushees were ushered into a Beauty parlor where they were manicured, massaged, and made beautiful by three of our girls dressed as French maids."[80]

The entertainment, favors, and refreshments provided at even an affair as simple as the Kansas Thetas' "rest party" increased the chapter expenses for the fraternity women of the 1890s and early 1900s. According to chapter reports sent to the Beta branch in 1907, the sisters of the Phi chapter at Stanford University spent $180 on rushing fees. In the Upsilon chapter at the University of Minnesota, each of the fourteen members was assessed $2.00 each per month, mainly to pay for the $250 worth of costs they racked up during rush. At the University of California, each of the twenty-two members contributed $2.50 per month and together paid $125 for rush expenses. In 1909, the chapter raised the cost of monthly dues to $3.00 and collectively paid $222 for rush parties and functions, an amount that at the time could have paid the monthly room and board for six sisters.[81]

The high price of rush functions on most campuses led the Theta sisters and their Greek letter peers to select early the women upon whom they would lavish such costly attention, to rule out wasting energy and money on those they did not want as members.[82] Indeed, whereas rush had taken place on an informal and fairly individualized basis in the early decades of the women's Greek system, in the decades surrounding the turn of the twentieth century, most chapters of Kappa Alpha Theta, Kappa Kappa Gamma, Pi Beta Phi, and other women's fraternities instituted more systematized methods for identifying likely candidates. By the early 1890s, most chapters adopted the practice of appointing "spiking committees" to work over the summer, to gather lists of the names of those women who would be enrolling at their schools in the fall and identify who among this group would be "promising" candidates. At the start of each fall term, most Theta chapters would assign each sister a list of "girls to be looked at," fining those who failed to meet with and assess their assignees. "Likely prospects" would then be entertained at "rush parties" and other "spiking drives," in the hopes that the fraternity would win them away from the other women's societies.[83]

In selecting their prospective members, the second generation of fraternity sisters took little time to learn anything of the academic abilities of their would-be pledges. In marked contrast to the practices of their predecessors, most chapters of Kappa Alpha Theta and the other women's fraternities picked and pledged their candidates in the 1890s and early 1900s without regard to academic performance but instead, based their decisions upon looks, amiability, and social performance. In Theta's case, once it had pledged a new prospect, if her grades proved below fraternity average, the fraternity adopted one of three stances: members either helped the desired woman make some improvement in her studies, waited for her to perform better, or simply waived the fraternity's minimum requirements for grades and initiated the chosen one anyway.[84] Picking and choosing their candidates based upon appearances and social graces exhibited at hurried rush functions, the second generation of fraternity women essentially altered the meaning they imputed to their organizations' ideal. Whereas the older sisters had foremost looked for evidence of intellectual capacity among the triad of qualities—intellectual, social, and moral—the Thetas, Kappas, Alpha Phis, and Pi Phis of the 1890s and early 1900s elevated social graces and introduced clothes and appearance as the main criteria for selecting members.

Kappa Alpha Theta, more so than some of the other women's fraternities, claimed "successful rushes" each year, in that its chapters managed to pledge nearly all the women they sought. "On pledge day," one Theta chapter noted, "we gave thirteen invitations and received thirteen enthusiastic affirmative replies. . . . Since then we have pledged another freshman . . . our fourteen freshman pledges are without doubt the pick of the freshman."[85] A survey conducted by Theta in 1914 found that while the chapters had pledged 135 women and initiated an additional 125, only twenty-one invitations issued were "lost," meaning that the person offered a bid had chosen not to enter Kappa Alpha Theta. In all, only twelve of Theta's thirty-five chapters had any of their invitations declined. Of the twenty-one students who chose not to become Thetas, twelve joined other fraternities and the rest remained non-Greeks.[86]

For many of the women being rushed by women's fraternities and sororities in the 1890s and early 1900s, Greek-letter membership would have proven attractive. The finest parties and most enticing social events on campus were sponsored by the Greek societies, and invitations to the best entertainments generally went to those wearing a fraternity badge, as did most of the honors, distinctions, awards, and positions.[87] Undoubtedly, many would have heard from friends and acquaintances about the social benefits accorded Greek-letter women. Likely many would also have read magazine articles and novels that contained descriptions of Greek life and the hold exerted by fraternities and sororities on campus social and extracurricular life.

Those who enrolled in college in the early years of the twentieth century would have arrived on campus expecting to engage in social as well as scholastic endeavors. *Harper's Bazaar, Good Housekeeping, Woman's Home Companion,* and especially the *Ladies Home Journal* published articles and pictures that detailed campus life, and numerous novels such as *The Bent Twig* also detailed the noncurricular endeavors of the day's "coeds." In a practice that historian Lynn Gordon linked to a conscious desire on the part of Progressive education reformers to portray collegiate women in a nonthreatening light and thereby quell societal concerns that they were harming the nation by becoming so engrossed in their studies and careers that they were refusing to take on the "proper" female roles of wife and mother, these articles and novels helped paint a portrait of "the college girl" as a "typical, fun-loving, middle class Gibson Girl." Establishing her in the popular imagination as pretty, sociable, and fun, these pieces helped construct an image of college women that was safe and attractive, a long and welcome replacement for the aggressive, manly, threatening scholar that previously had served as the popular model of women's higher education. Even while they undercut the scholarship of college women and reduced the complexities of their lives to jokes and frivolities, these pieces helped reassure a worried public that college was a good place for women.[88]

"College Girls' Larks and Pranks" served as the title for several installments in the *Ladies Home Journal* that recounted the social side of college life. "There is scarcely a girl, even the most sedate, who, having been through college, has not some excellent joke to tell if she would," one graduate wrote in her column, subtitled, "A Collection of New and Amusing Stories by Bright Students." Recounting tales of costume parties, pranks played on classmates, missed curfews, and midnight feasts, her article and the other pieces bearing the same name extolled the fun of college. "The College Scrapes We Got Into," "When College Girls Have Their Fun," and "Mapcap Frolics of College Girls" all served to underscore the importance of the social side of women's higher education. "What a Girl Does in College," a series of photographic essays published in the *Ladies Home Journal,* presented a strikingly playful image of collegiate females, offering images of women acting in plays and musicals, engaging in sports, posing alongside sorority sisters, and "at her fun and in her room." Only one installment of the series presented college as a place for study.[89]

Popular novels, too, stressed the nonscholastic side of college, and no female collegian appeared to benefit more from the social and extracurricular emphasis than the sorority member. As Shirley Marchalonis discussed in *College Girls: A Century in Fiction,* Greek-letter membership served as a defining characteristic in many stories published in the early twentieth century. Novels set on college campuses invariably presented sorority women as the most popular, as well as among the wealthiest and prettiest, of the "coeds." While some novels used the sorority sister as a foil against which to construct a serious, hardworking, poor, and/or morally righteous heroine, all served to reaffirm in readers' minds the link between Greek-letter affiliation and popularity on campus—popularity based on extracurricular and social involvement, rather than on intellectual or scholastic pursuits.[90]

For example, whereas *The Bent Twig* presented sororities as shallow and elitist in their selection processes, it, like nearly all other stories of the time period focusing on college life, posited sorority membership as a key to acceptability and peer recognition on campus. Even while damning them for their narrow-mindedness in not, for example, selecting a bright and charming rushee simply because she was poor, novels such as these still reaffirmed in readers' minds the link between fun on campus and Greek-letter affiliation.[91]

Popular magazines also fueled this link. The *Ladies Home Journal* published pictures of sorority chapters, along with articles glorifying the fun of college life for women.[92] An article in *Harper's Bazaar* carefully laid out the histories of several of the women's societies and likened the relationships shared by sorority sisters to Emerson's notion of the

In the early 1900s, fraternity members spent a great deal of their time planning and carrying out social affairs and outings. Butler University Thetas, like their peers in many other chapters, enjoyed picnics away from campus. (Courtesy of Kappa Alpha Theta Fraternity, © 2003.)

"perfect friendship," in which "each pair of friends is bound together by tender ties of intimacy to others."[93]

As in the case of novels about college life, even articles that painted unflattering portraits of sorority life testified to the powerful role these organizations played on campus. "Confessions of a Co-Ed," an anonymous article published in *The Independent* in 1907, noted the influential sway sororities held over newly arrived female collegians at the same time as it criticized the shallowness of the Greek system: "A sorority stands for social life, and its rating by the popular minds is made on that basis . . . the 'best' sorority is the one which represents the largest money backing and is formed of girls who make the best appearance in dress and are the most attractive on the ballroom floor." While the point of the article and others like it was to show readers that "it is the independent who alone can drink deep the democratic spirit of college life," the author still—perhaps unwittingly—reaffirmed in readers' minds the notion that sorority membership meant popularity, and thus desire for popularity meant rushing a secret society.[94]

An average of roughly one-third of the female students enrolled in college in the late 1890s belonged to a fraternity, and on some campuses, such as Cornell University, Allegheny College, and the College of Wooster, that number hovered above 60 percent.[95] In schools such as Northwestern University, where the Greek system claimed roughly 50 percent of the women students enrolled in the College of Liberal Arts, the pressure on new collegians to rush and win membership to a fraternity or sorority prompted one woman to write to her parents in September of 1890, "I hope that I shall be invited to join the fraternity . . . [because] a person is nobody at all if they are not a member of some frat." She added, "It will be very expensive to join, but I wouldn't go through the year for anything in the world hardly without joining if they ask me. It would be a thousand percent pleasanter if I could join that frat., than it would be to not."[96]

Kappa Alpha Theta's status as one of the oldest women's collegiate societies, as well as its reputation for taking in only the "finest material," helped it establish and maintain an aura of selectivity and desirability that similar organizations lacked. In 1895, a University of California campus newspaper, the *Berkeley Bulletin*, captured this image of the fraternity in its description of the Omega chapter at that institution:

> Of the three girls fraternities, the Kappa Alpha Theta is the oldest and has the best standing and most members. . . . It prides itself on being "nice" . . . nice in a quite particular and peculiar sense. All the members are pretty, flower-like girls, daintily dressed and coming from old, conservative intellectual families. They are recognized instantaneously. "Ah, that is a Kappa Alpha Theta, in the blue shirt waist with the golden hair and the graceful bearing."[97]

A letter written by a woman from Vermont also pointed up Theta's preeminence among women's fraternities. Advising a friend at Brown University whose small society was looking to merge with one of the national women's fraternities, Grace Bosworth recommended Kappa Alpha

Theta. "[T]here is only one other which is as large or as strong [as Theta], and that is Kappa Kappa Gamma, though there Kappa Alpha Theta takes the precedence because she is a little more select in her choice of girls; at least that is the rule in all colleges where they can be fairly judged, i.e. where there is a chapter of each."[98] Numerous letters sent to the fraternity by faculty members, administrators, and other parties throughout the country attested to popular belief in the "superior rank" of Theta and its great prestige both within and outside college walls.[99] An account written of campus life in the 1890s at the College of Wooster in Ohio noted that the "most popular" women on campus, the ones who "had beauty, wit, or more and prettier clothes than the others . . . were the ones for whom . . . the Thetas usually put on colors in the fall."[100] As testimony to the desirability many associated with the fraternity, the Theta women on several occasions discovered nonmembers wearing their badge in attempts to pass as sisters.[101]

While Kappa Alpha Theta had, since its inception, maintained an aura of selectivity and exclusiveness that made it desirable to far more women than it took into its number, the fraternity was not known in its early years as a bastion of wealth. Claiming the daughters of a professor, a minister, and a farmer among their founding members, the sisters of the first generation of Kappa Alpha Theta did not actively seek, nor did they specifically desire, wealthy women as their fellow members.[102] Yet the bolstered social concerns of the Theta sisters of the 1890s and early 1900s and the increased costs of fraternity dues and fees that accompanied these changes in focus meant that Kappa Alpha Theta began to attract, and to a certain extent sought, those women who could afford to pay for the lavish lifestyles pursued by most of the chapters. As a result, by the turn of the century, the fraternity had acquired the reputation of a "rich girls'" society.

A letter written by a non-Greek student at Northwestern University suggested this link between Kappa Alpha Theta and a moneyed element. The women who belonged to Theta, the young collegian wrote, were "all society . . . and that means a *good deal.*" She described the fraternity as a "rich girls' sorority," and somewhat wistfully concluded that she would never be asked to join, as her family lacked the financial means to make her a desirable candidate for membership.[103] Whereas prior to the turn of the century, the Delta chapter at Illinois, for example, had pledged women whose fathers worked as farmers, grain merchants, and nursery men, by the middle of the first decade of the twentieth century, the women who received Theta bids at that university generally hailed from the upper echelons of society, the daughters of company executives, bankers, doctors, and lawyers.[104] In 1905, an officer of Kappa Alpha Theta acknowledged the fraternity's predilection for wealthy rushees when, perhaps only partly seriously, she remarked that the fraternity should adopt the "Three C's" of character (which she equated with congeniality), clothes, and cash as its motto for selecting new members.[105]

This officer's perhaps playful comment pointed out in stark terms the changes that had taken place within Kappa Alpha Theta and its fellow Greek-letter societies. From organizations dedicated to helping their members make a place for their sex on campus, the women's fraternities by the turn of the twentieth century had become largely social entities. From groups that had taken months to choose their members and had done so mainly along academic lines, these societies now pledged their members based on little more than looks, money, and ephemeral social graces.

This changed focus in the women's fraternities mirrored and at the same time encouraged changes that were taking place in wider campus culture in the 1890s and early 1900s. As more affluent students were coming to campus, social class distinctions were becoming more apparent on campuses with and without Greek systems. As Horowitz showed in her study of women's colleges, even at places such as Vassar and Wellesley—institutions without formal Greek systems—class distinctions cleaved the student body. "Students divided themselves into sets, or cliques, which formed a hierarchical scale which 'the swells' sat atop." Some schools reinforced the divisions by setting aside special rooms for those with money and connections. Others sought to overcome the schisms by offering entertainments designed specifically to appeal to all students no matter what their backgrounds, looks, or personalities.[106]

While it may be easy to blame the Greek system for causing the rifts that increasingly divided students along class lines in the early twentieth century, it is more accurate to say that fraternities reflected divisions that were forming anyway and in some instances perhaps furthered those divisions. Certainly, the women's—and men's—fraternities, with their emphasis on lavish entertainments and over-the-top expenditures, helped delineate between the moneyed and their less-wealthy peers. Although it is not clear that, as some critics have argued, the Greek system caused divisions along social lines, it is abundantly clear that its members—as individuals and as fraternity sisters and brothers—helped reinforce divisions by pricing their entertainments high and by choosing as new members mainly those whose wealth and social manners matched their own.

This predilection for wealth and appearance did not go unchallenged within the fraternity world. Alumnae members, the collegians of the 1870s and 1880s, reacted strongly to the change in focus of their successors. Quick selection, coupled with the surface criteria of appearance, clothes, evidence of wealth, and social bearing brought with it the danger that a woman might be selected too hastily, before her character, background, morality, and virtues could be assessed. A "taking" appearance and a winning sociability were easy to manufacture, the older sisters recognized. Well accustomed to nineteenth-century advice givers' warnings that "confidence men" and "painted women" possessed the abilities to "manipulate . . . personal appearance in a calculated effort to lure the guileless into granting them confidence," many alumnae worried that the "wrong" kind of person possessing the "right" kind of appearance might sneak her way into the "mystic circle" of the fraternity before the sisters could uncover her true character.[107]

In an article in the *Kappa Alpha Theta,* for example, one first-generation Theta argued that the speed with which the collegiate members were selecting their pledges "gave no time either to the new student or the fraternity, for discovering each other's merits; for each fraternity was ever fearful lest it should wait too long to take the decisive step and thus suffer serious loss."[108] Another alumna warned her collegiate sisters that "girls who are the most 'taking' upon a short acquaintance are often undesirable in the close intimacy of sisterhood." Quick selection brought with it the danger of choosing individuals "as to whose standing, mentally, morally, and socially it may be somewhat posted, but is oftener ignorant." She continued:

> Only personal acquaintance can develop the fact whether or not a girl will be congenial in a sisterly relation. Mind, manners and morals may be entirely unexceptionable, and yet the broad, generous nature, the quick, sympathetic heart, which is the "sine qua non" of true fraternity, may be wanting. The feeling of genuine fellowship is fostered and developed by constant association in the same society, but is not "made to order." It cannot exist between acquaintances of a few days' standing.[109]

Other alumnae took up similar threads. In one treatise, a first-generation Theta declared that rushing, in addition to being undignified and boisterous . . . is also disastrous to the fraternity. It is impossible to form a correct judgment of a girl, to decide justly whether she will make a desirable and congenial Theta or not, when we have known her as a college girl only a few days; and especially as the circumstances of that short acquaintance are such that the real character of the candidate for membership cannot possibly be brought out.

Given the dire consequences of pledging someone who might turn out to be less than the fraternity originally thought, the woman reminded her sisters: "It is better to lose two girls we want, than, by over-hasty judgment, to initiate one whom we do not want, after we know her."[110]

Numerous and pointed, the critiques offered by the alumnae women regarding their successors' selections included explicit and implicit commentaries on the changing social class structure of late-nineteenth-century America. Running through their arguments were class-based fears that, unbeknownst to them, the fraternities might take into their number members of the "nouveaux riches" or the "petite bourgeoisie," both groups that lacked the proper background and pedigree to belong to Theta, but by copying the clothes and manners of the old establishment, could dupe the unknowing into accepting them as members. As these groups grew in number and influence in the United States, so too grew the danger that they would infiltrate the women's Greek system.[111]

Demonstrating their belief that money did not equal fine standing, many alumnae, in addition to critiquing the undergraduates for their speed and carelessness in selection, also took exception to the great expenses the collegiate chapters were taking on in their rush efforts. In an article entitled "Chapter Finance," published in the *Kappa Alpha Theta* in 1894, a member of the fraternity who had graduated in 1880 admonished her collegiate sisters to watch the costs they incurred. She reminded the active members that "the money which must be spent for chapter expenses does not properly belong to the individuals contributing it." Attacking the collegiate sisters for their "extravagance," "love of display," and "inordinate appetite for 'splurge,'" she wrote, "Unless we as Thetas make a determined stand against this tendency, we shall invariably lose the kind of women we wish to secure. That high-thinking and simple-living, which has in all times been the ideal of the cultured and the scholar, should be ours."[112] In another treatise on the same subject published several years later, the editors of the *Kappa Alpha Theta* penned their continued disapproval regarding the undergraduate sisters' penchant for costly displays. They wrote,

> When we count up the funds expended for rushing, flowers, refreshments, and other accoutrements to amusing ourselves and friends, we are face to face with the fact that our fun has cost a good deal. Usually the cost is out of all proportion to the fun, for is it the formal, elaborate—and expensive—function we really enjoy and recall with pleasure, or the genuine hospitality—with decorations, favors, etc., playing but a minor part?

While willing to acknowledge that some expenditures could be justified, the editors noted that there was "genuine rejoicing when [they had] the opportunity to call attention to the always present, though modest, other side of the shield."[113]

In their efforts to encourage their younger members to show greater "prudence" in their rushing and entertaining habits, the alumnae Thetas found allies among the older members of other women's fraternities and sororities. Across the board, Greek-letter women of the first generation found the behavior and customs of their successors both shocking and in need of reform.[114] So displeased with undergraduate chapter conditions were the alumnae of Alpha Phi Fraternity that, in 1902, they invited representatives of Kappa Alpha Theta and seven of the other most prominent women's societies to come together "for the purpose of discussing the question of pledging and rushing." Through collaborative agreements, the older women hoped, policies could be enacted to guide their collegiate sisters to change their ways.[115]

The early meetings of the Inter-Sorority Council, renamed the National Panhellenic Congress (NPC) in 1908, dealt almost exclusively with selection and pledging rules. The representatives who attended the meetings on behalf of the fraternities struggled to overhaul a rushing system that they as alumnae women considered both "hasty" and "extravagant."[116] They crafted recommendations calling for late pledge days, for better cooperation among the members of the different fraternities and sororities, and for a curbing of the "extravagant expenditure and excess of social function" that the rush period invariably provoked. They argued out the parameters and intricacies that would define rush.[117]

Alarmed by what they termed the "spurious growth" of the colleges and critical of the social conditions that existed on most campuses as a result, the representatives to the meetings struggled to enact legislation that would bind all Greek-letter women to abide by certain standards of conduct. As one woman told the gathered representatives in 1904, on college campuses of the day "there are no social regulations and the social standards are more those of the village than those approved by the best society in the respective States." To keep their collegiate members from acting in ways that would bring disrepute to their organizations, the women's fraternities needed to take action. "The true fraternity has for its purpose the betterment and improvement of its members," one sister argued. "This involves adherence to principles of living and conduct that society will respect and admire."[118] Bent on ensuring that the women who wore their badges would adhere to higher standards, the representatives enacted codes of behavior and drew up policies for conduct, all aimed at preventing their younger sisters from making "hasty" choices during rush, from engaging in "suggestive" or "indecent" conduct, and from taking part in "extravagant entertainment" or "the doing of anything for mere show."[119] They urged:

> By living up to the ideals established by their orders and by means of their organized strength, the College Greek Letter Fraternity can, by proper co-operation with faculties and with the non-fraternity men and women, not only disarm every criticism now so justly made against higher co-education, but can render a service to women and to the world of education such as it would be impossible to describe or even conceive.[120]

Earnest in their efforts and sincere in their intentions, the alumnae representatives to the congress who enacted these codes possessed little scope to enforce them and no means for punishing transgressors. In the NPC as in the individual member organizations, the alumnae sisters lacked the formal powers to force change in the actions and behavior of their younger members. Thus, like the missives of reprimand and disapproving articles penned by the Theta alumnae concerning the actions and behavior of the turn-of-the-century collegians, the codes and recommendations drawn up by the delegates had little effect in controlling the conduct of the undergraduates. Plead and admonish as they might, the older members of Kappa Alpha Theta and the other Greek-letter societies for women found their messages essentially ignored and their warnings largely unheeded.[121]

Indeed, with the sisters of the 1890s and early 1900s holding strikingly different ideas and attitudes than had their predecessors regarding what fraternity life ought to entail and how and on what bases new sisters ought to be chosen, Kappa Alpha Theta and its fellow women's fraternities faced challenges to their unity in the decades surrounding the turn of the twentieth century. As the undergraduate chapters expanded rapidly, the first-generation members, now alumnae, watched with alarm as newly pledged sisters who had been hastily picked for their looks or social graces went about their business with fraternity pins affixed to their chests but with little understanding of what this meant. They worried aloud, in journal articles and in letters, that their organizations risked infiltration by frauds, those with looks and money—or the appearance of money—who lacked the proper breeding and the morals and character that would make them worthy of fraternity membership.

In an article published in the *Kappa Alpha Theta* in 1906, one alumna gave voice to these concerns. She wrote, "Every chapter has experienced a barrier, variably slight or great, between its alumnae and active members. It comes inevitably from a misunderstanding of some sort. 'The girls now are not like those of our time. Do you think their standards are the same?' is a repetitional [*sic*] remark." To remedy this, she urged that a "specific code by which to choose and guide new members" be adopted by each chapter, so that "the relation between alumnae and active members would be improved."[122] An alumna officer of Theta voiced even more pointedly the older generation's fears of the type of woman being initiated in their fraternity by the collegians of the second generation. In an address to the 16th Biennial Convention of the fraternity in 1905, the officer admonished the collegiate chapters for their overly hasty rush and selection processes by commanding:

> Stop and think a moment. When you initiate, what does it mean? Forever, nothing less. For better and for worse, nothing less. You give her *our* pin, you give her *our* name. She stands as one of *us*, not merely as one of you. It is bigger than we realize, especially in the heat and nervousness of the rushing season. Therefore, take care . . . [that] not even the heat of competition in rushing-time blinds us to the fact that that girl who may wear our pin is going to be known all her life as a *Theta*; not in our little community, where she and her parents and the circumstances are known, but out in the world, where strangers judge our fraternity from one woman they see wearing our pin.[123]

Fearing that the sisters of the second generation held little understanding of the meaning of sisterhood or the obligation it placed on each member to act as a representative of the whole, the older fraternity women, those who had been collegians in the 1870s and 1880s, pushed to institute new rules and educational programs, so that all sisters regardless of age or chapter would hold the same understanding of the responsibilities, as well as rights, entailed in wearing a fraternity badge. As they would find, these attempts at uniformity would prove challenging, especially as the women's fraternities developed into nationwide organizations with branches on scores of collegiate campuses and memberships that represented different social, cultural, geographic, and generational worldviews.

3

A National Society to Rank with the First in America

Expansion and Exclusion in the Women's Greek System

Upon taking their oaths of loyalty to Kappa Alpha Theta, Kappa Kappa Gamma, or any of the other leading women's fraternities, new initiates became part of a nationwide fraternal network and not just of the particular chapter into which they were initiated. The vows required of sisters, that they pledge to "befriend and to comfort, to assist, support and defend the members of this fraternity in all their laudable efforts toward a higher intellectual and moral life and like-wise to have a due regard for their temporal wants, if occasion should require," covered all women no matter their age, geographic location, or place in society.[1]

In their ideal, the vows binding all sisters together served as the very basis of the fraternal relationship, enabling as they did extensive networks of support, assistance, and friendship. They fostered ties that brought rewards for those who took them, opening academic, extracurricular, social, and even vocational doors that otherwise may have remained closed.[2] At the same time, though, these bonds of sisterhood also brought complications, as their relatively broad-reaching nature—in encompassing members of multiple social, cultural, generational, geographical, and socioeconomic backgrounds[3]—created situations in which women sharing little in common other than a fraternity badge found themselves in "sisterly" relationships with one another, expected to support and nurture one another because all had taken a pledge of loyalty to the same organization. As Kappa Alpha Theta and its fellow women's fraternities developed into nationwide networks comprising many thousands of women, maintaining a sense of unity among members and common ideals for the organizations proved challenging.

By 1900, enough women had pledged themselves to a secret society that members of a particular group no longer came from similar social, geographic, and cultural backgrounds. Indeed, between 1879, the first year for which such statistics exist, and 1920, Kappa Alpha Theta alone ballooned from 275 members to a total of 8,133 members, 677 of them active collegians and the rest alumnae. During the same period of time, the average size of each college chapter expanded, from anywhere between roughly four and nine members in the first two decades of the fraternity's existence to between 33 and 46 by 1920. Kappa Kappa Gamma experienced even greater growth, expanding from 558 members in 1883 to 9,329 in 1920, a number exceeded only by Pi Beta Phi's 10,571.[4]

Along with this growth in membership, Kappa Alpha Theta, like its rivals, also expanded its reach by adding new chapters in a process the fraternity world called "extension." Between 1870 and 1880, the founding chapter of Kappa Alpha Theta helped form several other branches, four of which remained in operation at the close of the decade. In the next ten years, the fraternity added eleven more branches, for a total of sixteen chapters. By 1900, Kappa Alpha Theta boasted twenty-two active chapters comprising a collegiate membership of 401 women, and in the next ten years it added an additional eight branches for a total of thirty chapters. Theta's fiftieth year, 1920, marked the fraternity's growth to forty-three chapters, a number that brought Kappa Alpha Theta only one shy of Kappa Kappa Gamma's forty-four chapters.[5]

The soaring numbers of women pledging themselves to Greek-letter societies raised the profile of these organizations on campus and brought them greater networking capacities in social and vocational arenas. At the same time, such growth also increased tensions between different chapters of each fraternity and heightened conflicts over the meaning of fraternity membership. Opening a society to too many individuals brought the risk of weakening a fraternity's claim of including in its ranks only the worthiest female collegians. With so many women representing different viewpoints as well as social worlds united together under the banner of Kappa Alpha Theta, Kappa Kappa Gamma, or Pi Beta Phi, it was perhaps inevitable that conflict would develop over who among the collegiate women of the country should be allowed to join particular fraternities, what fraternities ought to represent, and what sisterhood and loyalty ought to mean.

Indeed, in Kappa Alpha Theta, from the time each chapter received its charter, the women who belonged to the different branches imbued their own particular group with a distinct identity, as dominant members who shared certain traits looked for the same characteristics in new members. While the influx of new Thetas each year occasionally caused the dominant motif of a chapter to change, each branch generally found itself known on its own campus for a particular set of characteristics. In their own colleges and universities, the Theta sisters may have thought little of their identities as chapters except in relation to other organizations or individuals on campus. Yet when brought together into larger Theta gatherings that included collegians of other chapters as well as alumnae members, the distinctions between the different groups of Thetas at times proved striking.

Especially with the fraternities' expansion and development in the early decades of the twentieth century, the Greek-letter societies began to show regional as well as campus-based differences. Faster methods of communication enabled these differences to be known, and friends and relatives as well as fellow Greeks proved eager to report to the fraternity women on their distant sisters' conduct. In addition, as improved transportation allowed for freer travel between locations and expanded opportunities for women in academic, extracurricular, and social settings increased the likelihood that fraternity members would be brought face-to-face with sisters of other chapters, differences in the character and identity of members of the same organizations came into striking relief. Issues of family background and religion joined concerns about sociability and class in the debates about who should and should not be admitted into their organizations. Geographical differences—in dress, social mores, and prejudices—complicated discussions, as sisters from across the country looked at the same people and the same settings and judged them differently, according to different standards and beliefs.

As more and more women looked to join Greek-letter societies in the decades following the turn of the twentieth century, latent beliefs about who was and was not worthy enough to be a fraternity member came roiling to the surface. As Kappa Alpha Theta and its fellow women's fraternities strove to expand their memberships and make themselves into national organizations with branches in all areas of the country, concurrent pressures mounted within their ranks to clarify and tighten the boundaries around whom and what they considered "appropriate material" for inclusion. Nationalization fostered increased conservatism within the women's Greek societies, as those who only a generation earlier had been campus outsiders because of their sex now looked to

preserve their newfound status as pillars of the collegiate—and societal—
establishment. With reputations now made or broken nationally and not
just in a single chapter on a single campus, organization-wide restrictions
and national policies designed to appeal to the most members became
standard practice in the female fraternities.

From the first, the women of Kappa Alpha Theta sought to form connections with members of other chapters. The first-generation Thetas exchanged lively correspondence with their sisters at other schools, detailing in their letters both fraternity business and news of their academic and
personal lives, and their successors had continued this practice through
their quarterly entries in the fraternity journal.[6] Eager to know more
about the women who comprised their sisterhood, the early Thetas
grasped at whatever bits of information they could find pertaining to far-
away members. "From two young men of Cornell and Leland Stanford,"
the Brown University Thetas reported, "we have learned what fine girls
are in our chapters at those universities." In a letter to a friend, another
sister stated proudly that the six Thetas she had met at a Y.W.C.A. convention "were all stylish, lovely girls."[7]

Strengthening the ties that bound sisters together served as the main
impetus behind the founding of journals for the women's fraternities. As
an editor of the *Kappa Alpha Theta* wrote in the first issue of the magazine, "We wish our chapters to learn something of the aims, objects, and
ideas of each. We expect to gain a broader information concerning the
colleges in which they are located . . . perhaps more than all else we wish
to gain an individual and social knowledge of our members."[8] Another
sister hoped for the journal that "it may prove a medium through which
alumna and under-graduate, chapter and chapter, may be more closely
bound together, thus promoting that perfect union which is essential to
our highest development."[9]

Yet, while word-of-mouth reports, correspondence, and entries to
their journals offered fraternity women glimpses into the personalities
and concerns of those who wore the same badge, they did not allow sisters to "know intimately" their fellow members. And so, from the first,
the sisters of Kappa Alpha Theta and other women's fraternities jumped
at the chance to meet and visit with one another. From the spring of 1870,
when members of the Alpha chapter of Kappa Alpha Theta traveled to
Bloomington to initiate a group of Indiana University students into the
fraternity, many members took opportunities to visit other chapters, to
see how Thetas on other campuses looked and acted and to form con-

nections with fellow sisters. The early meeting minutes of both Alpha and Beta chapters of Theta contain frequent references to sisters of different chapters being "in attendance" or "among our midst." As the fraternity grew, entries such as these increased in number, as did the frequency with which chapters wrote to the journal of visits and chance encounters shared by Thetas of different chapters.[10]

Initiations often brought members of various branches together, and in 1887, five sisters of the Alpha chapter and one member of the Delta chapter at Illinois Wesleyan met together in California, to take part in the installation ceremony of the Omicron chapter at the University of Southern California.[11] Traveling, too, served as strong impetus in prompting sisters to find fellow Thetas. In 1890, a sister from the Upsilon chapter at Minnesota sought out her fellow Thetas at the College of Wooster when her travels took her in their vicinity. The frequent conventions held by the Y.W.C.A. brought numerous Thetas of different chapters together, as many sisters—like their fellow members of other women's fraternities—served as both rank members and leaders for their campus branches of the organization.[12]

The growing popularity of intercollegiate football in the 1890s and early 1900s also helped create occasions upon which members of the same fraternity might meet one another. In a trend that developed singularly to the sport, female as well as male students began to travel with their teams to other campuses for games, forming spectator parties that often numbered in the thousands. Many Thetas—and Kappas and Pi Phis—took part in these activities, joining the members of other chapters for celebrations, dances, and socials when games were played at schools housing another chapter of their fraternity.[13]

During summers, sisters of different branches often met one another while attending summer school. In 1910, a group of fourteen Thetas, representing both alumnae and collegiate members of nine different chapters, found one another at Columbia University. A few years later, the University of Michigan Thetas opened their house to all sisters who might be attending summer school at Ann Arbor, and several members of multiple chapters took advantage of the accommodation by joining the Eta chapter for the term.[14] For those not inclined toward summer study, travel and visits to summer resort spots often brought them into contact with other sisters. In 1905, for example, two Thetas from Cornell met and visited with a Berkeley sister while overseas in Amsterdam. Back in the States, a member of the former group traveled to California, where she spent some time with the remainder of the Omega chapter Thetas at Berkeley.[15]

For the most part, the fraternity women found these interactions with sisters of other chapters both exciting and illuminating. At Y.W.C.A. meetings, at football games, in summer school, and on trips and visits together, Thetas of different chapters talked of fraternity customs and selection and initiation practices, and shared ideas for rush functions as well as for entertainments.[16] In letters to the journal and to their own chapters, they described joyful encounters with fellow members, often noting their pleasure at finding their faraway peers to be women whom they were proud to call "sisters."[17] Some women had friends and relatives who belonged to Theta on other campuses, and these ties helped strengthen the connections among chapters. Occasionally, the members of certain chapters shared particularly close bonds with those of another branch. In 1909, for example, the Tau chapter sisters looked upon the Illinois Thetas with such friendship and sense of trust that they asked the latter group to rush a prospective student for them while she visited the Illinois campus. In California, the Berkeley and Stanford Thetas shared such intimate connections throughout the 1890s and early 1900s that one chapter's actions concerning selection or rush strongly influenced the other chapter's decisions on similar matters.[18]

Conventions in particular provided opportunities for sisters of all ages and branches to meet one another. Held biennially for three to five days at different locations around the country, these gatherings brought together representatives from all the collegiate and alumnae chapters as well as numerous other attendees, both active and graduates. The topics addressed in the sessions covered immediate fraternity concerns such as rush procedures and extension questions; practical issues concerning vocations and technical training; and more philosophical issues such as whether there should be similarity or diversity among members of a chapter and whether the fraternity should remain a wholly secretive society.[19]

As a means of building greater familiarity among the chapters, the representatives of the collegiate branches brought with them collages of photographs, postcards, and clippings, as well as school banners, excerpts from minutes books, accounts of skits, and other adornments, which they arranged in one room at the convention. These displays remained up throughout the duration of the meetings as a means of offering a sense of each chapter and its life on its particular campus.[20]

Kappa Alpha Theta's 1887 convention, hosted by the Hanover chapter in southern Indiana, brought together delegates from DePauw, Indiana, Illinois Wesleyan, Wooster (Ohio), Simpson (Iowa), Kansas, Vermont, and Allegheny (Pennsylvania). One topic addressed was the "standardization of the badge." The group decided together that the "stars shall always be diamonds." (Courtesy of Kappa Alpha Theta Fraternity, © 2003.)

Designed to "build loyalty and fraternity spirit on an appreciative understanding of Kappa Alpha Theta," the Theta conventions, like those of Kappa Kappa Gamma, Pi Beta Phi, and other fraternities, aimed to bring chapters together, to foster greater understanding among members of all ages and regions, and to unify standards among the different branches of the fraternity.[21] And according to most accounts offered by convention attendees, the meetings indeed brought the desired effects. The experience of meeting sisters from across the country and seeing how members of other chapters operated proved extremely powerful to many women, and in letters to fraternity journals and to their friends, sisters of all chapters recorded their awe and genuine pleasure at finding themselves surrounded by so many women wearing the same badge.[22]

According to one Pi Phi member, attendance at convention meant "a new initiation" into her fraternity. "It is true that we were wont to speak of being loyal to the wine and blue, but after attending one of our conventions we are as loyal to one chapter of Pi Beta Phi as to another. The interests, the aims, the pleasures, the triumphs, the disappointments, the losses of every separate chapter, aye, of every individual member, we might say, become ours also." Another Pi Phi put it succinctly: "We are bound by ties—ties warmer and stronger than those of friendship—to noble, intellectual, womanly women all over these United States. For the dear little girl from the far West, for the gentle Quaker maiden of the East, for the stately sister of the North, and for the charming girl from the South, convention has brought us a warmer interest and love."[23]

The Theta members too wrote of the power of meeting sisters from across the United States. Upon joining a throng of sisters gathered in Minneapolis, one wrote, "the feeling that I belonged to them by a bond extending all over the country almost overwhelmed me at times. It was such a new and lovely thought to feel that here were more than a hundred girls, all wearing the kite, and although all but a handful were total strangers, all ready to welcome me as a sister."[24] Another Theta gleefully described her experience at the 1911 convention with the words, "Picture yourself on a train, moving through a most interesting country, and all filled with 180 girls—all a big family of Kappa Alpha Theta sisters! Think of all the 'gossip fests' between Thetas from Canada and Texas, Minnesota and Maryland! It was a great moving house-party, where the company remained, while the surroundings changed constantly."[25]

In addition to strengthening bonds between members of different chapters and providing sisters with an opportunity to meet others from around the country, conventions also served to open many members' eyes to the national character of their fraternity. The discussions and debates held at the meetings provoked especially the second-generation members to look beyond their own chapter and its concerns to the wider issues and meanings associated with fraternity membership. One Theta sister wrote in 1897: "Before the convention, the local chapter was to many of us our only experience of fraternity life and therefore seemed to be the most prominent part of the fraternity organization. In our isolated condition . . . it was difficult for us to grasp the idea of the unity of Kappa Alpha Theta." Yet at convention, "we met face to face, heart to heart, and then came the powerful revelation of what Theta really is. We feel now the deep meaning of our fraternity. We have come to comprehend its unity and are conscious of a feeling that binds us all together, chapter to chapter, Theta to Theta. 'There is a tie that binds our hearts in Theta love.'"[26] A sister of Theta's Upsilon chapter described a similar feeling in 1903:

Beginning in 1911, Kappa Alpha Theta arranged for special trains to carry delegates and visitors to biennial Grand Conventions. In 1913 more than three hundred delegates and visitors traveled to Lake Minnewaska in New York State to deliberate fraternity matters. (Courtesy of Kappa Alpha Theta Fraternity, © 2003.)

> Never, until a girl has attended a fraternity convention, can she know what her fraternity may mean to her. She has been "wooed and won" by a little circle of a dozen girls whom she has learned to love. They all reverence the same ideals; this she knows. But the national fraternity, the great organization of which her chapter is only a part, is a very vague reality to her.

Only upon attending a convention could a member feel the "importance, the dignity of a sisterhood which can hold the love and active interest of women long out of college."[27]

This broadening of outlook brought on by convention experience stood at the heart of the conventions' purpose. It enabled sisters to welcome "the sacrifice of individual chapter desires, if such desires conflict with the fraternity's broadest welfare" and to "keep on the ideal plane, with loyalty of chapters to each other."[28] As the officers of Kappa Alpha Theta argued, once members had attended convention they would "know, and love, Kappa Alpha Theta's ideals, and with this knowledge and love . . . [would] come together for many discussions, to gain the broadest point of view, and to work for the good of our whole fraternity."[29]

While most members came away from their conventions with positive impressions of their sisters and strengthened feelings of loyalty to their fraternity, on occasion encounters occurring at these meetings sparked rifts and divisions between members of different chapters. After one convention in the 1910s, the grand secretary of Kappa Alpha Theta, L. Pearle Green, included in a letter a damaging assessment of a representative of one of the collegiate chapters: "I am just a wee bit afraid of the __ chapter," she wrote. "They had a very ordinary girl as a delegate, quite different from other __ girls I have known and there were no other actives present from the chapter. We decided to get Gamma's delegate to make the motion from the floor because her personality was more winning."[30] At another meeting of the fraternity, the Grand Council members decided, upon meeting representatives of the Alpha Mu chapter, to "send some level-headed girl" to the University of Missouri to stay with the chapter through rush and help the members there select more fitting representatives for Kappa Alpha Theta.[31]

Poor impressions of the delegates of the Pi chapter at Albion College in Michigan prompted Theta's officers to launch an investigation of the branch, to determine whether the fraternity ought to revoke the group's charter. After visiting the small liberal arts college and determining that not enough "eligible fraternity material" existed there, the fraternity leaders recommended to the chapters that Theta revoke Pi's charter on the grounds that it fell "below Theta's standard." When all of the chapters voted in support of the officers' recommendation, the Albion Thetas chose to return their charter to the fraternity rather than suffer the humiliation of having it revoked.[32]

Negative views of the sisters of Theta's Lambda chapter, formed both at conventions and at visits to the University of Vermont, came close to concluding in a similar manner. Prompted by perceived differences in the manner and dress of the rural Northeasterners, as compared to their more stylishly adorned urban and Midwestern sisters, the fraternity's officers sent one of their number to investigate the status and conditions of the Lambda chapter. Her report proved damning. "With regard to the women students [at the University of Vermont], I cannot express too strongly how absolutely they fall below the standard of even the poorest sort of college girls I have seen elsewhere. The girls evidently come from

During the years when no national meetings were scheduled, the fraternity women often held district conventions that brought together alumnae and collegians from one geographical region. In 1912, Kappa Alpha Thetas from Oklahoma, Texas, and Colorado held their first district convention in Galveston, Texas. (Courtesy of Kappa Alpha Theta Fraternity, © 2003.)

crude, uncultured homes and in personality, mentality are a type I had never before met in college halls." While conceding that the Theta group included in its number "the best there is in the University, if one can draw any distinction in such a mass of hopeless material," the officer, herself a member of Barnard College's Alpha Zeta chapter, "earnestly and urgently" recommended that the leaders revoke Lambda chapter's charter.[33]

Whereas the Pi alumnae had supported the closure of their chapter, the Lambda graduates took the opposite stance, and once the officers put the Lambda matter before the fraternity, the older sisters stepped up to the fight.[34] Stung by the criticism of their active sisters, the alumnae members of the Vermont chapter wrote to the Grand Council of the fraternity, demanding an explanation.

> Now our ideal of a strong chapter is, and has always been, one made
> up of members chosen for character, intellectual ability, and womanly
> personality. It was because we believed these to be the standards of

Kappa Alpha Theta that we were led, twenty-six years ago, to merge into its membership our own flourishing local organization. . . . Today we have in our active chapter a full quota in numbers—nineteen in all—of young women who, in character, intellectual attainments and womanly personality, our Theta ideals, we can but feel would do honor to the best fraternity in any college.

Citing the fact that all of Lambda's graduates of the previous year had won entry into Phi Beta Kappa and that all had held the most prominent leadership positions in the school, the Lambda alumnae asked pointedly, "Now, where lies the difficulty? Have we, all along been mistaken as to the type of women Kappa Alpha Theta desires, or are her ideals changing? We sincerely believe that only by adhering strictly to our present standards can we continue to maintain a strong, influential chapter." Blaming the "baseless criticism from which Lambda chapter has so long suffered at the hands of our fraternity" for "sapping the life of a chapter, paralyzing its energies and weakening its allegiances to the fraternity," the Vermont alumnae called on Theta's officers either to admit that their ideals had changed or to cease their criticisms of the Lambda group.[35]

Theta's officers responded by holding their next meeting in Burlington and having each of them perform an individual study of the University of Vermont chapter and its standing on campus. The unanimity of their impressions surprised them all. "The chapter clings close to Theta's ideals of scholarship, noble living, and culture," and all the members of the group proved to be "sturdy, intelligent, cultured New England girls." While perhaps "less frivolous than college students some places" and possessing a "traditional New England disregard for latest fashion," the Lambda members constituted a friendly and fun-loving group, who, individually and as a chapter, measured up well against and could easily blend in with other groups of Thetas. As the Grand Council members noted, "What better test that they are the Theta type?"[36] Concluding that prejudices based on appearances and dress had stood at the root of the opposition to the Vermont women, the officers of Kappa Alpha Theta issued an apology to the Lambda chapter Thetas and asked the women to "bear leniently" with those sisters who continued to judge hastily.[37]

The near closure of the Lambda chapter and the vote to revoke the Pi branch's charter both stemmed from concerns on the part of both officers and regular members of Kappa Alpha Theta that certain women among

their group did not possess the qualities or traits considered desirable in
a Theta. While it rested upon the members of individual chapters to
choose their new initiates, the ramifications of a poor choice potentially
fell on the shoulders of all wearing the Theta badge. The weakness of one
chapter—and even of one member of one chapter—held consequences for
the entire fraternity, both because each sister bore responsibility for
Theta's reputation and standing, and, even more directly, because the low
status of such parties bore potential to harm other chapters, should of-
fending sisters choose to transfer or seek graduate degrees from other institutions where Theta had chapters.[38]

From the late 1880s, as increasing numbers of women chose both to pursue graduate work and to transfer to new institutions partway through
their college courses, the potential grew for chapters of the fraternity to
find in their midst Thetas initiated by different branches. By the early
1900s, the issue of transfers had become both common and controversial
enough to warrant discussion, as well as official monitoring and regulation.[39] Whereas the only record of affiliations in the 1890s had been the
informal notations provided by chapters in the *Kappa Alpha Theta*, by
the mid-1910s, in addition to commentaries reported in the journal, the
Grand Council began to keep official tally of the number of transfers as
well as documentation of those who formally affiliated with new chap
ters.[40]

Generally, the Thetas who transferred found themselves welcomed by
the branch on their new campus, eagerly taken in and made to feel at
home. The excitement with which the collegians bragged of their new arrivals in their chapter letters indicates their eagerness to take into their
number Thetas who had been initiated by other chapters. "We are very
glad to have Katherine Winans of Omicron with us this year," the Tau
chapter at Northwestern wrote in their quarterly report to the journal in
January 1895. An Iota sister from Cornell noted similarly, "We were glad
to welcome from Chi Miss Ada Parker, who is doing graduate work in
English."[41] A Pi sister at Albion College gushed enthusiastically over the
"treasure" Phi had sent them in Nellie McCaughan and concluded that
"[Phi's] loss is a great gain to [Pi]."[42] In November 1904, an Ohio State
Theta declared her chapter "most happy to have with us this year Mary
Louise Zurhorst of Delta," while the Chi sisters of 1909 labeled their ini-
tiation "especially pleasant" for the presence in their group of four Iota
Thetas who were pursuing work alongside them at Syracuse.[43]

While in most cases new chapters made transferring sisters feel welcome and at home, on occasion particular branches simply ignored an arriving Theta or refused to issue her an invitation to affiliate.[44] Because affiliation required chapters to take in as one of their own sisters who had been chosen by a different group of women, according to potentially different standards and for potentially different reasons than they themselves used in selecting their pledges, the question of whether chapters should be required by the fraternity to affiliate all transfers proved thorny.

"We cannot be responsible for what [another] chapter may see fit to take," claimed those sisters opposed to mandatory affiliation, while members in favor of it argued that the spirit of sisterhood required all Thetas to stand by those who wore their badge. Unless a woman proved "morally wrong" or had "renounced the respect due to good womanhood," each chapter bore the responsibility to take into its number all members of the fraternity, to honor the fact that each chapter constituted only a small part of the whole of Kappa Alpha Theta.[45] At the heart of this struggle over how to reconcile the issue of transfers lurked questions concerning the scope and meaning of the "ties that bound [all Thetas together]." In their efforts to determine the fraternity's policy regarding transferring sisters, the women of Kappa Alpha Theta were brought face-to-face with the question of what sisterhood really meant.

Indeed, the transfer issue brought to light the very real implications of what it meant for each sister to serve as a representative of the whole fraternity. It raised the bar for each chapter, placing on each branch the charge, "to use the greatest discrimination in her choice of members, that they may be representative girls whom she will not only be glad to send out herself, but whom other chapters will be glad to welcome."[46] At the same time, the transfer issue tested the very basis of the fraternal bond, for when chapters found themselves face-to-face with women whom they themselves would never have taken into the fraternity, they resisted lowering their own status by taking in, for all to see, one who represented "undesirable fraternity material."[47]

Numerous articles published in the *Kappa Alpha Theta* journal addressed the plight of the transfer and the issue of affiliation. Most of their authors took positions in favor of affiliation except in the most unusual or extreme cases.[48] One sister labeled the fraternity's nonpolicy on mandated affiliation "unconstitutional, un-ideal, imprudent, and unkind." Since expulsion from a single chapter meant expulsion from Kappa Alpha Theta as a whole, the woman argued that the corollary should also hold that entrance into one chapter should mean entrance into the whole fraternity and thus into all of its chapters. As she pointed out, "What else is the fraternity but the union of chapters?" Once a chapter initiated a woman into Kappa Alpha Theta, the rest of the fraternity "should stand by her choice of girls, until we see fit to withdraw the charter" of the initiating chapter.[49] As a fellow Theta put it, since "[t]he fraternity stands for unity . . . how could this be reconciled to any chapter's leaving one of the number out of their active life?"[50] Another member addressed the potential problems caused by a "non-fit" between transfer and new chapter, but argued that even in this case, "every presumption should be indulged in her behalf; instantly, every doubt should, if possible, be resolved in her favor." "The pin itself should remind us that there is something here that transcends chapter opinion . . . that our chapter is merely a part of a larger order from which it derives its power to be," an alumna wrote. Even should a transferring Theta prove "peculiar in ways, a little different from the girls in the chapter to which she comes, would it not be better to take her and keep her within the circle, to try to show her her mistakes and to minimize them in the sight of the outer world by our own lenience?"[51]

In 1915, the fraternity mandated affiliation, requiring that henceforth, "any Theta is entitled to active membership in any college chapter (active or alumnae), if she qualifies for active membership." This made it the responsibility of every chapter to "receive as active members all eligible members of the fraternity." "It shall be the duty of every college chapter, during the first month of every college year, to search out, welcome, and invite to affiliation, any Thetas entering from other institutions."[52] With this rule, the sisters of Kappa Alpha Theta brought to the surface issues that had simmered since the early days of the fraternity's existence.

Fear of what sorts of sisters other branches might send to them and what harm to their reputations these women might do if it were known that they were Thetas had led many chapters from the start to resist granting charters to certain schools. As early as the 1880s, stronger chapters such as those at the University of Michigan and University of Kansas had opposed the creation of branches in institutions they deemed inferior to their own. While in the 1880s the ranking of schools held sway in determining to what campuses Theta should spread, by the early 1900s the decision hinged more often on the backgrounds of the prospective charter members. In the 1910s, as more and different kinds of students were enrolling on campuses across the country, religion and the extent to which particular schools attracted mainly "American" enrollees proved the deciding factor. Indeed, as the fraternity grew in size and scope and drew its members from campuses with increasingly heterogeneous populations, concurrent concerns arose among some to limit diversity and make sure that all new members were palatable to the whole.

In the 1880s, conflict developed among the chapters of Kappa Alpha Theta over which campuses should be allowed to house branches of the fraternity. Spearheaded by the Eta chapter at the University of Michigan, the Alpha chapter at Asbury College (later, DePauw University), and the Iota chapter at Cornell University, this group of Thetas argued that the fraternity should exist only on campuses with superior academic reputations. This group—which had its parallel in Kappa Kappa Gamma, Pi Beta Phi, and other women's fraternities—disparaged the size and paltry resources of some of the smaller institutions where the fraternity had branches. Arguing that the fraternity should exist only in colleges "of well recognized standing and exceptional endowment," these sisters both refused to grant charters to groups in smaller institutions and actively strove to take away the charters of those chapters whose campus reputations they considered especially weak.[53]

The schools opposed by those attending the more elite colleges were the small, denominational schools—the very ones Theta populated early on—and the newly established Land Grant universities. Believing that such institutions could not possibly rank among the "best schools of the country," this group virulently opposed expansion to such campuses as Hanover College, Allegheny College, Purdue University, and Ohio Wesleyan College. When another Theta chapter went ahead and initiated the new groups anyway, an irreparable chasm formed.[54]

Even the formation of a Grand Chapter, in which was vested the power of granting and withdrawing charters, was unable to bridge the gap. The Michigan and Cornell chapters decided to break away from Theta and merge instead with Alpha Phi Fraternity, a plan that they hoped would allow them to affiliate only with those attending more prestigious institutions. The Cornell group then reconsidered and agreed to remain with Theta under the condition that the fraternity withdraw the charters of "several chapters to which we object."[55] Arguing that they "could not affiliate with girls in institutions where attendance was so small" and did not want to belong to a fraternity that took in "too much . . . 'small-town stuff,'" the Thetas of Cornell and the Universities of Vermont and Kansas pushed for a special meeting, to decide the matter once and for all. In

1886 that meeting took place. With the goal of saving those they considered their best chapters, sisters of Kappa Alpha Theta collectively agreed to cut off their "weaker links" and thereby strengthen the "chain of Kappa Alpha Theta." They revoked the charters from Ohio University and Butler University. At the same time, they withdrew the Michigan branch's charter, thereby freeing the fraternity of the disloyal chapter that had wanted to break away rather than working to strengthen Kappa Alpha Theta.[56]

The closing down of chapters on smaller, less prestigious campuses enabled Theta to consider itself an elite organization with branches on only the finest campuses. It also set a precedent for extension to campuses of only a certain rank and reputation.[57] Similar moves in Kappa Kappa Gamma brought about the same effect. In 1884, the fraternity revoked the charter of its chapter at Franklin College, deeming the school of "low standard" and its students unworthy of Kappa membership. It followed the same practice at Simpson College, again ridding the fraternity of a chapter on a smaller, less prestigious campus.[58]

Other women's fraternities followed similar practices, choosing to populate only those campuses that were popularly considered elite. Excluding out of hand any institution "where coeducation . . . ha[d] recently been questioned,"[59] most adopted rules requiring that chapters be formed only on those campuses in which students performed "college work in the accepted sense of the term." So concerned were the fraternity women with the status of particular campuses that together they came up with a list of appropriate schools for their organizations to consider as sites for expansion. They singled out the higher-ranked campuses for inclusion and barred all agricultural, technical, and vocational institutions out of hand.[60]

Still, the debate did not end. As the nineteenth century rolled into the twentieth, and the women's fraternities raced against one another to establish branches on an increasing number of campuses, battles continued within each organization, again over the question of fitness of certain campuses to house chapters of the fraternity.[61] Yet, while the debates in the 1880s explicitly hinged on the academic reputation of particular campuses, those taking place in later years had as much, if not more, to do with the type and class of students enrolled at certain campuses than they did with the schools in general.

In Kappa Alpha Theta, the Kansas chapter members of 1911 refused to grant a charter to a petitioning group at nearby Washburn College.

Their opposition stemmed in large measure from the fear that those who would become Thetas at Washburn would not be the same caliber of women as those selected by Theta at Kansas: "A Theta from Washburn might very probably come to the University of Kansas to do her higher work. Kappa might be glad to see her, and again she might not." The newer chapter might take in "undesirable material" in order to maintain its numbers, and while "'[w]e all make mistakes,'" the Kansas Thetas stood "willing and ready to make the best of [Kappa's] own mistakes but [they did] not want to suffer from a Washburn chapter's mistakes."[62] Likewise, at prestigious Swarthmore College, the Alpha Beta sisters for many years refused to support an application from a group at the University of Pennsylvania due to the differences they saw between themselves and the petitioners. Only "a few [of the petitioners] would ever by any chance be Thetas at Swarthmore," the Alpha Beta members argued. If allowed into Theta, these new women would tarnish the fine reputation that the Swarthmore chapter had for many decades cultivated throughout their state.[63]

Two cases of extension demonstrate particularly clearly the Theta members' concerns with the kinds of women who might be taken into their fraternity, should charters be granted to petitioning groups on new campuses. In discussions in the late 1890s concerning whether to grant a Theta charter to the Tri Kappa society of Brown, the class and background of the petitioning members played as much a role as their academic abilities did in persuading the fraternity to welcome them in.[64] The officer sent to Brown to evaluate the petitioners questioned the dean about "the scholarship, social and general standing of the girls" in Tri Kappa. She was pleased to learn that the petitioning group had made "very judicious selections" in choosing members and that this had given them "very good standing in every way" on the Brown campus. "The Dean showed me his book containing marks of standing, and I found that each and all were exceptionally good students; many had received the highest mark given by the faculty in nearly all their work. . . . The three seniors he said were all eligible to Phi Beta Kappa so far as scholarship was concerned."[65] But while years before, this would have been enough, by and large, to ensure admittance to Theta, by this time academics were only one of a number of factors Kappa Alpha Theta considered.

Indeed, after a discussion of the fine reputation of the college, the Theta investigator moved on to an analysis of the women comprising Tri

Kappa Society. "I met every member of Tri Kappa at Miss Waite's home which, by the way, is very lovely and she evidently has abundant means. I was favorably impressed with each one. They are typical college women, and give evidence of large culture and refinement. Many are from old Conservative New England families and are truly delightful girls." Based on this assessment of the background and class of the petitioners, the evaluating officer concluded that "Brown University is beyond all question an institution which we should enter because of its national reputation," and that "the Tri Kappa girls are pre-eminently desirable as charter members of Kappa Alpha Theta." In 1897, six visiting Thetas installed the Alpha Epsilon chapter at Brown.[66]

The pains taken by Kappa Alpha Theta to evaluate both the institution of Brown University and the women of the Tri Kappa Society demonstrate changes in the qualities sought by the fraternity. Not only did Theta inquire after the academic abilities and institutional reputation of its petitioners and their school, but it also looked into the class status and family background of the women seeking affiliation. Implicit in the officer's assessment of the Brown petitioners ran a class-based evaluation that rendered the Brown women more favorable due to their backgrounds in "old Conservative New England" and their affiliation with a woman who "evidently has abundant means." As an organization that mandated the outlay of constant and sizable amounts of money, Kappa Alpha Theta sought to ensure that those considered for the fraternity could afford membership and, through their own wealth, add literally (through donations) and figuratively (through social prestige) to the fraternity's standing.[67]

The 1915 evaluation of a petitioning group from Randolph-Macon pointed up this concern with class and background to an even greater extent. Grand Secretary L. Pearle Green, sent to assess the would-be Thetas, raved to the fraternity about those she had met: "Individually the members are attractive girls, well poised, with a fair amount of good looks, well dressed, charming mannered, well bred, and delightfully womanly, as well as popular socially . . . and its members' antecedents are unquestionably all right families."[68] Further, she reported:

> In the Dean's opinion, and from his records, all are exceptionally good students but one girl. She hasn't the brains though she works hard—but she has got "family" no end and is a dear child. . . . The background of all of them who are from Virginia is O.K. and rest may be, but not so

well known about by people of VA. Beside family, there is much wealth in said families . . . most all of them are eligible easily to the Daughters of the American Revolution and also to the Colonial Dames.[69]

Green offered details on each applicant's personal attributes and family background in support of her claims to their superior social standing: "Lucy Ames, sophomore, Pungoteague, VA. Pretty, charming. 'Ames family one of VA's best and her Mother of equally desirable clan.' . . . There isn't a single one of them but whom most every chapter of Theta would be delighted to have."[70] Despite some resistance from other chapters—whose members challenged the evaluating officer's assessment of the petitioners' superior social standing—the group at Randolph-Macon won admittance to the fraternity. Impressed by the social standing and family connections of the women, the fraternity leaders chose to ignore the dissenting members and installed Beta Beta chapter in 1916.[71]

Other extension decisions rested on similar concerns. At Purdue University, the University of Cincinnati, and Oregon State University (formerly Oregon Agricultural College), social class and family connections also played major roles in the sisters' decisions to grant charters. In recommending the petitioners of the V.P.C. sorority at Cincinnati, one Theta officer listed the last names of several of the women, noting that one belonged to "a family of Virginia 'planters' and their name ranks throughout the South with that of Fairfax and Lee." To assuage concerns among some members as to the fitness of the petitioners to belong to Theta, she hastened to assure them that, "the girls in V.P.C. were socially 'our class.'"[72]

While the 1890s and early 1900s were notable for their focus on social class and family connections, the 1910s brought additional concerns of religious affiliation and "Americanness." Having solidified their positions among the establishment of campus and society, Kappa Alpha Theta and the other prominent women's fraternities now looked to maintain those positions by keeping their organizations free of what some among them considered the "taint" of ethnic and religious diversity. By the middle of the decade, nearly all the women's fraternities were experiencing internal disagreements over the question of whether to admit non-Protestant students. While some resolved the issue by crafting blanket statements on the question, such as those that banned all non-Christians from membership, others engaged in delicate balancing acts with their groups, reluctant to force disparate chapters to adopt uniform policies but at the same time hesitant to take in as members those whom many would refuse to acknowledge as sisters.[73]

Founded at a Methodist institution and, from its early days, taking for its moral code a passage from the New Testament, Kappa Alpha Theta nevertheless did not adopt an official position on religion.[74] Although in its first two decades of existence the members of the fraternity judged prospective and current sisters in terms of their "moral standing," neither in their minutes nor in their letters and other documents did the Theta women associate morality with church affiliation. Religion played little part in decisions regarding who would or would not receive an invitation to join Kappa Alpha Theta in its first four decades.[75]

In the 1910s, however, the Theta women's position toward religion changed, and the policies—written and unwritten—of other women's fraternities changed as well. This likely occurred in response to increased enrollment of Jewish and Catholic students in colleges and universities and the concurrent rise in religious intolerance in many areas of the country. In the nineteenth century, few female Jews or Catholics attended college. Of the less than 2 percent of women aged eighteen to twenty-one who attended college in the 1870s and 1880s, nearly all came from Protestant backgrounds. Small numbers of Catholic females did pursue higher education, but for the most part they attended their own church-affiliated institutions.[76] If any Jewish women attended college, they did so without comment, either hiding their religious identities or else blending in with their fellow collegians.[77]

The first identifiable Jewish female collegian, Amelia D. Alpiner, attended the University of Illinois in the mid-1890s. Alpiner played a prominent role on campus, taking part in many activities and serving as a charter member of Pi Beta Phi Fraternity.[78] Shortly after her graduation in 1896, another identifiably Jewish female, Gertrude Stein, graduated from the Harvard Annex, or Radcliffe College, the women's division of Harvard. Other than these two prominent women, however, the Jewish females attending college during the latter decades of the nineteenth century and the first decade of the twentieth century did so in relative anonymity.[79]

In the 1910s, things changed noticeably. Fueled by the massive wave of immigration that increased more than tenfold, to 3.3 million, the Jewish population in the United States between 1880 and 1917, the number of Jewish students enrolled on college campuses increased dramatically.

Hailing mainly from eastern Europe, the new immigrants to America proved poorer, less educated, less cultivated, and more ostentatious in their habits and behaviors than their better-assimilated German predecessors.[80] When the children of these recent immigrants began to arrive in number on college campuses in the 1910s, their presence attracted greater societal and institutional notice and comment than had earlier Jewish students.

Yet even with their increased numbers in the 1910s, Jewish women still constituted only a tiny percentage of their age and religious cohorts. A 1916 Intercollegiate Menorah Association survey reported that although Jewish men attended college in a higher proportion than did their non-Jewish counterparts—3.6 for every thousand Jews as opposed to 2.2 for every thousand non-Jews—female Jews comprised only one-ninth the number of male Jews enrolled on campus. In addition, they were 50 percent less likely to attend college than were their non-Jewish counterparts. Although at the all-women's colleges of the Northeast such as Barnard, Radcliffe, Smith, Wellesley, Vassar, and Bryn Mawr, 335 Jewish women held 5 percent of the enrolled places, in the rest of the country, they accounted for only a tiny fraction of the number of higher-education matriculates.[81]

Still, the large numbers of poor, uneducated eastern European Jews, combined with the millions of Italian, Greek, Slavic, and Polish immigrants and those of other eastern European countries streaming into the United States in the early decades of the twentieth century, prompted concerns on the part of many Americans, including novelist Henry James, Harvard president A. Lawrence Lowell, and University of Wisconsin Progressive reformer Edward Alsworth Ross, that the "unwashed masses" were taking over their institutions.[82] The elimination of Greek and Latin as entrance exams at many colleges and universities in the 1910s helped open the doors to members of particular social and ethnic groups who had heretofore not been represented in the realm of higher education. The increasingly diverse population of schools located in cities and other ethnically mixed communities served to exacerbate fears on the part of many white Protestants that "foreigners" were overrunning American higher education. As historian Lawrence Levine noted of such concerns, "These were not the views of extremists but those of polite society whose members were pained at the people they now had to share space with."[83] While it would not be until the 1920s that schools such as Harvard and Columbia—along with their female counterparts—would institute quotas, "intelligence tests," and other overt restrictions, by the 1910s enough concern about the extent to which Jewish enrollment was tarnishing the Anglo-Saxon character of campus life, that students, alumni, faculty, and administrators of many institutions began to discuss openly ways to restrict the numbers of Jewish students enrolled in their schools.[84]

At the same time as public fears were augmenting over the number of Jewish students matriculated in America's colleges and universities, the number of Catholic women attending nonsectarian schools was creeping upward as well, as all-male Catholic schools proved reluctant to coeducate. Habitual objects of prejudice in both public and private nonsectarian institutions, Catholic women, with the arrival of Jews, became, in the words of one historian, "the most acceptable of the newcomers."[85] Though the recipients of less outright prejudice than their Jewish peers, Catholic women—especially those with ostensibly Irish names, ethnic appearances, or cultural affiliations—still attracted the disdain of some observers and found themselves excluded from many campus organizations, especially the women's fraternities.

Despite their increases in numbers, Jewish and Catholic collegians, especially women, still did not hold many places in American institutions of higher education prior to 1920. Most institutions, especially the country's state schools, continued to reflect their surrounding populations, which remained largely white, American-born, and Protestant. Yet in places such as New York and Chicago, public perception told a different story.[86] Many observers took stock of the increasing ethnic populations at city schools such as Columbia and Barnard, and multiplied in their minds the logical outcome of such a trend.

A handful of Jews in the collegiate Greek system would be fine, many believed, but more "would be an entirely different matter." And since it was likely that opening the door a crack would lead to a flood, it was better to oppose the initial entry. As one women's fraternity member put it in registering her opposition to allowing Jewish organizations to join the National Panhellenic Congress:

> The Jew will never be an American. He has only technical citizenship. He gets all the benefits, all the opportunities American life affords, and yet he maintains a race separate and distinct in our nation, and when the Jew in our country comes into position of sufficient power we find him turning on us the same intolerance that he has been subjected to in other nations. That is, in return for the benefits and opportunities he gets here

for advancement he doesn't award us a like liberality. And if we were to have a body of six or seven Jewish organizations I fancy we would soon begin to feel some of the effects of that intolerance.[87]

The fraternity women of the 1910s worried about the effects on unity of taking in women whom some members would refuse to acknowledge as sisters. According to the few recorded statements on the topic, Kappa Alpha Theta's little mentioned and unwritten policy discouraging the pledging of Jewish and Catholic students stemmed as much from fears of prejudice within their group as it did from opposition to having Jews or Catholics in their sisterhood. As one fraternity woman noted in a speech to the 1923 meeting of the National Panhellenic Congress, "We ought to look at this question from the standpoint of the whole country. As far as any personal prejudice against [Jews] is concerned, I have none. However, in different sections of the country I know it is different, and we must try to look at it from the standpoint of the whole country."[88] Believing that some of their members would react negatively to any affiliation with Jewish or Catholic women, the sisters of Kappa Alpha Theta, Kappa Kappa Gamma, Pi Beta Phi, Alpha Phi, Chi Omega, and other organizations largely barred women of these faiths from entry.[89]

It is important to note that the historically white and Protestant Greek societies were not the only organizations to practice discrimination. Both the Jewish organizations and their African American counterparts did as well. Founded in the 1910s largely in response to the refusal of the more established groups to admit women of their background, the Jewish and black sororities—and most of these were indeed called sororities and not women's fraternities—also adhered to discriminatory practices, many of them using criteria such as ethnic background or skin color to determine eligibility for membership. Perhaps in a quest to establish themselves as closely as possible with the more powerful historically Christian organizations, historically Jewish Alpha Epsilon Phi and Sigma Delta Tau, for example, both practiced discrimination against recent immigrants and other students who looked or acted in ways that the Greek members deemed insufficiently "Americanized." Concerned with the assimilation of Jewish students into mainstream campus culture, these organizations and others like them strove to counter negative stereotypes of Jews by teaching etiquette, manners, dress, and upper-middle-class American behavior and mores. Their primary mission was to make themselves quintessential American collegians; in the process of fulfilling it, they excluded anyone whose appearance, manner of speech, or background bore any taint of the Old Country.[90]

The historically black sororities, too, practiced discrimination against members of their own race. Codes that prohibited admissions for any woman whose skin color was darker than a paper bag were common among the more elite of the African American groups. While the officers of groups such as Alpha Kappa Alpha Sorority have denied that their organizations ever used what has been called "the paper bag test," anecdotal evidence, especially provided by insiders, is so great as to suggest that if not adhered to as part of a national policy, appearance-based admissions tests, including those regarding the way prospects wore their hair, were most certainly a widespread, if localized, practice.[91]

Discrimination, thus, was not limited to the historically white and Protestant organizations, though in general they applied more blanket standards in their selection processes and in all cases wielded far more power on campus and in society than did the historically Jewish or African American groups. In a survey released in 1926 regarding the admissions policies of organizations belonging to the National Panhellenic Congress, most of those surveyed admitted to having some form of restricted membership. Five of the seventeen women's fraternities taking part in the study acknowledged having written policies that limited admission to members of the Christian faith. Three additional groups followed "unwritten rules" nationally, while nearly all of the others either followed informal exclusionary practices or allowed their chapters to follow unwritten policies along racial and religious grounds. Some were explicit in their restrictions: "National policy to limit to white race and exclude Jews." Others followed more nebulous guidelines: "Membership based on congeniality, which itself tends to bar other races—probably national policy an 'unwritten law.'" Some organizations adhered to specific quota: "In a few chapters, certain proportions of religious faiths must be kept. In one instance a number limit was placed." In other groups, "experience, and in certain situations the advice of national and local officers . . . limited, or even curtailed, for a time, admission on religious grounds."[92]

In most of the historically white Greek organizations for women, policies excluding Jews and Catholics went into effect in the 1910s rather than at the time of their founding. "In recent years chapters have had serious problems because of large numbers of Catholic girls," one fraternity woman noted. "Girls of different religious beliefs have not worked in harmony, and fraternity standards were not upheld." Whereas the question of admitting non-Protestant women rarely arose in earlier years, by 1912 and 1913 many organizations reported a dramatic increase in discrimination within their organizations. "Prejudice evidently growing," one Kappa Kappa Gamma representative noted, "There now seems to be prejudice against both Jews and Catholics."[93]

In Kappa Alpha Theta, religion became a determinant when choosing desirable pledges and selecting potential sites and groups for extension. In an examination of the backgrounds of prospective members at Sophie Newcomb College in New Orleans in 1913, for example, an officer of Kappa Alpha Theta noted that the father of one woman in the group was a "reformed Jew" and that her mother was highly involved in the Catholic Church. "I care less for her than for any of the active girls," she declared. While not specifically stating that her assessment stemmed from the religious background of the young woman, the woman suggested the connection by dedicating half of her description to the prospective member's religious background.[94]

Religion played an even more prominent role in another extension case. While investigating a group of potential petitioners at Hunter College in New York City, which by this time had become home to a large number of the Jewish immigrants flocking to the country, a major question upon which the decision hinged was whether the group admitted Jews into its number. While satisfied that the answer was no, the Theta sisters decided to bypass the group anyway: despite the restricted nature of the organization, the popular association of Hunter College with Jews, Catholics, and immigrants, as well as general perception that the school "doesn't draw from what we recognize as the distinctive American classes," fueled a "very stubborn prejudice" against the school. Fearful that Kappa Alpha Theta might tarnish its reputation by entering an institution considered by many to cater "mostly [to] Jews" and to the children of second- and third-generation immigrants, the fraternity determined in the end that Hunter was "not a place for Theta."[95] They made the same determination about a group at New York Teacher's College at Albany, dropping their interest in a prospective organization upon finding out that several of its members were Irish Catholics.[96]

At the University of Pittsburgh, the studious nature and limited means of the students paled in comparison to the school's reputation as one containing "little of the Jewish, foreign element." Despite the "questionable ranking" of the institution among first-class universities in the country, the officers of Kappa Alpha Theta decided to pursue their quest to charter a group that took in "only Christian girls."[97] Only when the alumnae Thetas of Pittsburgh classified the petitioners as lacking in unity, distant from one another, and wholly disorganized did the fraternity officers determine that the University of Pittsburgh women were "not ready to apply formally for admission to Kappa Alpha Theta."[98] Never abandoning their quest, they continued to cultivate the petitioners, and the following year installed the Alpha Omega chapter on the Pittsburgh campus, a place whose "American" nature they considered appealing.[99]

The eagerness of the Theta women to establish a chapter at the largely American-born and Protestant University of Pittsburgh campus and the reticence they displayed to pursue an opening on the Jewish-friendly Hunter campus suggest that religion played a significant role in determining eligibility for membership in Kappa Alpha Theta in the 1910s. Whereas little evidence exists concerning the decisions made by the individual collegiate chapters, it is clear that in matters placed before the entire fraternity for a vote, being Jewish or Irish Catholic worked against petitioners' causes, rendering them "hopeless" in the words of one sister and off-limits for acceptance in the views of many.[100]

The Theta women left few explanations for their resistance to taking Jewish and Catholic women into their fraternity, but one likely cause is that they and the members of the other women's fraternities may well have felt threatened by the changes that were taking place in the student bodies and in the broader society around them. The new kinds of students enrolling on campus in the 1910s often looked, dressed, spoke, and even thought differently than did their most established college peers. They took their studies more seriously; they eschewed the more social extracurricular activities in favor of jobs or co-curricular pursuits. Some came from families that had socialist leanings. Many brought an intellectual curiosity and willingness to debate that were rare in the typical college classroom of the day. In all, their presence had the potential effect to change the feel of campus and social climates. While they lacked the organized power of the Greeks, these newcomers' increasing involvement in campus affairs nevertheless may have presented a psychological challenge to the status quo.[101] For the members of the women's Greek system, who only a generation before had been outsiders and still, because of their sex, did not hold nearly as much power as did their male counterparts, the Jewish and Catholic arrivals may well have threatened their conceptions of what a college campus was supposed to look like and what an ideal

America was supposed to be. Having now taken their place as part of the campus and societal elite, the fraternity sisters may well have been resistant to any change from what they knew.

If they held this fear, they would not, of course, have been alone. As historian Levine wrote of Henry James, who returned to New York City from Europe in 1907 only to find himself surrounded by "'a row of faces, up and down, testifying, without exception, to alienism unmistakable, alienism undisguised and unashamed,' which made him gasp 'with the sense of isolation,'" "In spite of his obvious privilege and position, James professed—and obviously really felt—himself to be displaced and rendered impotent by the new immigrants."[102] Ordinary white, middle-class Americans shared this concern, enough that popular books, magazines, and newspapers regularly ran articles that referred to immigrants in derogatory tones and warned, in the words of the chairman of the New York Zoological Society and trustee of the American Museum of Natural History, that "the day of the 'Great Race' that had built the United States . . . was coming to a close [as a result of rampant immigration]."[103] Fear of ethnic incursion on Anglo-Saxon power helped fuel anxieties about "race suicide" among the white Protestant elite. The same concern led to the passage just a few years later of laws that severely restricted immigration to the United States.

While it is impossible to know to what extent these fears, conscious or unconscious, caused the fraternity women to erect the barriers they did against Jews, Catholics, and the children of recent immigrants, it is likely that they, as members of the old white, Anglo-Saxon, Protestant middle and upper-middle classes, were motivated at least in part by the same sentiments that worried James and other prominent thinkers. To maintain their privileged roles in society and ward against the increasing presence of newcomers who potentially threatened their power and status may well have been what prompted the women's fraternities to tighten the restrictions governing their memberships and allow their groups to settle only on those campuses that remained untainted by the wave of new arrivals.

In addition, another concern prompted the increased restrictions instituted by the women's fraternities. In a letter sent to the Alpha Beta chapter at Swarthmore College, Grand Secretary L. Pearle Green characterized the fraternity's resistance to accepting Jews into its number as the product of pressure on all Thetas to take in only women whom other members would accept as sisters. Referring to a Jewish woman from Chicago whom the Swarthmore Thetas were considering bidding, Green wrote to the group:

> [I]f you initiated this girl you would create [embarrassing] situations for Tau [at Northwestern University], Delta [at the University of Illinois] and other chapters (who each year initiate Chicago girls) and probably hamper their future rushing of Chicago girls; also would raise a problem for the hundreds of Theta alumnae who live in Chicago and vicinity. They would have a life time of the problem which for you would exist, if at all, for only nine months out of each of four years (if the girl stayed at Swarthmore for her full course).[104]

Should the Alpha Beta women persist with rushing the Jewish woman, Green warned, their actions would irreparably harm the Tau sisters' chances of winning desirable students from Chicago during Northwestern's rushing period. "It is just because Thetas over the country had faced such embarrassing, unpleasant, and harmful situations, just because some chapter would find some city or school closed to its successful rushing after it had built up a strong background there," that the fraternity discouraged chapters from admitting women whom other chapters would not acknowledge as sisters. Thus, rather than condemning the Tau sisters for "local prejudice," Green urged the Swarthmore Thetas to "look at the matter impersonally" and respect other Thetas' opinions as to the "desirable local fields for rushing."[105]

Based on the belief that "the social division between Jews and gentiles ha[d] a fundamental background as its real origin," the anti-Semitism displayed by the sisters of Kappa Alpha Theta and other women's fraternities in the 1910s and for decades thereafter thus stemmed at least partially from the reticence of the fraternities to allow any chapter to admit to its number women to whom other chapters would object. Because Kappa Alpha Theta's very existence rested on the fundamental ideology that each Theta was bound to all others by a vow of loyalty and a bond of sisterhood, if a sizable or vocal segment of the fraternity would not accept Jewish or, to a lesser degree, Irish Catholic women as sisters, then either the basic core of Theta would disintegrate, or the entire fraternity had to unite as a whole against the initiation of those whose presence might prove divisive to the sisterhood. Faced with these two options, the women charged with determining Theta's policies chose the latter. They urged each chapter to respect the beliefs and perspectives of all members to the greatest extent possible and to place above all else the opinions of those sisters who would be affected most by any one chapter's decisions.[106]

In their reaction to the diversification of the campus fields in which they operated and from which they chose their members, the women's fraternities of the early twentieth century thus adopted positions designed to attract the least amount of resistance or opposition from their memberships. Believing that their national scope required a certain cautiousness in approach, especially with respect to whom they took into their number, the leaders of Kappa Alpha Theta and the other women's fraternities adopted strikingly conservative stances. The paths they pursued were those that would reinforce their positions as bastions of established society. Wary of any move that might jeopardize their reputations as elite organizations, the women's fraternities showed the new arrivals to higher education the same cold welcome that many of the male students of the nineteenth century had shown to the earliest female fraternity members.[107]

No doubt many Greek sisters themselves opposed this conservatism. Statements by individual members, for example, suggest that not all shared their groups' opposition to Jewish and Catholic members. Most, however, believed that fraternity unity was predicated on cautiousness with respect to social issues.[108] When it came to another heated debate of the day, that regarding woman suffrage, an equally conservative attitude held sway among the women's Greek system.

One fraternity's decision not to embrace the suffrage cause in many ways ran counter to its conception of itself as a key promoter of women's progress. While its pro-working stance and glorification of independent, strong women invited many parallels to the goals promoted by the suffrage movement, Kappa Alpha Theta Fraternity refused to lend its name or support to the cause. Despite the central role that college-educated women played in propelling the Nineteenth Amendment to passage and even while many of its own members served at the forefront of this effort,[109] the organization as a whole resisted taking a position. Because it claimed as its members thousands of women of different age groups who came from disparate social, geographic, and cultural backgrounds, Theta's officers felt that taking up any cause that might prove divisive ran counter to their and the fraternity's best interests. They argued that the fraternity's continued stability and success depended upon its members' belief that it stood for ideals that they, as an increasingly large and diverse group of individuals, embraced. Supporting a sensitive cause might upset the delicate alliances formed from a balancing act between local interests and fraternity loyalty. Because Theta's continued existence depended so thoroughly on the sustained loyalty and efforts of its many members, its leaders chose to act cautiously on the suffrage issue and refused to take a stand.[110]

Indeed, although they supported most of the policies for which the suffragists were fighting and throughout their history elected their own leaders by membership vote, many Thetas recoiled from involvement in the movement because of its association in their minds with what they considered "unwomanly" individuals. In a stance loaded with class-based assumptions, many sisters disassociated themselves from the suffrage cause because, as one member put it, "We know that the militant suffragette does not typify ideal womanhood." Yet the same women who denigrated the suffragists also showed affinity with their goals: "The woman who holds herself aloof from all civic interests on the theory that woman's sphere is limited to her home, is just as far from the realization of our ideals."[111] Reluctant to oppose the women's vote but equally unwilling to associate themselves with "unwomanly" women, those who spoke for Kappa Alpha Theta refrained from engaging its name on either side of the suffrage question. Many of its members supported the cause of suffrage and prominent sisters—such as Martha Evans Martin, associate editor of the Richmond (Indiana) *Daily Telegram* and vocal suffragist, and historian Mary Ritter Beard, founding member of the Congressional Union for Woman Suffrage (later, the National Women's Party) and editor of the American Woman Suffrage Association's journal, *Woman Voter*—labored long and hard for its passage. In a move that demonstrated the widespread popularity of the cause among members, Kappa Alpha Theta even chose as an honorary member the Reverend Dr. Anna Howard Shaw, at the time vice president at-large and later president of the National American Woman Suffrage Association.[112] Even so, the preoccupation of many members with allying themselves only with the "right kind" of people kept Kappa Alpha Theta from joining with other prominent women's clubs—Sorosis, the New England Women's Club, the Association for the Advancement of Women—and supporting a cause that shared its fundamental belief in women's rights.[113] For many members of Kappa Alpha Theta and other Greek societies, maintaining fraternity unity meant disassociating from people and causes that potentially threatened the elite status of their organizations.

On the question of suffrage as on that of ethnic diversity, Kappa Alpha Theta and other women's fraternities thus in many ways adopted the paths of least resistance.[114] In adapting strategies designed to appeal to the views of the many, however, it was still impossible to quell internal debate. Despite the moves made to smooth over differences in belief in the name of unity, dissension rocked the women's fraternities throughout the 1910s, as social, cultural, and geographic distinctions among members compounded those caused by age and social environment to create a myriad of different views among the various branches of each organization. Faced with contests over who should belong to their organizations as well as what membership ought to mean and what rights and responsibilities it ought to entail, the fraternity women of the 1910s recognized that they needed to bring their members more in line with one another and with the fraternal ideal if they were going to remain strong. In the form of another challenge, this one posed from the outside by opponents to the Greek system, the leaders of Kappa Alpha Theta and their fellow women's fraternities found the impetus they needed to rally their chapters to work more closely together.

4

In Search of Unity

Fostering "High Ideals" in the Face of Antifraternity Sentiment, 1910–1920

The early years of the twentieth century saw enormous growth in the women's Greek system. Between 1898 and 1912, the number of women pledged to fraternities skyrocketed, from nearly 12,000 to almost 40,000. Within ten years, the number had expanded still further, to 113,000 by 1923.[1] Yet even as they blossomed, the women's fraternities faced challenges from within their memberships. Generational and geographic differences threatened their unity, and clashes over the class and religion of potential members pitted member against member. By the mid-1910s, prejudice was so rife in some organizations that their leaders enacted restrictive policies to pacify those who would not acknowledge Jewish or Irish Catholic women as sisters. Across the United States, members of Kappa Alpha Theta, Kappa Kappa Gamma, Alpha Phi, and other women's fraternities looked at their sisters on different campuses and in different settings and wondered aloud if each was as worthy as they were to claim membership in their organization.

At the same time as internal struggles plagued the women's fraternities, external assaults in the form of increasing opposition also threatened Greek life. A steady though essentially powerless undercurrent throughout the nineteenth century, antifraternity sentiment swelled on campuses and in state legislatures in the early 1900s, while its proponents strengthened in number and influence. At the same time as increasing numbers and percentages of students were joining Greek-letter societies, growing groups of students, administrators, and wealthy alumni were railing against what they labeled the secrecy, elitist selectivity, antidemocratic nature, and anti-intellectualism of the fraternities. On campus after campus in the 1910s, fraternities found their purpose and value questioned, and, especially in places where critics held monetary or positional influence, their activities curbed or even prohibited. How did the women's Greek system respond to growing opposition? In what ways did antifraternity sentiment shape the actions and behavior of fraternity members in the early decades of the twentieth century?

Opposition to the Greek system was not new, but prior to the 1910s, the opponents had won few gains. Since the founding of collegiate fraternities, individuals opposed to their selectivity, suspicious of their secrecy, or envious of their unity had mounted protests against them, charging members with everything from elitism to anarchy. Evangelical religious figures had spoken out against societies that privileged secrecy above revival confessions. Faculty members had taken exception to organizations that bound members to secrecy and required a pledge of loyalty that placed fraternity before college. Campus intellectuals had decried the undemocratic nature of the organizations, while students left unaffiliated also spoke out in opposition to the Greek system. Still, fraternities prospered.[2]

By the end of the nineteenth century, with the rapid growth of both male and female fraternities and the resultant increase in the Greek domination of campus activities, those opposed to fraternities began to speak out. They charged the Greek organizations with elitism and disruption and blamed them for negatively impacting the campuses on which they existed. In trustee meetings and in state assemblies, those opposed to the Greek system strove to convince those with monetary and political power that fraternities were "pernicious [organizations] against the highest and best development of the student and as American youth."[3]

In 1901, for example, a protest submitted to the state legislators of Wisconsin likened the state university's Greek system to the poisoned spring in Ibsen's play, *An Enemy of the People.* "Your attention as a legislator is invited to the fact that the state of Wisconsin is maintaining a *poisoned spring. . . .* The poison is that of *aristocratic exclusiveness,* mainly introduced through certain associations known as Greek Letter fraternities." Noting that "Wisconsin bears one of the worst reputations . . . [as a fraternity-run school] of any western institution," the author called on the state legislators to join Princeton and Yale in "purging" the campus of its "poison" by banning its Greek system.[4]

While "A Poisoned Spring" did not capture immediate attention, eight years after its publication the state legislators called for an investigation of the University of Wisconsin's Greek system. Labeling fraternities extravagant, elitist, and destructive to campus morale, state officials charged the Board of Regents to conduct an inquiry "for the purpose of remedying the antidemocratic and cliquelike tendencies of these organizations." After months of close study, a faculty investigating committee appointed by the Regents arrived at the conclusion that fraternities engendered poor scholarship and undemocratic conduct among their members, but that they were "not extensively antidemocratic, snobbish, or clannish."[5] Moreover, the committee argued, Greek-letter societies helped ease the extreme housing shortage wracking the Wisconsin campus: "In the absence of dormitories and student commons, this service [provided by the fraternities] cannot be overestimated."[6] Subsequent investigations ordered by the state legislators arrived at similar results. Faced once again with the fact that fraternities provided room and board for hundreds—perhaps as many as a quarter—of the university's students, those charged with determining the fate of the Greek system chose to call for reform of the "antidemocratic" fraternities but declined to bar them from existence on campus.[7]

While in Wisconsin the legislative ban on fraternities failed to pass, the Greek-letter organizations in other states were not as lucky. In South Carolina, Arkansas, Mississippi, Missouri, Ohio, Indiana, Texas, Kansas, Washington, and California, governmental authorities approved investigations of fraternities on publicly funded campuses. In at least four of these cases, state legislatures passed bills that effected bans on the Greek system.[8]

In South Carolina, for example, the state legislators in 1897 passed "an act to prohibit Greek letter fraternities or any organization of like nature in State institutions." A few years later, Arkansas passed a similar bill, though its campus authorities did little to enforce the measure.[9] In 1912, the Mississippi state legislature voted to prohibit fraternities at the University of Mississippi and at other institutions supported by the state. Although fraternity members challenged the constitutionality of this law, both the State Supreme Court and the U.S. Supreme Court approved its scope.[10]

In Texas the issue proved especially divisive. Student opponents of fraternities at the state university brought the legislators a petition to outlaw

Greek societies, calling such action "absolutely necessary to insure united popular support of the University and a united student body." They wrote: "We, the Executive Committee, representing the non-fraternity students . . . believe that fraternities at the University of Texas are an evil; that their presence in the University presents the most serious problem that confronts us at the present time; and that their abolition is the only solution of this problem." Arguing that even reforming the Greek system would not eradicate its faults, the nonfraternity students of the University of Texas condemned the Greek societies for their "artificial distinctions," their extravagant expenditures, their penchant for bloc voting in campus elections, and the divisiveness they caused on campus.[11]

As at Wisconsin, the opponents of fraternities at Texas failed to win the ban they sought from the state. On several private campuses, however, places where policy could be determined without oversight from state officials, opponents of the Greek system met with greater success.[12] At Brown University in 1911, for example, Lida King, a newly hired Dean of Women, declared fraternities harmful to her ideal of college life as "one family sharing everything in common" and so embarked on a crusade to expel them from the campus. In a setting in which two-thirds of the women students belonged to Greek-letter organizations, King's position proved wildly unpopular. Still, her view resonated with Brown's president, who, while a supporter of Greek life for men, nevertheless agreed with King's position that the women's organizations were detrimental to academics. In pursuit of a campus environment in which students would be "grouped not along lines of social cleavage, but on the basis of definite interests and purposes," Dean King and President William H. P. Faunce announced their decision to close Brown's women's fraternities. Despite protests waged by fraternity alumnae and officers, the administrators stood firm, and the ban went into effect.[13]

Shortly after the expulsion of fraternities from the Woman's College at Brown, the College of Wooster in Ohio followed suit. Spurred on by a wealthy trustee who tied a one million dollar donation to the banishment of fraternities, the leadership of Wooster debated what to do about its large Greek system. The need for funds won out. In 1913, the university accepted the donation and that same year erected a ban on Greek societies, threatening expulsion for members who did not return their charters to their national organizations.[14]

Other schools also witnessed fierce battles over fraternities. At Barnard College, several years of antifraternity agitation wore down pro-Greek administrators, and in 1915 secret societies were banned. Adelphi College, the University of Washington, and Sophie Newcomb College also experienced strong waves of opposition, allowing their Greek societies to remain only after exacting promises of reform. On campus after campus, non-Greek students rallied faculty, administrators, and outside agitators to their cause. They bolstered their arguments with claims that the Greek system was "undemocratic"—a powerful accusation on the eve of World War I—and thus won converts to their cause in state legislatures and on boards of trustees throughout the country.[15]

Not all college administrators opposed Greek societies, however. Out of eighty-eight college and university presidents who spoke publicly on the question in 1913, only seven expressed themselves opposed to national organizations. But even those who publicly supported or spoke neutrally on the topic argued that changes were needed to strengthen the benefits that fraternities and sororities provided to campuses. And even with official administrative support, student and faculty opposition to the Greek system often held sway.[16]

Alarmed by the waves of opposition confronting them on campuses throughout the country, the leaders of the major women's fraternities recognized that drastic steps had to be taken if the female collegiate Greek system was going to survive. Cognizant that their own calls for reform had gone unheeded in years past, they now saw the antifraternity movement as their cause to rally around. It was one thing for younger members to conduct themselves in ways that worried their alumnae; it was quite another when these actions provided fodder for the Greek system's opponents. "'[We must prove ourselves] such an influence for good that the general movement against fraternities will cease,'" the women argued.[17] "It behooves us . . . to examine with equal seriousness the conditions which have combined to develop an increasing criticism and opposition to national fraternities," a member of Delta Gamma pointed out. "One cannot readily believe that an institution that has lived in perpetual youth and vigor for almost one hundred years can be overturned by act of legislature, but neither can one readily believe that this growing opposition is anything less than the result of accumulated irritation because of years of error and unreasonableness on our part."[18] Recognizing that their own members' attitudes and behavior had played key roles in arousing the anti-Greek sentiment swirling around them, the leaders of Kappa Alpha Theta, Kappa Kappa Gamma, Pi Beta Phi, Alpha Phi, and other women's fraternities came together to enact reforms that would bring their collegiate members into line, quash the antifraternity movement, and solidify the Greek system's status as an American college institution.[19]

The first critique of fraternity life that the officers addressed—the facet most often raised by critics—was the excessively social nature of the collegiate Greek system. "We must put a stop to the excessive social life, and we must make the girls do it," a Zeta Tau Alpha alumna stated. At the biyearly gatherings of the National Panhellenic Congress, the fraternity leaders urgently addressed the growing opposition around them. "We must tell our chapters to stand for different things, we must insist on individual as well as general fraternity scholarship, for our enemies take the individuals to hold up to the public."[20] Recognizing that even one bad apple could spoil the reputation of the entire lot, the leaders of the women's fraternities cast about for ways to limit the excessive socializing of their collegiate members. "If we could come to some agreement on rules that would limit the number of parties, and the expense of them, we would really begin to accomplish something worthwhile," a Chi Omega sister urged.[21] Others advocated a "reasonable and sane limitation of expense" for sisters actively involved in campus life.[22]

Curbing excessive social life would also improve academics, and poor scholarship was a charge the fraternity leaders desperately wanted to refute. Schools such as the University of Texas were instituting scholarship standards for the Greek-letter societies, banning social events for those groups whose cumulative grade point averages fell below certain standards, and prohibiting the initiation of students with poor scholarship records.[23] An in-depth study of antifraternity agitation concluded that poor scholarship represented the most often-stated complaint against the Greek system.[24] That campus administrators had to force collegiate Greeks to perform better in their studies was an embarrassment to the women's fraternities, especially those that prided themselves on having been founded as organizations privileging scholarship and intellectual ability. In response to the curbs placed by some campuses and in the hopes of preempting others, the officers of the major women's fraternities rushed to institute new scholarship requirements and minimum grade point averages for their collegiate members. They hoped that improving the scholarship record of their organizations would lessen and even diffuse criticism leveled against them by faculty, students, and administrators. They hoped, too, that it would help restore to their organizations some sense of the early focus on intellectual ability.[25]

Indeed, while the casual attitude toward their studies displayed by fraternity members had for years drawn the ire of their professors, many within the women's Greek system—especially the alumnae belonging to the more studious first generation—concurred in their disapproval of the collegians' approach to academic matters. While it was one thing to encourage sisters not to focus too narrowly on scholarship, as many of them had, standards still needed to be set and met, and the initiation of poorly performing women needed to be banned.

Across the board, the women's fraternities put in place "severe legislation" on chapters whose cumulative averages fell below a certain standard. Some banned members with low grades from participating in collegiate activities. Others prohibited active participation in fraternity events of any sister not maintaining a set average.[26] The National Panhellenic Congress sent delegates onto campuses to check up on the scholarship records of collegiate Greeks. In addition to checking grades, it authorized its representatives to investigate the conduct of sisters in areas such as "limitation of social life," "social expenses," and "sane interest in college activities."[27]

In Kappa Alpha Theta, in an effort to raise the profile of scholarship among the undergraduate branches, fraternity leaders instituted formal grade-checking policies.[28] They opened the collective performances of each chapter to scrutiny by the rest of the fraternity and made comparisons against national averages for other fraternities and for nonfraternity students. In an effort to improve the "spirit of respect for scholarship" among the collegiate sisters, Theta's leaders published accounts of "Scholarship Honors to Kappa Alpha Theta Members" throughout the 1910s, and included in their lists the names of members receiving Phi Beta Kappa honors, fellowships, and other awards each year.[29] To work toward extending the list of honors, the fraternity required each college chapter to appoint a scholarship committee and charged its members with checking on sisters' grades and speaking with professors concerning performances and class absences. They collected the information gathered by the scholarship committees and disseminated it to alumnae advisers, district presidents, and other officers.[30] Fraternity leaders also collected reports on each chapter's average grades and ranked the branches in descending order of performance, publishing the results in the *Kappa*

Alpha Theta journal or in the Grand Council bimonthlies, so that all members could see where each chapter ranked.[31] In some surveys, the officers published the ranking of each chapter in relation to other fraternities and sororities in its institution. In others, the leaders offered averages on each campus for fraternity and nonfraternity students, and then situated the respective Theta chapters' within the context of their peers' performances.[32]

Groups that earned poor records received letters of reprimand from the fraternity officers, who sternly warned them to improve their scholarship. When, for example, the Tau chapter sisters earned marks ranking them ninth out of the eleven women's fraternities on their campus, the fraternity ordered them to implement more stringent rules to improve their scholarship. The sisters responded by creating a "blacklist" for those members whose grades fell below a certain minimum, forbidding blacklisted members from keeping midweek dates and prohibiting those who failed "to maintain a satisfactory standard of college scholarship" from voting on chapter affairs or taking part in fraternity-centered activities.[33]

Other chapters of Kappa Alpha Theta also heard their records disparaged as "mediocre" and were told by their leaders that their performances were "cause for shame."[34] In 1916, the undergraduates as a whole found themselves at the receiving end of a barrage of criticism for producing the poorest record Theta had ever received. Alarmed and embarrassed by their younger sisters' performances, the Grand Council of the fraternity admonished the undergraduates to "ponder over and resolve not to help repeat" the record that had caused Kappa Alpha Theta such terrible embarrassment.[35] While overall performance improved marginally over the next few years, Theta leaders still complained of "too many poor grades" and chided the collegians for falling more often below, rather than above, the average ranking for their respective colleges.[36]

The policies instituted by the women's fraternities to improve grades and rankings may have restored scholarship to a slightly more prominent place in the collegiate Greek system of the 1910s, but they did not necessarily evoke a corresponding degree of concern from undergraduate members. The collegians dutifully reported grades and cuts at their chapter meetings, but when left to their own devices frequently voted to waive fraternity rules designed to uphold scholarship standards, such as those prohibiting the initiation of any student with lower than a C average or those barring blacklisted members from enjoying midweek dates and partaking in social activities.[37] The reports of the activities they engaged in and the descriptions they provided of their lives reveal far different interests and concerns than the fraternity officers held. For many of the younger fraternity women of the early twentieth century, college represented a place to spend a few years engaged in pleasant social activities more than it did a site of learning and intellectual engagement.

Still, the renewed emphasis on scholarship did succeed in lessening the force of some opposition to the Greek system. On campuses such as the Universities of Texas and Wisconsin, improved grades on the part of Greeks won concessions from faculty and administrators. Witnessing the efforts the fraternities were exerting to make their members adhere to certain standards, campus leaders found themselves more willing than ever to work with the Greek system, believing that, through "mediation and surveillance over . . . members," fraternities could "aid the college in the maintenance of discipline."[38]

The women's fraternities had for many years been interested in closer relationships with school authorities across the country. They were well aware that on many campuses, groups of nonaffiliated students, faculty, and administrators maintained an impression of the Greek system as subversive of campus community, a theme that had simmered among opponents of fraternities in the nineteenth century but that had risen to the surface during the Progressive Era.[39] Prominent female administrators such as Marion Talbot at the University of Chicago had made their opposition to fraternities public, believing that Greek societies detracted from campuswide loyalties by drawing their members' attentions away from all-women's groups and concerns.[40] Quick to respond to these charges by showcasing the high levels of participation fraternities members maintained in all-campus activities, particularly in women's groups such as the Y.W.C.A., the female fraternities nevertheless recognized that if they were going to quell the rising tide of opposition, they needed the support of campus administrators, especially the powerful deans of women.

Since 1907, the NPC fraternities had urged their members to interact smoothly and politely with their campus leaders, but with the stakes now raised, the organizations ratcheted up the pressure they placed on collegians to maintain good relations with administrators.[41] In matters of dress, entertainment, and custom, the fraternity leaders pledged their members' support for all campus policies. "Kappa Alpha Theta expects cooperation with college authorities and self-governing bodies," its officers wrote. "We as a selected body of students should have qualities that make us useful in the college world." The leaders of the other women's fraternities agreed, mandating cooperation with deans of women for members of all NPC organizations.[42] "We do not believe that the fraternity should be responsible for the entire social system, for the different kinds of dancing, and so on," an officer of Chi Omega noted. But fraternity women must cooperate with faculty and administrators "for the amelioration of conditions."[43]

By placing curbs on socializing, mandating scholarship requirements, putting alumnae in greater charge of fraternity matters, and stressing the importance of smooth relations with administrators, the women's fraternities strove to alleviate many of the problems that both their leaders and their critics saw in the collegiate Greek system of the early 1900s. In many cases they succeeded in winning the understanding—if not always the respect—of administrators. By the 1920s many deans of women and other campus authorities were looking to the organized bodies to help establish customs and set limits on behavior. This movement on the part of administrators across the country to work with and not against the Greek system in many ways marked the full acceptance of fraternities as permanent facets of American campus life.[44]

While eager and willing to reform their organizations in the hopes of saving the campus Greek system, the alumnae officers of Kappa Alpha Theta, Kappa Kappa Gamma, Pi Beta Phi, Alpha Phi, and other organizations did not—perhaps could not—address the key issue underlying much opposition to the Greek system: its lack of democracy. In general, the women's fraternity sisters dismissed this critique as "socialist propaganda" and brushed aside charges of exclusivity: "The outstanding charge of those hostile to fraternities is Lack of Democracy. The system is all wrong because there should be equality on the campus. So say the Socialists of Life everywhere." It is human nature to be selective, they argued: "It is inherent in the human race to form cliques and class distinctions . . . and however idealistic a democratic foundation of human society may be, that is, nevertheless, something that does not exist." Unless women's fraternities wanted to "choose the communistic basis," selectivity would ever be a part of fraternity admissions. Even with their undemocratic manner of selecting members, the fraternities' approach was still preferable, they argued, to the "Bolshevikism" of forcing organizations to take in anyone who wanted to be a member.[45]

Certainly, many sisters realized that the more selective the Greek-letter organizations were, the more likely they were to arouse opposition. The problem of having "so many good girls coming in and so few sororities" was one of which the fraternity leaders were particularly conscious: "It would make the whole situation more democratic in the college," one argued, if more organizations could be founded to take in those left out by the existing fraternities and sororities: "[T]hey have either got to run the number up [in each chapter] or they have got to let out girls." The latter approach, they recognized, would "bring a strong criticism on fraternities."[46]

Bypassing the essential challenge that they selected their members, the fraternity women believed that if they simply took in better members—smarter, more committed to campus life, more gracious—and trained them to act more in line with their organizations' ideals, then they would diffuse the critique that their selection process rested solely on wealth and popularity. "If we *live* our ideals we cannot justly be abolished," fraternity leaders declared. "Loyalty to fraternity means, in its truest sense, loyalty to fraternity ideals."[47] To their active collegiate members, the women's fraternities directed missives warning of the immeasurable harm one careless sister could cause by not adhering to fraternity ideals. Any ill-considered action could bring dire results. "One snobbish, conspicuous, silly, indiscreet, loafing fraternity girl can lower the position of all fraternities in any one college more than four hundred sane, wholesome, charming, scholarly girls can raise it." In order to ensure not only that Theta or Kappa or Pi Phi's position remained strong but also that opposition did not lead to the banning of all fraternities on still more campuses, each fraternity sister bore the responsibility of abiding by her organization's stated ideals. "It is by fraternity undergraduate chapter life, not by fraternity ideals and plans . . . that fraternities will stand or fall."[48] But the question of how to ensure appropriate behavior among fraternity members did not have an easy answer.

Waving the specter of antifraternity agitation, the women's fraternities instituted new systems for influencing and controlling the conduct of their members. In Kappa Alpha Theta and in other organizations, these systems took the form of educational programs and training practices, designed to iron out discrepancies in beliefs and mores brought about by the geographic, cultural, social, and generational diversity of their memberships.

In the early 1900s and 1910s, the collegiate members of most women's fraternities operated without much involvement in national affairs. While

most sought out and greatly enjoyed opportunities to interact and socialize on their own terms with sisters on other campuses,[49] their participation in wider fraternity mechanisms was limited. Alumnae largely controlled and managed the organizations, and when campus crises arose or
other events required fraternity representation, such discussions often
took place without collegians present.[50] Unlike their predecessors who
had debated fraternity policy and played active roles in extension, the collegiate Greeks of the twentieth century focused their attentions mostly on
their own concerns, hosting the best parties and rush functions and making their own chapter the most popular and sought-after group on campus. With only occasional visits from overworked district officers to in-
trude on their autonomy, members of individual chapters went for
months and often years with little more than an official notice or report
from their Grand Councils. In a striking change from the missives of the
previous generation, the collegians' letters to their fraternity journals
dwelled on decidedly localized issues, and little sense of fraternity loyalty
beyond the individual chapter—except for social engagements with sisters of other campuses—showed in the chapters' dealings with their national bodies.[51]

In Kappa Alpha Theta, both officers and perceptive members alike recognized that this fragmentation threatened the strength and stability of
their organization, as well as their ability to show the anti-Greek world a
unified face.[52] "People judge a fraternity by each girl's actions, so how
careful we should be always to conduct ourselves like true Thetas," one
sister noted.[53] To bring the collegiate chapters more firmly into the fold,
the leaders of Kappa Alpha Theta in the early 1910s set about tackling
the discrepancies in practice and behavior that were causing many of the
conflicts. "It seemed to us that the most urgent need was to make the fraternity a unit; to do what we could to create an atmosphere of trust and
appreciation in place of the very critical atmosphere present in many sections," the Grand Secretary noted.[54] Since the different methods each
chapter used to identify and select new members incited the most criticism and bad feelings on the part of alumnae and collegiate members, the
leaders of Kappa Alpha Theta turned first to this area in their quest to
make the fraternity more unified in practice and feeling.

To curb what they perceived as the collegiate members' lack of care
and at times questionable judgment in selecting "good Theta material,"
the officers of Kappa Alpha Theta began to press for and later to require
the use of recommendation letters when identifying candidates for rush.

They urged their members, particularly the alumnae, to write to the relevant chapters when women they knew were matriculating at college. "The watchful eye and careful inquiry of a Theta, meeting such girls, might lessen much anxiety and prevent many mistakes in securing new members for our fraternity," the sisters argued.[55] Within a short time, a practice that had been taking place informally for decades became de rigueur in Theta and in other organizations, as chapters began to place heavy weight on the recommendations of other sisters when choosing from among the large numbers of women enrolling in their respective colleges. The letters proved so helpful that in the 1920s, they became mandatory.[56]

By urging the use of recommendation letters to screen potential candidates, the older members hoped to influence their collegiate sisters to choose more judiciously in their mad rushes for new initiates. Too swift selection, they feared, would lead to the mistaken pledging of individuals who appeared attractive, yet who upon closer inspection and longer acquaintance lacked "social eligibility," the pedigree, or even the religious affiliation necessary to make her a "desirable girl."[57] A Theta recommendation, particularly one sent by an alumna, would alleviate such situations, as the older Thetas would know both what "qualities the desirable girl should possess" and what particular types of women would best suit their former chapters.[58] Whereas the undergraduates often displayed a tendency to value appearances and sociability in their selections, the older Thetas would possess the "worldliness" and "foresight" to choose sisters based on the more lasting and, in most cases, influential factors of family background and reputation in their home communities.[59] As Grand Secretary L. Pearle Green explained, a national fraternity such as Theta depended upon its members making their choices with the wishes of other Thetas in mind.

> Grand Council urges chapters to give greater consideration to other chapters' territory in pledging stray girls from a distance. A chapter should consult Thetas in a girl's home vicinity before pledging her, as by not doing so a chapter may destroy with one pledge the carefully built up position of another chapter in a city from which it draws regularly.[60]

Another way to ensure that new prospects would prove good sisters was to take in mainly the daughters, cousins, nieces, and sisters of fraternity members—in essence, to practice as much of a "closed shop" as possible. Stressing that the "family background" of such candidates was already "known" and thus less of a risk was inherent than in cases of those of "unknown parentage," officers and alumnae pushed the collegians to expedite their evaluations of Theta relatives, even treating the candidacy of such rushees as essentially pro forma. Most of the collegiate chapters willingly did so, taking in the relatives of current and older members and often making special rules for them that waived waiting periods and other evaluation procedures.[61] Many chapters bragged of the number of daughters, sisters, and cousins they had won, calling themselves fortunate to have so many "Theta families" to keep their chapters strong. One year, for example, the Kappa sisters at Kansas extended ten bids for membership, six of them to Theta sisters. Another year, the Alpha Lambda sisters at the University of Washington bragged of having been "especially fortunate this year, in the number of sisters and daughters [the chapter has] had the opportunity of welcoming in to fraternity life."[62]

Most chapters heeded their alumnae recommendations, even at times placing their officers' predilections for familial relations over their own judgment in issuing bids for membership. Yet not all chapters adhered so willingly to this system, particularly in cases in which a Theta relative arrived at a chapter far different in custom and style than her mother's or sister's. In these situations, the sisters of the collegiate chapters balked at having to take in those they considered awkward or weak, simply based on sometimes-distant family relationships. They asked why a woman should gain easy entrée to Theta simply due to perhaps distant ties to someone who, years before and on a campus far away, had pledged herself to the fraternity.[63] To the alumnae leaders of the fraternity, the answer seemed simple—sisterhood demanded it:

> The obligations of the fraternity tie demand that a chapter extend every possible courtesy to matriculates related to Thetas, and judge them with the greatest possible leniency. . . . The younger sister, or the daughter of a loyal fraternity member has a better fraternity background than has any freshman from a non-fraternity family, and the advice of the fraternity members in the family can weld her to the chapter ideals as can no other one influence. It is always saner chapter policy to invite into Theta, girls whose family traditions are known than to take a charmingly appearing girl of whom nothing is actually known. Sisters and daughters a chapter can afford to take more on trust because the family tradition is known to be right.[64]

The leaders of the fraternity worried how rejection of a relative might affect particular Theta women who may have sent their daughters, nieces, cousins, or sisters off to school primed to become Thetas, only to learn that the students had not made the cut. They warned the collegians, "A Theta relative has to be very uncongenial and impossible indeed, not to do more harm outside of a chapter than in, for it is a grievous harm to put the loyalty of a member to the test of telling her, her own people are unworthy, and the alienation of loyalty does not stop there, but affects all the true fraternity friends of the hurt Theta."[65]

With large numbers of women about whom the sisters knew little enrolling in colleges and seeking membership in Kappa Alpha Theta, the older sisters considered taking in as many known entities as possible the safest means of guarding the reputation of their fraternity.[66] When undergraduate sisters veered from the recommendations and suggestions of their alumnae sisters, the Grand Council members simply issued policy resolutions to the chapters and sent strongly worded letters of reprimand. And in the case of new or weaker chapters, the officers sent "girls who are good rushers to help out . . . chapters during the rushing season, to see that they take the right kind of Theta material."[67]

To enforce more uniform practices and results, the officers of Kappa Alpha Theta also began encouraging alumnae members to take more active roles in rush and in selection decisions. Although from the earliest years alumnae sisters had played key parts in the day-to-day functioning of their college chapters, most of this involvement had taken place on an informal and individualized basis.[68] By the early 1900s, however, fraternity officers began to urge the chapters to formalize their relationships with particular alumnae and to turn their roles into more permanent positions by assigning them specific advising responsibilities and requirements.[69] They believed that undergraduate chapters would derive great benefit from the advice of an alumna whose role would entail guiding the collegiate members in their rush, selection, and training activities, and thus ensuring the formation, development, and perpetuation of a solid Theta branch.[70]

Not only did the officers press the undergraduates to look to their alumnae, but they also urged the alumnae sisters to respond to the needs of the collegians. "*To work for, rush for,* and *aid financially* the nearest active chapter is surely the *biggest* and most *vital* work [alumnae could do]," Theta's officers declared. In the pages of the *Kappa Alpha Theta* and in other fraternity publications, articles such as one entitled "Things

New chapter installations gave cause for fraternitywide celebrations. Whenever possible, officers and members of other chapters conducted the installations and attended the celebratory teas and banquets. Theta's Alpha Phi chapter at Sophie Newcomb College was installed in 1914. (Courtesy of Kappa Alpha Theta Fraternity, © 2003.)

Alumnae Should Be Doing" delineated both the need of the collegians for tangible support from their alumnae, and the obligation the older Thetas bore to offer such assistance. "The undergraduates need the wisdom, sympathy, and the aid of the more experienced, more tolerant alumnae," the fraternity leaders wrote. "Since you are a Theta for all time, the fraternity believes you should be an *active* Theta for all time." Not only was postgraduate participation in fraternity affairs vital to the continued strength of the fraternity, but it was also the only way the alumnae could pay the debt of loyalty they owed to Kappa Alpha Theta.[71]

Many alumnae members heeded the call and involved themselves actively in the rush events and decisions of their undergraduate sisters.[72] In nearly all college towns, resident sisters organized to influence and materially aid their local collegiate groups.[73] Chapter minutes reflect frequent interactions between collegians and their graduates, as the younger sisters solicited suggestions from their alumnae regarding fraternity matters and sought their advice and aid in planning and implementing rush functions.

Indeed, on several occasions, when faced with a debate concerning what to do about particular rushees, the sisters chose to consult their alumnae and learn their opinion on the matter before making any final decisions.[74] Younger alumnae often attended chapters' rush events, while older and more established alumnae sisters opened their homes to collegiate members for use during cotillions, luncheons, and other rush-related gatherings.

Most chapters found their alumnae sisters willing to aid them with hosting rush functions and making selection decisions, as well as with chaperoning and providing funds for their social affairs.[75] Dismayed and occasionally shocked by the undergraduate Thetas' methods and conduct, the older fraternity members willingly embraced the opportunity both to assist their younger sisters and to help mold the collegiate members to adopt more "Theta-like" behaviors.[76] The quest on the part of the fraternity to find, furnish, and establish a suitable chapter house for each of its collegiate branches provided just such an opportunity.

In the fraternity's early years, many Thetas, like their peers, lived near their schools and thus resided at home during their college courses. The few who lived beyond easy travel distance lodged in boardinghouses, either alone or in the company of fellow Thetas. The chapters held their meetings in one another's homes, or, when the numbers grew too large, rented rooms or halls at which they would gather for their weekly or biweekly sessions.[77]

In the late 1880s and early 1890s, growing acceptance of women's higher education as well as improved systems of transportation contributed to larger numbers of students attending campuses beyond easy travel distance from their homes. The influx of students seeking room and board in many college towns created a housing crisis that school administrators lacked the financial resources to address. In response to members' needs for room and board as well as to a fundamental belief shared by many in the fraternity of the value of a chapter house, Kappa Alpha Theta, like other men's and women's fraternities, strove to lease, purchase, or build houses for its chapters where members might live in a self-contained unit.[78]

Not only did the chapter houses help ease the pressure on school administrators to provide housing for the growing numbers of students attending their institutions, but they also served other functions of equal or greater importance to many Thetas: they helped strengthen the bonds

Although colleges and universities started admitting women in increasing numbers in the late 1800s, rarely did they provide housing to matriculating students. Fraternity women solved that problem by renting houses and hiring chaperones. Around the turn of the twentieth century, Kappa Alpha Thetas at the University of Nebraska lived and studied together in a house near the campus in Lincoln. (Courtesy of Kappa Alpha Theta Fraternity, © 2003.)

between sisters and aided in the enculturation and training of members. In the confines of a house defined by its Theta associations, members were surrounded by their sisters on a constant basis and thus subject to conscious and subconscious reinforcement of Theta values and beliefs. Grouped together without the addition of outsiders, sisters experienced firsthand the values of harmony and unity, if not homogeneity, among members. Close living also allowed for subtle influence and overt correction. Houses helped members keep an eye on one another and thus prevented deviations in individual members' behavior.

In urging their fellow Thetas not to rest until they had secured a chapter house, many sisters predicted the uplifting influences and solidifying effects such group living would bring. "The responsibility a chapter house imposes upon each inmate is an excellent thing in every way," one sister wrote. "The influence of the more studious and cultured members would be quickly felt. In the constant intercourse with minds largely centered upon the same duties and ambitions lies much of the pleasure and profit of college life."[79] In chapter houses, "the girls are brought into closer touch with each other and the fraternity means more in their lives thereafter for it is an influence present at all times."[80] By the 1910s, the fraternity leaders considered a chapter house "a beneficial aid in the attainment of [Theta's] ideals and in the securing of the fullest, symmetrical development of her members." They wrote, "A chapter house furnished—however scantily—only with things of quality and taste, presided over by the proper type of chaperon, can do more for culture . . . for genuine noble womanhood, than can any other one thing in the college environment." They charged alumnae with providing the means and the effort for creating such a wholesome and proper setting for their younger sisters.[81]

To assist Kappa Alpha Thetas at the University of Nebraska in furnishing their "home away from home," the men's fraternities sent the sisters vases, artwork, and chairs. Each of the Theta members also provided Christmas gifts for the house: pillows and pennants to decorate the rooms. Ca. 1902. (Courtesy of Kappa Alpha Theta Fraternity, © 2003.)

Prior to joining Kappa Alpha Theta as the Alpha Rho Chapter, members of local society T.B.D. at the University of South Dakota spent time together in their parlor, working on their needlework, ca. 1908. (Courtesy of Kappa Alpha Theta Fraternity, © 2003.)

In working to improve the conditions of the chapters and in seeking to influence and oversee both the conduct of the collegians and those they selected to join them as sisters, the alumnae sisters acted in their own interests as well as for the good of the younger members. Because in accepted fraternity parlance each member of the fraternity bore responsibility for the strength of the whole, the wayward actions of one undergraduate branch posed a threat to the fine reputation of all Kappa Alpha Theta members. Thus, the need for active alumnae support and involvement felt very real to many of the older women, and they perceived their intervention in collegiate matters as vital to their fraternity's continued success.[82] Time and again, fraternity leaders told the collegians that "the strength of the fraternity lies in its members" and "The rank of a fraternity . . . depends upon the innate traits of the individual members composing it."[83] They stressed to new and old members alike that, above all, the fraternity demanded loyalty and that "as soon as the pin is put on that they must do their part."[84] They singled out the older collegians, the juniors and seniors of each chapter, and told them, "You are an example to all of your younger sisters . . . [and thus] should be ever willing to lend a helping hand, advise, and, best of all, set a good example. . . . At no time can a Theta afford to sit with folded hands and quiet mind, and feel that her work and responsibilities are over."[85] They urged all collegiate members, "Let us remember, once a Theta always a Theta" and preached the attitude that "if the world is to judge my fraternity by me, then no act of mine shall ever cast the faintest shadow on the brightness of its name."[86]

Even while stressing the importance of each sister upholding the fine name of Kappa Alpha Theta, the older fraternity women recognized that in order for the young collegians to learn what such actions entailed, they needed training mechanisms and educational programs in which new sisters would be taught how to act like Thetas and how to hold proper respect for fraternity life and its demands. As one alumna put it,

> Rushing season simply furnishes the raw material to work with in our endeavor to build up what we believe to be the noblest type of womanhood. Of course we cannot too carefully scrutinize the offered material, but that is far from being the whole duty of a fraternity girl. There are very few "born Thetas." Most good ones are constructed with infinite pains on the part of the chapter and of the girl herself.[87]

Fearing that the collegiate sisters lacked a significant enough understanding of what Theta meant, to train their new pledges and initiates effectively, the older fraternity members in the early 1900s created a formal educational program designed to inculcate Theta's values into the women wearing its badge.

The sisters of Kappa Alpha Theta had, since the fraternity's founding in 1870, instructed their initiates on the basic tenets of fraternity life. They designed their initiation ceremony to teach new sisters that fraternity membership entailed responsibilities as well as rights, and that it bore costs as well as benefits.[88] As one sister noted, "In the beautiful ritual of Kappa Alpha Theta are the elements that may make Thetas true and noble." Yet one initiation ceremony was not enough to instill in sisters a full enough appreciation of the meanings and responsibilities that came with Theta membership. They needed frequent repetition of Theta's

ritual and moral code, so that the ideals they contained could truly become "a part of every Theta's life."[89]

With the chapters of the 1870s and 1880s often numbering fewer than
ten women and the order of business to be conducted left entirely to their
determination, the first generation of sisters of Kappa Alpha Theta often
took time in their meetings to reaffirm their vows to one another and to
remind themselves and one another of the central place that the fraternity
held for each of them. At the close of each of their meetings, sisters regularly positioned themselves in a circle, hand in hand, as a reaffirmation of
the bonds between them as members of the "Mystic Circle of Kappa
Alpha Theta."[90] They used songs as a means of reaffirming the important
role the fraternity played in each of their lives, joining together at the
close of their meetings to sing tributes to the love they felt for one another
and for Kappa Alpha Theta.[91]

The songs written and sung by the collegiate sisters of the first generation mostly entailed tributes to loyalty, sisterhood, and love as inspired by
the fraternity. Lyrics such as "Love the sisterhood / And to yourself be

When performing their rituals, sisters of Kappa Alpha Theta often wore their
fraternal robes, as did these Stanford sisters, ca. 1892. (Courtesy of Kappa
Alpha Theta Fraternity, © 2003.)

These four women from Sophie Newcomb College in New Orleans shared their fraternity songs at the 1915 Kappa Alpha Theta Grand Convention, held on the coast of Oregon. (Courtesy of Kappa Alpha Theta Fraternity, © 2003.)

true / And in the end she will defend / And ever honor you" and "We gather in our mystic home / Where loyal 'Thetas' gladly come / And here once more our vows renew / Unto each other to be true" strove to rein force in the minds of sisters new and old the goals of the fraternity as taught to them in their initiation ceremonies. Frequent repetition of songs, it was hoped, would reaffirm in members' minds the values the founders of the fraternity had imputed to Kappa Alpha Theta.[92] Through song as well as ritual and ceremony, early members of the fraternity sought to transmit to the women on whom they pinned the Theta badge the key roles that love and support for sisters, as well as honor and loy-alty to fraternity, played in defining what Kappa Alpha Theta meant.[93]

Yet while songs, initiations, and other ritualized ceremonies may have helped transmit Theta's values within the small and rather tightly knit chapters of the 1870s and 1880s, the growth in size of most branches by the 1900s and the rapid rate at which the sisters added to their number meant that the informal and rather localized methods of training collegiate members no longer sufficed.[94] With growing rifts dividing chapters and evidence of fragmentation mounting on all sides, the Theta sisters realized that more formal training methods were necessary. In order to successfully counter an opposition movement that was looking for every weakness or sign of disunity, the fraternity needed a Committee on Education to outline appropriate material for each Theta to know and to make sure that it got learned.[95]

The early years of Kappa Alpha Theta's educational program brought mixed returns. Some chapters embraced the training urged by officers and noted that, "a deeper love, a truer understanding, and a keener sympathy . . . [might] be obtained at least in part by study and discussion together of Theta's ideals." But more than a few chapters brushed off their leaders' prescriptions, choosing instead to spend their time on more enjoyable activities. When an examination was scheduled in 1910 to test the undergraduates' mastery of what the Theta officers considered important for them to know, four chapters earned marks of 90 percent, while twenty fell between 80 and 89 percent. Ten earned grades in the mid and low 70 percents, while one chapter scored only 64 percent. Papers submitted in subsequent years yielded similar results.[96]

Such failure to embrace the educational program left Theta's leaders alarmed at the state of their fraternity. "The papers are disappointing and in many cases show a sad lack of interest and study. . . . The ignorance on many vital matters was positively startling. Some of the papers, particularly from one or two chapters, were very flippant in tone. If such an attitude is characteristic, poor records are accounted for and a grave danger to the unity and strength of Kappa Alpha Theta made apparent."[97] Unhappy that their gentle attempts to bring the chapters together had not succeeded, alumnae leaders worried that the lack of loyalty shown by some sisters would open the fraternity to further challenge and critique. After all, they believed, a failure to conduct oneself as a "true Theta" could have very real ramifications—especially when the behavior was rash enough to arouse opposition among administrators.

And so Theta's leaders issued a new set of regulations regarding fraternity education. No longer would they trust the undergraduates to decide when and how to teach fraternity policy and train themselves in Theta's history and ideals. A new Committee on Education was formed, its members drawn from the alumnae sector. It assumed total power in deciding what ideals and aspects of fraternity history should be taught.[98] The group issued yearly prescriptions in the form of a "syllabus" and included details on how, in what order, and for how many minutes per week the sisters should study the required material.[99] The Committee on Education detailed which aspects of the fraternity's history the collegians should study, what elements of Greek life should be held up as exemplary, and what characteristics and traits the sisters should strive to embody. It devised an exam, which it issued yearly, and publicized the results for all in the fraternity to see.[100] It issued strongly worded warnings to those who failed to perform well: improve or face requests for resignation. The committee joined with the broader Theta leadership in threatening expulsion for "intractable" members who did not improve.[101]

The formal educational program instituted by Theta in the 1910s was mirrored in other Greek-letter organizations for women. In fact, all of the National Panhellenic Congress societies instituted similar training and control mechanisms during this time period, and the cumulative efforts at reforming campus conduct did help bring the collegiate Greeks more in line with their organizations' ideals and therefore helped quiet some of the opposition that had swelled in the early years of the decade. The men's fraternities too instituted strong reform measures, such that by 1920 it was possible for one sister to proclaim, "Many of the evils which have been laid at the doors of the fraternities in the past have been eradicated, viz., low scholarship, lack of broad college viewpoint, failure to cooperate with the college authorities and exclusiveness in the sense of circumscribed interests." At this point, not only was the Greek system solidly entrenched on most campuses where it had existed in the 1910s, but it was spreading rapidly to other schools, its influence growing and its legitimacy proclaimed even by those not members of a Greek organization.[102] Struggles certainly continued to make the undergraduates focus more on academics and less on socializing, but by this time school administrators recognized the power of the Greek system to set campus mores. Smart administrators chose to work with the men's and women's fraternities rather than against them, to use the groups, with their internal controls and mechanisms for enforcing certain behavior, to help control conduct on campus.[103]

In their quests for reform in the face of their own concerns and those of their critics, the women's fraternities restructured themselves in many ways. Whereas collegians had served as the main players in the early decades of the women's Greek system, by 1920 very little fraternitywide work took place outside the realm of alumnae oversight. Indeed, the formal education programs instituted by Theta and its peers solidified trends that had been gaining in strength since the mid-1890s. Alumnae now heavily influenced the training and educating of members, in addition to rush and selection, and they also controlled the face these organizations presented to campus officials and even state legislators.[104] In their efforts to make their organizations more unified, the women's fraternities in essence removed power from the undergraduate sisters and placed it in the hands of alumnae who would, it was hoped, serve as more mature, steady, and responsible fronts for organizations that wanted to think of themselves as at the forefront of modern womanhood.[105]

Given the power of the alumnae sectors and the responsibilities placed on them by the women's fraternities, it was crucial for the continued success of the organizations that they turn out involved and committed alumnae. Thus, in their efforts to improve their organizations, fraternity leaders specifically targeted for intervention the growing segments of their memberships that were leaving school after only a year or two without earning a degree. In the 1910s, more and more women were coming to school only for short stints, and unlike those in past years who had left mainly for reasons such as illness, family responsibilities, or financial hardship, this new breed of women was wholly intent upon a limited course of action. They were arriving at college without any intention of remaining until graduation, some leaving to get married and others to pursue other ventures. This meant that they had less invested in fraternity life and less to lose if their behavior brought shame or bad light on their sisterhoods.[106]

Despite their lack of concern for education and resultant lack of concern for grades, these short-term students—often of wealthy and influential backgrounds—tended to hold great appeal for the second-generation fraternity sisters.[107] In 1910, for example, 111 out of 1,197 Theta sisters failed to return to school for reasons other than graduation, and in 1916, this number increased to 200, constituting nearly one-fifth of the entire collegiate enrollment. By 1920, the number of Theta members departing early increased still further, to the point that the fraternity lost more than

300 of its nearly 1,100 collegiate members, one-third of whom gave reasons other than graduation for their departure.[108]

Not only worried by the behavior these transient women were exhibiting on campus, the leaders of the fraternity were even more concerned that the short stints in active chapters would not inspire the devotion and lifelong loyalty that served as the very core of a fraternity's purpose.[109] Departing sisters, fraternity leaders fretted, would leave "one-fourth equipped; one-fourth finished," to go among strangers without the proper molding in how to conduct themselves as Greek women should. As one Kappa Alpha Theta officer warned, "Unfinished and shallow women wearing a pin we respect, uncharitable and malicious women wearing a pin we respect, careless and indifferent women wearing a pin we respect—what shall we say of the college, of the chapter, that gave them the rights?"[110]

In Kappa Alpha Theta, many members young and old argued strongly against early departure from college and worried what would happen to their organizations if large numbers of their sisters continued to do so:

> [Kappa Alpha Theta] cannot hope for the continued power, strength and interest that our alumnae have always given us, if our college chapters of the present continue to initiate large numbers of the transient college students. . . . A large, constantly changing membership will undermine fraternity strength which is based on unity and lasting friendship. If our college chapters are to be true to their trust, they must look carefully after the character of their membership and cultivate conservatism.[111]

In the officers' and alumnae members' view, it rested on the undergraduate sisters to recognize and make known to their new initiates that membership in Kappa Alpha Theta constituted a privilege, which in return demanded loyalty and service to fraternity. At the same time, it rested on the older women, the alumnae who had greater experience and broader outlooks, to train the undergraduates to hold and transmit such values.[112]

Herein lay the gravest danger to Kappa Alpha Theta and the other women's fraternities experiencing the same problem. Because these organizations relied on their alumnae to either perform or oversee much of the selection, training, and molding of their younger members, they needed loyal alumnae who were willing to dedicate time, energy, and money to build up and strengthen the sisterhood. Yet apparent in the losing battle to keep sisters in school loomed the indisputable fact that those who departed school before completing their fraternity training showed less interest in fraternity welfare once outside of school and worked less diligently for their organizations' advancement. As one Greek member warned her sisters,

> Many of our college chapters have lost an unprecedented number of their active members the past year; that is, far too many of our girls leave college without degrees. And far too many of these ex-members, as well as far too many of the graduates of the last few years, take no interest in the fraternity after they leave college. The loyalty among the younger alumnae is in no way comparable with that shown constantly by the older alumnae.[113]

This lowered degree of interest in and willingness to work for fraternity welfare was worrisome to the Greek-letter organizations. Without the willingness of their older sisters to serve as advisers and mentors, the whole notion of training would suffer and with it the ability of future members to understand and live up to fraternity ideals. Without the sustained loyalty of their members, the principle of each sister representing one "link" in a "mystic chain of sisterhood" would crumble, as would the underlying philosophy of the lifelong vow as the very basis of fraternity membership.[114]

Recognizing the need to retain the involvement and dedication of the collegians in the years after leaving college, the officers of Kappa Alpha Theta and the other women's fraternities in the late 1910s consciously strove to offer more tangible and explicit forms of aid to their young graduates and others leaving school. They hoped that such efforts would help kindle the lasting appreciation of the younger sisters and, consequently, inspire their active and continued involvement in fraternity matters. As they aptly realized, the future strength of the women's Greek system rested on keeping second-generation sisters involved, especially in the years after college.

5

Once a Sister, Always a Sister

Fraternity Membership
in the Postcollege Years

By the early 1910s, fraternity alumnae outnumbered their collegiate sisters by as many as seven to one and played vital roles in the governing, training, and general management of their organizations. The leaders of Kappa Alpha Theta, Kappa Kappa Gamma, Alpha Phi, Pi Beta Phi, and other women's fraternities relied on alumnae members to provide financial and emotional support to the chapters; to attend, host, and oversee rush functions; to lend their presence and weight to initiations and installations; to investigate and recommend sites for possible charters; and to uphold the ideals of their respective fraternities and represent their interests in all of their pursuits. They pressed the older sisters to donate time, energy, and money to support students whom they had never met and of whose activities they often disapproved. In the name of sisterhood, they asked alumnae, busy with jobs, families, and projects, to remember and uphold vows of loyalty they had made to their fraternities during their often-distant college days.

In numbers that ebbed and flowed through the years and finally soared in the late 1910s and early 1920s, the alumnae of Kappa Alpha Theta and other fraternities responded to the call. Yet why? What motivated thousands of Greek-letter members to remain active in their fraternities long after the memories of chapter meetings, rush parties, and educational evenings had faded, and what rewards did they reap as a result of their involvement?

In the later decades of the nineteenth century, large numbers of fraternity alumnae—up to 25 percent—remained actively involved in their Greek-letter organizations. Loyalty, the desire for social outlets, and personal interests inspired continued participation, as did appreciation for the support the fraternity had offered during their struggle to make a place for themselves on campus. Those who resided near their colleges sought the social ties that involvement offered, remaining active in their chapters even while starting their own families, and joining in with rushes, initiations, and other fraternity celebrations. For many graduates, their sisterhoods provided sustained bonds of friendship as well as opportunities for continued social and intellectual engagement in the years following graduation. For women who might otherwise have lacked peers who shared their educational and social expectations, rejoining their chapters for meetings and social gatherings provided a welcoming and much-appreciated outlet that likely added a great deal to existences that otherwise may have seemed dull after the fullness of campus life.[1]

For those who moved away from home and chapter in the years after leaving school, fraternity affiliation provided continued support and sustenance. Countless letters written by the early sisters attest to the warmth and camaraderie that came with Greek-letter membership. One Theta sister reflected back on her experiences in the Mu chapter at Allegheny College, noting, "The short time I have been away from regular meetings has only served to strengthen the fraternity bonds and deepen my interest in fraternity matters. . . . It is, indeed, the remembrance of the good old times, and the dear old friends, that makes the 'black and gold' the emblem of happiness."[2] Another Theta wrote longingly from her teaching post in rural Minnesota of her "beloved Upsilon" chapter at the University of Minnesota and promised "distance cannot . . . detract from its power of this absent member."[3] An alumna who left school in 1875 concurred, noting, "It has been twenty-five years since I left college . . . but the old love is strong within me and whatever I can do for my fraternity will be done *eagerly*."[4] For decades after graduation, sisters continued to write earnestly of their deep affection and appreciation for their organizations. As one woman wrote more than sixty-five years after her initiation, "Throughout the years I have met so many wonderful Pi Phis and I feel so fortunate to have so many dear Pi Phi friends today—so Pi Phi has been a great part of my life for years."[5]

Numerous sisters shared stories of how their Greek-letter pins won them immediate friends in new surroundings. As one Theta sister told her story, "I well remember my feelings as I journeyed toward the west, having bid adieu to friends and sisters at Allegheny. I felt, indeed, like a stranger in a strange land. But what was my delight on arriving at my destination . . . to be greeted by the sight of a Kappa Alpha Theta pin, worn

Many sisters remained actively involved in fraternity life even after graduation. Edna Wickson (Kelley) (top), for example, who was initiated into Kappa Alpha Theta at the University of California at Berkeley in 1894, went on to serve as the national fraternity's Education Chairman from 1897 to 1901; as a District President and Grand Council Vice President from 1899 to 1901, and as Grand President from 1901 to 1905. (Courtesy of Kappa Alpha Theta Fraternity, © 2003.)

143

by [a] member of the faculty."[6] Another Theta described a similar encounter, upon her arrival at the town where she was to teach:

> What a hot day it was when I arrived in the small town of P—, where I was to bury myself far from the giddy whirl and pleasures of college life! I was a full-fledged "school ma'am," with my contract tucked under my arm and sternness enthroned on my brow; but, oh, such a homesick tugging at my heartstrings. . . . After much wandering, I found the president of the board, who immediately offered to tell me where to look for rooms. I tried to appear grateful, but my heart sank again at the thought of the vicissitudes always attendant upon that quest. I must meet the English teacher, he said, who could probably direct me to rooms. . . . Cheerful prospect! But I was glad to see anyone who could be company in my misery. Shall I ever forget that meeting? Her first greeting was, "Just look at that Kappa Alpha Theta pin!" Sweetest words on mortal tongue! We were friends from that moment, bound by a tie which we all love and which never was so dear to me as on that hot September day.[7]

In these stories and in others recounted in letters sent to the fraternity by former collegians, the alumnae of women's fraternities suggested that their membership served them well, not only by providing support and friendship while inside the college walls, but also by easing their way once outside of them.

For second-generation sisters, too, fraternity affiliation helped smooth their paths into their postcollege lives. To the more socially oriented sisters of the 1890s and early 1900s, the networking capacities the organizations enabled for their members represented one of the greatest benefits provided by Greek-letter membership.[8] Known since its inception as one of the most selective and therefore most prestigious of the women's organizations, Kappa Alpha Theta virtually ensured those who wore its badge entrée into the "best homes" in cities throughout the country.[9] In account after account, both public and private, numerous Theta sisters testified to the social connections the fraternity enabled. Some wrote of using their "Thetahood . . . to get intimate with or at least invited to the homes of [prominent citizens]" in given cities. Countless others noted that membership in Theta provided sisters, "whether [they] be traveling or permanently away from home, of a ready-made circle of friends . . . for 'once a Theta, always and everywhere a Theta.'"[10] Theta sisters were not alone, of course, in finding entrée through their fraternity connections: "Being a member was great help to me in making fast friends wherever I moved," one Pi Phi wrote. "I was always proud to be a [member]."[11]

In many respects, the women's fraternities served as social connectors for their alumnae members. They helped sisters on the move find hospitable hostesses; they assisted new graduates in acclimating themselves to unfamiliar environs. In Berlin, Germany, seven Kappa sisters formed what they called the "Berlin Chapter of Kappa Kappa Gamma," their network serving as a welcoming society for those sisters who found themselves abroad and in need of connections from home.[12] Back in the States, groups of alumnae members also made it their business to seek out and welcome any new arrivals or visitors to their areas. "We wish . . . that the chapters or individuals would let us know when sisters come to Philadelphia to live or visit," a group of older Thetas wrote to the *Kappa Alpha Theta* journal. "We have a social committee appointed to call upon any such, and we wish all Thetas living near Philadelphia to join [our group]."[13] A collection of Thetas living in Southern California issued a similar plea, as did a group of New York Thetas, who requested that "the corresponding secretaries . . . make it a point to inform us promptly in regard to their alumnae who may have come to New York to live, or to pursue courses of study for the winter."[14] In 1915, the Theta women made it the duty of all alumnae members to call on sisters newly arrived to their towns, to provide assistance to the newcomers and to invite them to join local alumnae branches.[15] Pi Phi sisters reported the same practice, one member noting, "I [have] lived in Philadelphia, Chicago, Kansas City, and . . . Rockford. In each city a Pi Phi would call and invite me to a local alumnae meeting. . . . Pi Phi has been a great part of my life for years."[16] To help sisters find one another and increase their abilities to use their fraternity connections, the organizations published updated catalogs every few years, listing the names, addresses, and relevant details of sisters. Most grouped their listings according to both chapter and geographic region, so that members might easily locate one another.[17]

Testimonies written by sisters attest to the frequency with which they drew upon their fraternity affiliations. Bernice Hall Glass, a 1912 initiate of the Gamma Chapter of Kappa Alpha Theta, kept a copy of the fraternity catalog as her personal address book throughout her life, marking on its pages the married names, family details, and new addresses of nearly all of her chapter contemporaries.[18] Other sisters used the catalogs to broaden, rather than keep up with, their social circles. Especially for those who moved away from their homes and chapters in the years following college as a result of marriage, new jobs, or husbands' occupations, the catalogs provided an easy way to locate sisters and form new social connections. As one Theta alumna noted, not only did the social gatherings that resulted prove "enjoyable from each one's selfish standpoint," but also they served to "further . . . the ideals of Theta sisterhood in that, through them, many strangers in town, brides particularly, have formed real friendships."[19] As an elderly Pi Beta Phi sister wrote more than a half-century after leaving school, "Wherever I've lived—U.S. or Canada—I have met wonderful 'sisters' and have been so proud to be a member."[20]

Many alumnae women wore their fraternity pins regularly, in the hopes that chance meetings might result. One Theta sister in Denver wrote excitedly of her encounter with another member one afternoon, the meeting a direct result of each sister's Theta badge. She reported, "Two young women coming face to face, each with eyes glued to the Theta pin above the other's heart. Amazement, disbelief and joy, as Psi and Phi literally fell into each other's arms, asking 'Who are you? What is your chapter?'"[21] Another sister, a young newly-wed, vividly described the loneliness and worry she felt upon moving to a small town in the Northwest, fears that were assuaged upon meeting a fellow Theta:

> And then I heard of another Theta in town, a dear, generous, wonderful girl from a near-by chapter. . . . She was *almost* as glad to see me as I to see her, as we constituted the Theta quota in the town. It was she who offered us wonderful hospitality until we were settled, loaned us silver until our wedding gifts were sent from home. In true Theta spirit she made me welcome and I knew I had made one really worthwhile "tie" in the new town.[22]

One member wrote of wearing her pin while abroad in Berlin. "At a reception given to our recent Ambassador . . . I spied a Theta pin. I rushed to the girl and gave her the grip before I could find voice to say a word, so great was my joy. . . . I never fully appreciated [the privilege of wearing the pin] until, far from home, I met a stranger who was not a stranger, sharing my interests, striving for a true and noble womanhood, brought near to me the mystic tie that binds."[23] Many years after her attendance at college, a Kappa Kappa Gamma member noted the importance of her pin: "I still have my pin and when I take summer trips I wear it. [Another

Kappa member] introduced herself to me years ago, going down the Hudson River, when she saw the little key."[24]

For the thousands of sisters who lived their lives without spouses or companions, fraternity connections likely proved especially important. A significant number of first generation sisters, like their nonfraternity college-educated peers, either chose not to marry or else entered into marriage at a later age than their non-college-educated peers. In a survey conducted in 1916 by Kappa Alpha Theta Fraternity, more than 30 percent of the sisters who joined the fraternity prior to 1900 reported that they had never married. For those initiated between 1900 and 1916, the percentage of unmarried sisters was even higher—55 percent—but it is likely that many of this group subsequently married, as the survey included those who had left college only that year.[25] Still, for those who never married, married late, or found themselves widowed early, women's fraternities such as Kappa Alpha Theta may well have served as an especially important source of support, both emotional and financial. The organizations provided for their members irrespective of marriage status, and offered belongingness and assistance without any of the accusations that unmarried women would have heard from other sources, that they were selfish, career-obsessed, unfeminine, and responsible for "race suicide."[26] While it is true that many collegiate chapters had rituals to mark the engagement of members—chocolate sent to the group from prospective grooms in one chapter, a gift of silver spoons given to engaged sisters in another—Kappa Alpha Theta, like its fellow Greek fraternities, made no distinction between married and unmarried sisters and held up members of both groups as models for emulation by the rest of the sisterhood.[27] Many high-ranking fraternity officers remained unmarried, and they helped set the tone for their organizations. For those who went through all or part of their adult lives alone, knowing that they belonged to a sisterhood that was bound to "befriend and to comfort, to assist, support and . . . have a due regard for their temporal wants, if occasion should require," would no doubt have been comforting, especially as they read novels such as Dorothy Richardson's *The Long Day* and other depressing accounts of the lives of unmarried working women.

Indeed, to sisters who suffered from illness or material need—a group that often included either unmarried or widowed sisters—all of the women's fraternities provided assistance and support. After an incident in 1913, in which Kappa Alpha Theta learned of an ill sister being cared for by a Kappa Kappa Gamma member because no Theta money was available for her assistance, Theta's leaders made it a priority to see that their pledge of temporal aid to fellow members be "something more reliable than empty talk."[28] With this move, they fell into line with Kappa Kappa Gamma, which had from earlier years pledged to care for its sick and bury its dead. Through money-generating drives and appeals to alumnae, the fraternities raised the resources to follow through with their pledges and by the 1920s had specified funds earmarked to "aid [sisters] in need of temporary assistance and without other friends upon whom to depend."[29]

To sisters wanting to continue their education but lacking the money to do so, their fraternity affiliations gave them access to much-needed means. A Scholarship Fund, created in 1902, provided money to needy Thetas who sought to complete their college courses. Numerous alumnae members labored on behalf of the fund, selling cookbooks to raise money or otherwise holding drives for its support. Unaffiliated alumnae offered individual contributions, such that by 1915, the fraternity had enough money to pay the tuition and expenses of twelve members. In 1916, Theta increased the number of recipients to eighteen, and by 1922, the Fund contained more than $15,000 to use for the sole purpose of aiding sisters in completing their college and postgraduate degrees.[30]

Kappa Alpha Theta was not alone in granting scholarship money to needy sisters. At their 1907 convention, the sisters of Pi Beta Phi authorized money to pay for fellowships for graduate study in America or Europe, in addition to the money they were already setting aside for undergraduates, and Delta Gamma, Alpha Omicron Pi, and Gamma Phi Beta—to name just three other organizations—offered scholarships to their needy sisters as well.[31] Kappa Kappa Gamma also maintained a scholarship fund, which provided money to any Kappa requiring financial support to continue her studies. Founded in 1902 and used little in its first few years, by 1920 the fund had helped 120 sisters and money was so plentiful that the Kappas opened the scholarship up to needy students outside of the fraternity.[32]

The increasing numbers of sisters seeking paid employment after college found just as tangible and forthcoming support from their fraternities. As early as 1914, representatives to the National Panhellenic Congress discussed the need for vocational training for their collegiate members.[33] With surveys showing a stronger interest in paid vocations on the part of college graduates, fraternity officers began to introduce more vocationally related materials into the fraternity journals and other publications in the mid-1910s. The *Kappa Alpha Theta*, for example, ran, "Opportunities for Vocational Training in Boston," "Special Training Centers for Vocational Work for Women," "Life Insurance as a Business for Women," "Nature Study and Children," and "Nursing and Its Opportunities for the College Graduate," and offered a feature entitled "Vocation Notes" that ran in all the issues.[34] For those graduates unsure of what vocation to pursue, the editors offered "Vocational Suggestions for the Trained Woman" and "Various Vocations for Women" to help them find appropriate paths.[35] Fraternity officers developed job banks, listing the titles of jobs available as well as relevant contact information, and encouraged their members to draw from their resources. In articles such as "Are You Hunting a Job?" Theta's leaders disseminated information on how sisters should best approach their job searches. As extra assistance, they offered information on national vocational bureaus for college women and offered special advice to sisters interested in particular, specialized fields.[36]

Large numbers of fraternity members, both alumnae and collegiate, took advantage of these vocation-related offerings. Most Thetas, for example, pursued some type of employment for at least a few years after their graduations.[37] As both cause and effect of their members' interest in career planning, the leaders of Kappa Alpha Theta increased the tangible and emotional support they gave to helping their ex-collegians find paid employment. Prior to 1900, although more than half of their graduates entered some kind of profession, the fraternity offered little acknowledgment that a Theta might be interested or actively engaged in a vocation.[38] By the 1910s, on the other hand, with more opportunities open to women after college in fields such as social work, library science, teaching, and nursing, the leaders of Kappa Alpha Theta stepped up not only their openness to students pursuing explicitly practical fields but also the support they offered for such endeavors.[39]

For example, in addition to increasing the amount of time they spent addressing undergraduates' and alumnae sisters' vocational concerns in the fraternity quarterly and in other publications, the Theta leaders also put ideas into action through the formation of a fraternitywide Vocational Committee. Charged with gathering lists of jobs in fields other than the most common one, teaching, and sending these to all interested sisters, the committee members helped advise the collegians and young graduates on which courses would best prepare them for careers in particular fields.[40] In addition, they helped recruit alumnae to serve as advisors for younger sisters who wished to enter their fields of work.[41] Their stated objectives entailed "[to] help individual Thetas, either active or alumnae, in practical and definite ways; to help with advice and information of many kinds; to promote individual and national efficiency; and to broaden the scope of Theta sisterhood."[42]

Anticipating the fact that many of their graduates would pursue careers in the business world, social service, and teaching, the leaders of Kappa Alpha Theta and the other women's fraternities advised their younger sisters to prepare themselves early for postcollege employment by taking courses in vocationally oriented areas such as domestic science, education, and business.[43] Whereas in its first forty years, Theta's constitution had prohibited students enrolled in any course other than liberal arts from winning membership inside its circle, in 1914 the sisters voted to overturn this rule and even moved to consider agricultural and technical colleges as potential sites for charters. Whether of their own volition or due to their fraternity officers' encouragement, more than half of the collegiate Thetas by 1917 were actively pursuing some kind of vocational work in their collegiate training.[44]

At their biennial conventions and at National Panhellenic Congress gatherings, the leaders of the women's fraternities also arranged for more vocational and career-oriented sessions. Rather than holding panels entirely dedicated to issues such as rushing and pledging, as in former days, fraternity leaders introduced sessions on vocations and employment training.[45] At the 1915 convention of Kappa Alpha Theta, for example, the officers engaged a lecturer on commerce to come and "give advice to any Theta who wishes to enter the field of secretary work." At the same meeting, the fraternity also brought in an actress to meet with "any Theta who has longings for the stage."[46] Officers organized sessions on household management and instructed sisters on balancing budgets. In publicizing these offerings, the fraternity leaders took great care to point out the practical and lasting applications that the sessions would have for those attending.[47]

This advice and guidance resonated with the large numbers of the fraternity sisters who pursued some form of employment after graduation. Indeed, despite their overly social outlook during their college years and the reputation of women's fraternities as organizations for the rich, a significant proportion of sisters did choose to engage in paid work after leaving school. In Kappa Alpha Theta the percentage of members who en gaged in paid employment rose from 52 percent before 1900 to more than 75 percent in the late 1910s.[48] A survey conducted in the winter of 1919 of the previous year's graduates revealed that of the 164 sisters who responded to the questionnaire, 65 held teaching positions at various levels, 27 were engaged in war-related work such as nursing or assisting in governmental activities, eight were employed in businesses such as advertising or brokering, four held secretarial positions, four worked in some form of literary endeavor such as writing for the news media, six were involved in science as either laboratory assistants or chemists, three worked in libraries, and two in philanthropic fields. Fifteen others were enrolled in graduate programs, while five more sisters attended some form of business college. Overall, 119 of the respondents, or 73 percent, were engaged in some form of employment after graduation, while an additional twenty sisters, constituting 12 percent of the total, were pursuing higher degrees. Only 15 percent of the sisters who graduated from college in 1918 eschewed either further training or paid employment, and of those, most cited marriage as their reason for opting to stay outside the workforce.[49]

In their occupational choices and rate of employment, the Theta sisters essentially mirrored those of their fraternity and nonfraternity counterparts. Roughly 85 percent of women's college graduates during this time period entered the workforce, and over 65 percent of these women pursued teaching as their vocation.[50] Like their cohorts in Kappa Alpha Theta and other women's fraternities, the nonaffiliated collegians of the late-1910s largely considered paid work both a desirable, and in some cases necessary, pursuit. Depending on their personal situations, however, their access to these jobs would have fallen short of that of their Greek-letter counterparts. Nonfraternity women would have had to struggle harder to gain access to vocational networks and job banks than did their Theta, Kappa, or Pi Phi peers, and thus their entrée into particular fields would have taken greater effort and required them to draw upon more personal resources than did their fraternity counterparts. Whereas the fraternity sisters could rely on connections fostered through their individual organizations' resources as well as through those of the highly networked National Panhellenic Congress, what few resources did exist for nonaffiliated women, namely the Appointment Bureau of the Women's Educational and Industrial Union in Boston and the Intercollegiate Bureau of Occupations in New York, cost money to use and took several years to get up and running. Books such as Mary Caroline Crawford's

The College Girl in America, published in 1905, offered the nonaffiliates some guidance, but they lacked specific details, became outdated within a few years, and therefore provided no concrete leads concerning employment openings. Thus, the nonfraternity women searching for jobs in the mid and late 1910s would in most cases have found themselves largely alone, dependent upon their own personal connections, resources, and luck, both in securing employment and in making the transition from college life to the working world. Greek sisters, on the other hand, in most cases found doors opened to them and paths paved, largely as a result of the badges they wore.[51]

Once engaged in professions, too, fraternity women found their Greek affiliations helpful. At teachers conferences, such as the Convention of the National Teacher's Association, and at other vocational meetings, fraternity sisters gathered together, reinforcing the connections between them and re-creating these ties vocationally as well as socially.[52] Some alumnae sisters used their collective power to take up battles that, if won, would benefit thousands of fellow Greeks. The Seattle Alumnae chapter of Kappa Alpha Theta, for example, wrote to the School Board of their city in 1919 that they "wish[ed] to go on record as favoring a raise in salary for the grade teachers" so that "college girls" would continue to find teaching an attractive pursuit.[53]

No statistics have been preserved regarding the number of fraternity women who availed themselves of the different vocationally oriented services provided by the Greek-letter organizations, but the consistency of these types of offerings as well as the comments made by different groups' representatives concerning the frequency of employment-related requests suggest that a large number of sisters did take advantage of the career training, counseling, and advising offered to them in the latter half of the 1910s.[54] Yet in analyzing the implications of the vocational orientation of many of the women's fraternities, as significant a fact as the number of sisters who partook in the services offered is the entirely positive and supportive message that Kappa Alpha Theta, Kappa Kappa Gamma, Pi Beta Phi, and other organizations sent to their members regarding paid work for women. Through frequent advice columns as well as practical suggestions and offerings, the leaders of the major women's fraternities created an environment favorable to their members' pursuit of paid employment. In an article in the *Kappa Alpha Theta* that surveyed the paths pursued by Theta's alumnae members, one sister wrote, "Careers appeal to us first. We are proud of those women who have worked their way to

fame and brought renown to the name of our fraternity." Fraternity historians included the names and occupations of "outstanding members"
in their histories of their organizations, including in this number those
members who earned advanced degrees and those engaged in the professions.[55] In countless other writings as well, Greek leaders celebrated as
"outstanding" those sisters who pursued careers in paid vocations.

In particular, Theta member Estelle Riddle Dodge and her fellow fraternity historians gathered and listed the names of those Thetas involved
in professions in which few women were represented. The pages of
Dodge's "What Some Thetas Are Doing" in her *Sixty Years in Kappa
Alpha Theta* provided details on Theta professors, scientists, lecturers,
writers, editors, "experts," politicians (in the western states), physicians,
administrators (in and outside of academia), and executives. Without
sorting or ordering the list, Dodge and Grand Secretary L. Pearle Green
presented to their fellow members those sisters whom they considered
worthy of mention for their outstanding accomplishments. In their esti-
mation, and in those of other fraternity leaders who published lists and
compilations such as reprints of pages from the *Woman's Who's Who of
America,* the sisters who deserved particular mention were those who had
forged into previously closed or difficult-to-enter fields and had risen to
national and international distinction because of their vocational endeavors.[56]

This is not to say that those members who eschewed remunerative
jobs in favor of charitable enterprises found themselves without support
or encouragement. In fact, the leaders of the women's fraternities bestowed equally high praise and attention on their members who took up
benevolent activities.[57] Alumnae groups that worked together in support
of settlement houses, hospitals, and schools received frequent notice and
commendation from their fraternities. Most organizations adopted pet
causes, from sending money and goods to families in Appalachia to
opening an orphanage in France, and these works generated a good deal
of press, both inside the individual organizations and in the wider fraternity world.[58] So public were the women's fraternities about the charitable works their members were doing that even people outside the
Greek world took notice. Allegedly, reports of the charitable works done
by the Pi Beta Phi sisters in the mountains of Tennessee were influential
in convincing the state legislators of Wisconsin not to follow through
with their threats to outlaw fraternities on the University of Wisconsin
campus.[59]

Especially during the First World War, fraternity leaders made long mention of those sisters who sent packages of homemade goods to far-away soldiers or who knitted or sewed for troops abroad. Many members served overseas, some funded by their organizations, and those who remained home raised an estimated $50,000 for the war effort.[60] Both collegians and alumnae engaged in war-related work, and the women's fraternities helped publicize their members' projects, supplying both ready-made lists of names upon which to call for support and free advertisement on behalf of pet causes. With the fraternity's help, for example, Kappa Alpha Theta alumnae raised $3,800 for the Red Cross to fund the Base Hospital in France and an additional $3,900 to supply nurses with needed clothing and equipment. Countless orphans were supported and displaced persons cared for.

Kappa Kappa Gamma alone sent clothes and money to support three hundred families in one war-torn area of France, and all of the organizations assisted the Red Cross and Y.W.C.A. in providing relief for those injured or left destitute by the Great War.[61]

The women's fraternities were abundantly proud of their members who adopted charitable enterprises, both for the works they did and for the positive way that their efforts reflected on their organizations. In the leaders' eyes, the good works performed by their members was the best possible answer to those who criticized fraternities. They wrote:

> Ask Belgium if sorority effort has not been the means of bringing comfort to homeless multitudes and starving babies; ask the Red Cross if willing hearts, tireless fingers, and generous gifts have not been worthwhile; ask the Y.W.C.A. if hostess houses would have been so easily achieved without the material aid of sorority women; ask foreign lands if the hospital nurses and corps of reconstruction workers have not met more than a passing need. If—after this world wide demonstration of altruistic endeavor—the sororities are still forced to defend their existence, where will they find a better argument than the continuation of the same whole hearted service which meant so much not only to the world but to the organizations.[62]

In their efforts to ameliorate the ills they saw around them, those members who chose to perform charitable works received both aid and praise from their Greek-letter organizations. As a result of a pledge of loyalty made years before, the sisters of Kappa Alpha Theta, Kappa Kappa

Gamma, Pi Beta Phi, and other fraternities found themselves supported and assisted in all their endeavors, be they personal, social, charitable, or vocational. Guided throughout their college years by fellow members bent on their success; trained for their desired careers and assisted in their procurement; welcomed to new cities and granted access to socially desirable circles, the members of women's fraternities lived their lives bound to one another by far-reaching fraternal ties.[63] The opposite in nearly every respect to the isolated, anonymous working women described by historian Joanne Meyerowitz, the Greek-letter sisters of the late 1800s and early 1900s received throughout their collegiate and postcollegiate careers assistance, support, and friendship in exchange for their continued involvement in fraternity matters. Unlike the "women adrift" of Meyerowitz's study, the sisters of Kappa Alpha Theta, Kappa Kappa Gamma, and other secret societies found members literally clamoring to welcome them to new environs, to help them locate employment, and to provide assistance in support of their chosen endeavors.[64]

In the support members received from their fraternities as they worked to forge a place for themselves in postcollegiate society and in the assistance they provided to their sisters as they embarked on their own particular social, vocational, and personal pursuits, the reciprocal ties of the Greek-letter fraternities took on a tangibility that gave form to the organizations' chosen symbols: the kite of Kappa Alpha Theta helped members soar above their peers in academic, social, political, and vocational pursuits; the key of Kappa Kappa Gamma gave members access to homes, institutions, and jobs that they otherwise might have found closed to them; and the weight of Delta Gamma's anchor kept sisters connected to one another and to their fraternities, preventing each sister from being torn away and left to float without the backing of her organization. The price they paid was loyalty—to their fellow members, to their organizations, and to the sometimes amorphous entity they called "sisterhood."

6

Bound by a Mighty Vow
The Costs and Benefits of
Fraternity Membership, 1870–1920

From the time of their founding through the first decades of the twentieth century, the women's Greek-letter fraternities used metaphors such as Theta's "linked chain" to describe the relationship between their members and the organizations. "Bound together" by a "mighty vow of sisterhood," each fraternity woman drew strength from the force of the whole chain, yet at the same time owed her sisters the obligation to keep her own "link" strong. Implicated in, as well as responsible for, one another's conduct and behavior both in and outside the classroom walls, the sisters of Kappa Alpha Theta, Kappa Kappa Gamma, Alpha Phi, Pi Beta Phi, Sigma Kappa, and other women's fraternities played key roles in shaping one another's collegiate and postcollegiate experiences. From the moment each new member was initiated, she found herself charged with preserving the exclusivity of her sisterhood. Her academic performance now received scrutiny from her fellow members; her social habits merited constant regulation and even critique. Her personal habits attracted the attention and control of others, and even her choice of career—or lack thereof—drew comment from her organization. In monitoring one another's academic and social performances and training one another to act in certain narrowly prescribed ways, Greek-letter women, both active and alumnae, strove to regulate one another's behavior, both to ensure the academic and social success of their sisters and to make certain that no member violated the tenets of the fraternity ideal.

In many respects, the women's fraternities played markedly supportive roles for their many thousands of members. From assisting them in making a place for themselves and for other women inside the walls of academia to encouraging them to pursue vocations in arenas other than the

TIFFANY & CO.

At the 1907 Kappa Alpha Theta Grand Convention, the fraternity's first official coat of arms was adopted. Prior to 1907, various insignia representing individual Theta chapters were used in publications such as college annuals. The 1907 coat of arms incorporated elements representing the fraternity's ideals and principles, especially the symbols of the links in a chain. It is still used by the fraternity today. (Courtesy of Kappa Alpha Theta Fraternity, © 2003.)

traditionally female-centered world of schoolteaching, the female fraternities acted at the forefront of women's progress, even while retaining largely conservative notions of how "true women" ought to act. They posited high scholarship and intellectual achievement as both the ideal and the norm for women, while simultaneously helping them cultivate the traditionally feminine traits so valued by society. They treated married and unmarried women alike as role models, presented paid employment as desirable and virtuous, and linked efficiency and leadership—both characteristics of professionalism—to the achievement of fraternity ideals. In offering models of behavior that challenged certain social expectations while fulfilling other feminine ideals, Kappa Alpha Theta and its fellow women's fraternities helped stretch their members' conceptions of what sorts of endeavors women of their education, background, and class might pursue. They helped them push against barriers even while serving as bastions of proper society. They enabled members to be both traditional models and social movers, both representatives and challengers of traditional notions of womanhood.

In this respect, they were very like the voluntary associations and clubs to which so many white, middle-class women belonged during the decades surrounding the turn of the twentieth century. Nineteenth-century clubwomen, as historian Karen Blair argued, "utilized the domestic and moral traits attributed to the ideal lady to increase autonomy, assert sorority, win education, and seize influence beyond the home in the forbidden public sphere." Often selective and defined by class as well as culture, the literary clubs and charitable associations of the nineteenth century were to a large extent built upon the tenets of "true womanhood," even while they promoted "practical methods for securing to women higher intellectual, moral, and physical conditions, with a view to the improvement of all domestic and social relations."[1] Using language similar to the women's fraternities and with memberships that had a good deal of crossover, literary clubs and voluntary groups, while maintaining the traditional parameters of domesticity and morality, helped enlarge woman's sphere both metaphorically and in very real, economic terms. "The preservation of conventional appearances in the implementation of Domestic Feminism," Blair argued, "permitted the opening of new public avenues to women."[2]

Through social connections and networking access, fraternity affiliation helped members navigate the complex and at times threatening social worlds of America at the turn of the century. The closing decades of the 1800s had brought radical changes to everyday life for most Americans, as immigration, urbanization, and industrialization altered social relations, changed work expectations, reorganized space, disrupted patterns of interaction, and broke down the "island communities" that had heretofore characterized the nation.[3] Money no longer signaled class, and for those concerned with others' pedigree, the right clothes and the right manners no longer signified the right breeding. It was harder to know one's neighbor in twentieth-century America, and, indeed, improved transportation systems and increased opportunities for work and travel made it less likely that individuals would settle in the same geographic areas in which they had grown up and more likely that those they ended up next to would have different values and different customs. Massive immigration to the United States meant new and different kinds of people with whom individuals had to interact. Even the universities, the preserves of the middle and upper-middle-class white Anglo-Saxon males, saw their gates opened to women, followed shortly by Jews, Catholics, ethnic minorities, and others who in the past had been kept out.

Turn-of-the-twentieth-century American life may well have been stressful for many Americans, especially for the white, Protestant establishment. Challenges to their status from above by the newly rich entrepreneurs and industrialists combined with challenges from below by new immigrants and the "petite bourgeoisie" to create a real fear that the world as they knew it was spinning out of control.[4] In this environment of anxiety, as historian Mark Carnes argued, the fraternal organizations served to "re-create the face-to-face relationships and values" that were interrupted by the rapid changes taking place in America. "A source of stability amidst the social chaos of modern life," secret societies offered their members "cohesive social networks" that turned strangers into "brothers" or "sisters" and individual burdens into shared ones.[5] Both literally, through the networks they enabled, and figuratively, through the support and solidarity they provided, Greek organizations helped their members negotiate their roles and identities, as individuals, as women, and as members of the white Protestant middle and upper-middle classes, in a period of changing social rules and expectations.

Yet at the same time as they enabled certain achievements for members, women's fraternities also served as constraints upon their many thousands of members. The tight restrictions on access to fraternity membership helped re-create, on campus and beyond, many of the social and socioeconomic divisions that higher education in other contexts helped smooth over. The all-encompassing nature of the fraternity experience encouraged the development of patterns for social interaction and social cleavage that members would bring with them and reconstitute in their adult lives, thereby institutionalizing practices of exclusivity and elitism that brought potential ramifications, both for those excluded from the groups and for those who lived within their confines. The national character of fraternities and the pressure this placed on sisters to mold behavior to certain agreed-upon patterns and to limit associations to certain "known" and "approved" entities posed dangers to sisters' social, personal, and even moral development. The oft-touted efforts sisters exerted to comport themselves as "ideal Thetas" or "ideal Kappas," complete with the carefully delineated boundaries such conduct entailed, brought with them the potential to curb individual expression and suppress unorthodox or just plain different behavior.

Indeed, even while prizing leadership among their members and making much of their history as pioneers of women's advancement, the female Greek-letter organizations at times acted conservatively rather than proactively. On the question of suffrage, for example, even though many of its members held leadership positions in the movement and it included a list of these members among its roster of "outstanding Thetas," Kappa Alpha Theta Fraternity refused to put the weight of its membership behind the cause. Out of fear of taking a position that might alienate a segment of its membership, Theta remained cautious and conservative and therefore missed the opportunity to join with other powerful women's organizations in working toward woman suffrage. In addition, with respect to the ethnic diversification of college campuses, even while they themselves were founded to provide support for outsiders in the realm of higher education and held up for emulation sisters who worked to improve the lives and options of those less fortunate, the women's fraternities turned their backs on prospective members whose races, religions, family status, or backgrounds the sisters deemed unacceptable.

Indeed, compared to their male counterparts and campus opinion in general, the women's fraternities dragged their feet on the issue of whether to recognize the historically Jewish sororities as full members of the national Greek system. Even though some of them included Jewish members in their own organizations, it was not until 1951 that they allowed Alpha Epsilon Phi, Sigma Delta Tau, Delta Phi Epsilon, and other historically Jewish organizations membership in the National Panhellenic Congress.[6]

They also resisted pressure exerted from within and outside campus walls to drop their written and unwritten restrictive admissions clauses. As one Pi Beta Phi member argued, "We believe in . . . the right of a fraternity to limit its membership if it wishes to do so. We have both Jews and Catholics and members of many races and religions. We have no national policies against any race and religion . . . [but] [t]he local chapter is expected to include only persons acceptable to the fraternity as a whole."[7]

Importantly, it was the undergraduate chapters of the 1940s, 1950s, and 1960s, spurred on by campus legislation that withheld recognition from organizations with discriminatory memberships, that finally pushed those Greek-letter fraternities with restrictive clauses to drop them. "We . . . are in the majority opposed to discriminatory clauses in constitutions and national laws of fraternities against minority groups," a group of Greek chapter leaders at the University of Wisconsin wrote, voicing sentiments echoed on campuses across much of the United States. "[W]e believe that corrective measures must ultimately be taken by the national organizations. Local chapters are urged to exert every possible pressure on their national organizations to this end."[8] While resisting the efforts of outsiders to force the organizations to change their policies, many undergraduate sisters, along with their brothers in the men's fraternities—especially returning veterans of the Second World War who had fought alongside black and Jewish men in the trenches and so recoiled from blanket policies that excluded them—nevertheless struggled long and hard to do away with their respective groups' restrictive clauses. Upon meeting resistance from more conservative alumnae, some undergraduate chapters reluctantly disaffiliated from their national organizations rather than going along with the restrictive policies.[9] But most continued to uphold their organizations' policies, even while they may have labored to do away with them. By 1960, many schools throughout the East, Midwest, and West enacted legislation—often with the support of the Greek chapters on campus—prohibiting groups that had charters that discriminated on the basis of race or religion. By the middle of the decade, the last of the Greek-letter organizations caved to public opinion and pressure from their undergraduates and did away with their discriminatory policies, an act that brought them in line with the 1964 Civil Rights Act, which called for an end to discrimination on the basis of race, creed, color, or national origin.[10]

In this matter as on the question of suffrage, the women's fraternities acted conservatively rather than proactively. They resisted action out of fear of taking a position that their broad memberships might not find palatable. Indeed, although many undergraduate members supported the removal of restrictive clauses from their groups' constitutions and many fraternity women not only supported suffrage but also served as leaders of the movement, the goals of the individual in these cases got subsumed under what fraternity leaders considered the good of the whole. Greek-letter women, most believed, especially the alumnae, were simply not ready for religious and racial inclusion, either in the 1910s or decades later, into the 1960s. And those same fraternity women, many also believed, were not the sort to want to associate with the kinds of people who would get involved in messy political causes. Thus, the organizations retained their discriminatory clauses long after public and campus opinion (shared by many undergraduate Greeks) had recognized the importance of eradicating restrictions. They also remained aloof from one of the most important social and political movements of their day, even though this stance ran counter to so many of their ideals. In both of these cases, the positions adopted by the women's fraternities represented a lowest-common-denominator form of thinking, a paradox for organizations that in other ways were key promoters of women's advancement.[11]

In many ways, as much as a study about college life, this examination of the early history of the women's Greek system in general and Kappa Alpha Theta in particular provides a close look at the establishment and maintenance of a collegiate and societal elite. And in the process, it offers an inquiry into the relationship between individual and society. For those who claimed membership in a women's fraternity, the bonds of sisterhood that brought them great benefits at times required the subordination of the self to the whole. In exchange for its advantages, members at times placed their own agendas and concerns below those of their fraternity. The large numbers of women who willingly did so, who took pledges of loyalty to a secret society, who came of age through the filter of fraternal ties, and who, as a result, reaped the rewards of lifelong membership suggest that, for many, the benefits of sisterhood far outweighed the costs. For the thousands of women who belonged to fraternities in the early decades of their existence, their Greek-letter badges and the backing of their networks truly helped them live their lives bound together by a mighty vow of sisterhood.

Notes

NOTES TO INTRODUCTION

1. Kappa Alpha Theta, like nearly all of the prominent women's organizations founded before the turn of the twentieth century, was chartered as a "women's fraternity" rather than as a "sorority." The latter word did not exist until 1882, when female students at Syracuse University founded Gamma Phi Beta and called it a "sorority" after one of their Latin professors suggested the term as a female equivalent to the masculine-sounding term, "fraternity." The new term gained rapid acceptance on campuses across the country, to the point that most accounts of college life after 1890 used the word "sorority" to refer to all Greek organizations for women. Some Theta sisters and those of other prominent female fraternities proposed changing the title of their organizations to reflect the growing acceptance of the new word. Yet those women interested in preserving the historical accuracy of their sisterhoods insisted that the original term, "fraternity," be continued. In 1915, the traditionalists won an important battle over the name of their society when, at their annual convention, the sisters of Kappa Alpha Theta amended their constitution to read, "Inasmuch as the word fraternity is derived from 'fraternitas,' an abstract feminine Latin noun, meaning brotherhood, applying to both men and women, and inasmuch as there is no corresponding word from 'soror,' we shall avoid 'sorority,' an incorrect word, and instruct freshmen to this effect." Most of the other major women's fraternities made the same decision. See Constitution of Kappa Alpha Theta, amended, 1915; Minutes of National Panhellenic Congress, 1908; also, interview by the author with Mary Edith Arnold, Kappa Alpha Theta fraternity archivist, March 1996.

2. This initiation scene is described in the Alpha minutes, May 17, 1875. All chapter minutes, labeled according to the Greek letter by which they were known, contain proceedings of branches of Kappa Alpha Theta Fraternity. They are housed in the Kappa Alpha Theta Archives, Fraternity Headquarters, Indianapolis, Indiana. The process of assigning a Greek name to each new initiate was followed by every chapter of Kappa Alpha Theta and by other Greek-letter societies. The Greek names assigned to each sister were considered secret, though the members did refer to one another by these titles in their meeting

minutes. All references to Kappa Alpha Theta's ritual are based on the fraternity's historical accounts. They do not refer to practices followed at the time of this writing, as Kappa Alpha Theta's leadership has changed both the language of and the practices associated with the fraternity's ritual in the past several decades. Interview conducted by the author with Lissa Bradford, former president, Kappa Alpha Theta Fraternity, May 21, 2003.

3. William Raimond Baird, *Baird's Manual of American College Fraternities,* 7th ed. (New York: By the editor, 1912), 718–734; also, 10th ed., 1923, 756–758.

4. Baird, *American College Fraternities,* 10th ed., 756–757. According to this edition, published in 1923, twenty-one women's Greek-letter societies existed as of 1920. This number, however, excludes those organizations, such as Alpha Kappa Alpha and Delta Sigma Theta, which pledged and initiated only African American women and organized themselves into a different system. It does include the so-called Jewish sororities such as Alpha Epsilon Phi and Sigma Delta Tau, which were founded in the 1910s in response to the spoken or unspoken bans in most of the women's organizations against Jewish students. See Paula Giddings, *In Search of Sisterhood: Delta Sigma Theta and the Challenge of the Black Sorority Movement* (New York: William Morrow, 1988); Diana Turk, "College Students," in Paula E. Hyman and Deborah Dash Moore, eds., *Jewish Women in America: An Historical Encyclopedia,* vol. 1 (New York: Routledge, 1998), 259–260; Marianne Sanua, "Jewish College Fraternities and Sororities in American Jewish Life, 1895–1968: An Overview," MS with accompanying notes, 1995.

5. Kappa Alpha Theta Ritual, codified 1897; "Fraternity Ritual" box, Kappa Alpha Theta Archives.

6. John Robson, *The College Fraternity and Its Modern Role* (Menasha, WI: George Banta, 1966).

7. Beverly Sgro, "The Evolution of Fraternities for Women," unpublished paper, Virginia Polytechnic Institute and State University, August 1985, 2, Northwestern University Archives.

8. Robson, *College Fraternity,* 23.

9. Ibid., 23. According to fraternity critic historian Helen Lefkowitz Horowitz, the adoption of "serious, high-minded purpose" constituted mere "rhetoric," and the "real concern of each fraternity was to create within the larger college a small group of compatible fellows for friendship, mutual protection, and good times." See Helen Lefkowitz Horowitz, *Campus Life: Undergraduate Cultures from the End of the Eighteenth Century to the Present* (Chicago and London: University of Chicago Press, 1987), 29.

10. As both Horowitz and Frederick Rudolph showed, faculty members had good reason to distrust their students, since on the late eighteenth and early nineteenth century campuses, revolts against authority, mutual suspicion, and antipa-

thy characterized faculty-student relationships. See Horowitz, *Campus Life*, 28–29; Frederick Rudolph, *The American College and University: A History* (New York: Alfred A. Knopf, 1968), 98, 102.

11. George B. Manhart, *DePauw through the Years*, 2 vols. (Greencastle, IN: DePauw University Press, 1962), 134; Sgro, "Evolution of Fraternities," 2.

12. William Baird, *American College Fraternities: A Descriptive Analysis of the Society System in the Colleges of the United States* (Philadelphia: J. B. Lippincott, 1879), 160–161.

13. Frederick Rudolph, *Curriculum: A History of the American Undergraduate Course of Study since 1636*, prepared for the Carnegie Council on Policy Studies in Higher Education (San Francisco, Washington, London: Jossey-Bass, 1977), 101; Mabel Newcomer, *A Century of Higher Education for American Women* (New York: Harper and Brothers, 1959), 46. Data taken from both *The Reports of the Commissioner of Education* and *Biennial Statistics of Education*, Office of Education. See also Lynn Gordon, "Coeducation on Two Campuses: Berkeley and Chicago, 1890–1912," in Mary Kelley, ed., *Woman's Being, Woman's Place: Female Identity and Vocation in American History* (Boston: G. K. Hall, 1979); Gordon, *Gender and Higher Education in the Progressive Era* (New Haven: Yale University Press, 1990); Barbara Solomon, *In the Company of Educated Women* (New Haven and London: Yale University Press, 1985), 63.

14. For a discussion of familial language as used in the nineteenth century by women's groups, see Nancy F. Cott, *The Grounding of Modern Feminism* (New Haven and London: Yale University Press, 1987); Linda K. Kerber, "Separate Spheres, Female Worlds, Women's Place: The Rhetoric of Women's History," *Journal of American History* 75 (June 1988): 9–39; Carroll Smith-Rosenberg, *Disorderly Conduct: Visions of Gender in Victorian America* (Oxford: Oxford University Press, 1986); and Barbara Welter, "The Cult of True Womanhood: 1820–1860," *American Quarterly* 18 (Summer 1966): 151–174.

15. The founders of Kappa Alpha Theta and their fellow female Greek societies based their organizations closely on the models of the men's fraternities around them. They relied heavily on the advice and support of male professors and advisers, themselves fraternity men, and copied many of the rituals and practices that they saw the fraternity men perform. See Manhart, *DePauw*, 136; Dodge, *Sixty Years*, 19, 28. For a discussion of the pervasive nature of secret clubs and societies in nineteenth-century middle-class American life, see Mark Carnes, *Secret Ritual and Manhood in Victorian America* (New Haven and London: Yale University Press, 1989; also Rudolph, *The American College and University*, 147.

16. As discussed previously, the secrecy that characterized the collegiate Greek system grew out of the mutual distrust that pervaded faculty-Greek member relationships during much of the late eighteenth and early nineteenth centuries. It persisted (and continues to persist in the twenty-first century) because

many members believed that the true meaning of fraternal bonds is increased in weight and importance if kept for members only. Since the founders of the women's fraternities used the male societies as their model, they chose to adopt secrecy as well. In the late 1890s and early 1900s, the sisters of Kappa Alpha Theta debated the issue of whether to remain a secret society. They resolved in the affirmative, and thus the fraternity has remained a secret society. See Horowitz, *Campus Life,* 28–29; Bertha L. Broomwell, "A Plea for Non-Secrecy," *Kappa Alpha Theta* 8 (July 1894): 7; "Non-Secrecy," *Kappa Alpha Theta* 10 (May 1896): 65–66; Isadore Gilbert Mudge, "Secrecy," *Kappa Alpha Theta* 11 (November 1896): 1–7; Lydia M. Mather, "Theta Aims and Benefits," *Kappa Alpha Theta* 13 (January 1899): 84–85; Kappa Alpha Theta Bi-Monthly 4, no. 2 (April 1913); Kappa Alpha Theta Bi-Monthly 4, no. 4 (December 1913); Constitution of Kappa Alpha Theta, 1914; and Kappa Alpha Theta Bi-Monthly 5 (February 1914).

17. Alpha minutes, May 17, 1875. The metaphor of each sister serving as one "link" in the "mystic chain" was used by each chapter of Kappa Alpha Theta, as was the phrase of being "bound" together for life by their vows of fraternal loyalty. The early minutes of nearly all the chapters contain constant references to new sisters "adding one more link in the chain" of sisterhood or being bound with the "ties that bind in Theta love." Beginning informally and then codified in 1893, each member, upon initiation, received a silver link with her Greek name engraved on it, and she added her link to the chapter's chain as part of the ceremony, thereby literally as well as figuratively "binding" her link to the chain of the fraternity. For discussion of the ritual and the use of the links and chain, see Fraternity Ritual, codified in 1897. Copies located in "Ritual" box, Kappa Alpha Theta archives. Ritual also included in a book entitled *Beta Records,* undated, preceding minutes from 1881, Kappa Alpha Theta Archives. For members' frequent usage of the terms "link," "mystic circle," and "vow," see minutes from Alpha, Beta, Epsilon, Sigma, Phi, Tau, and Alpha Beta chapters, 1873–1920.

18. For an overview of some general differences and similarities among the first generations of female collegians, see Solomon, *Company of Educated Women,* 95; Gordon, *Gender and Higher Education,* 5.

19. In using generation as my means of categorizing the fraternity women, I recognize that I am in fact constructing a somewhat artificial division that in some ways suppresses strong elements of continuity. My use of two generations, 1870–1890 and 1890–1920, derives from my reading and interpretation of the behaviors, concerns, and values of the Theta sisters, and while I am aware that it contradicts the traditional manner of regarding the early history of women's education as comprised of three distinct generations, the "pioneers" (1865–1890), the "undefined" middle group (1890–1910), and the "gay coeds" (1910–1920), my own evidence suggests a different story. Like historian of women's education

Lynn Gordon, I see more similarity than change in the conduct of and values expressed by women collegians between 1890 and 1920, and thus, in the context of this study, I consider a two-generation construct more valid than the three-part rubric used by most other scholars of women's higher education. See Gordon, *Gender and Higher Education,* 5. For a study that uses the three-generation approach, see Solomon, *Company of Educated Women.*

20. The year 1920 is a common beginning and end date for histories that look at turn-of-the-century American life. Within the context of the history of women's higher education, this date marks the closing of the Progressive Era and so serves as a neat boundary for studies linking female campus cultures to Progressive Era concerns. For others, it serves as a marker of a new period, one characterized by new trends and ideas that would organize campus life in the decades to follow. For an example of the former approach, see Gordon, *Gender and Higher Education*; for an example of the latter, see Paula S. Fass, *The Damned and the Beautiful: American Youth in the 1920s* (Oxford and New York: Oxford University Press, 1977).

21. Kappa Alpha Theta constitutes an appropriate organization upon which to focus as a case example because in terms of its size and geographic range, the fraternity mirrored other female collegiate organizations of this time period. In addition, the composition of its membership, in terms of class, race, ethnicity, geographic origin, and religion, was relatively typical of women's fraternities of this period. See "Admission of Limited-Membership Groups to N.P.C.: Summary of Questionnaires," survey conducted by Committee on Eligibility and Nationalization of Social Groups of the National Panhellenic Congress, June 11, 1925. Contained in Report to the 19th National Panhellenic Congress, 1926, Student Life and Culture Archives, University of Illinois, Urbana-Champaign.

22. Baird, *American College Fraternities,* 10th ed., 756–757.

23. Survey conducted by the author of Greek-letter membership at twenty of the twenty-two colleges and universities at which Theta had a chapter at the turn of the twentieth century. This percentage was arrived at by comparing the numbers of women enrolled in each college during the year 1896–97 to the numbers of women belonging to Greek-letter organizations on these campuses. The former figures were gathered from registrars' records, or, in the cases where few or no records exist, were gleaned with the help of university archivists, while the statistics on women belonging to fraternities were published in the chapter reports of the April 1897 issue of the *Kappa Alpha Theta*. See Chapter Letters, *Kappa Alpha Theta* 11 (May 1897): 160–193. See also Horowitz, *Campus Life,* 132; L. Pearle Green, "The Fraternity and the College Today," *Kappa Alpha Theta* 28 (January 1914): 165–166.

24. Solomon, *Company of Educated Women,* 106–109.

25. Gordon, *Gender and Higher Education,* 61.

26. Horowitz, *Campus Life,* 17, 131–140, 292.

27. Giddings, *In Search of Sisterhood*, especially 48–52.

28. One group of histories defies this categorization: those performed by members of fraternities and sororities themselves and published on behalf of their organizations. These works do not reflect scholarly approaches, however, nor do their authors provide any real analyses of their findings. Rather, these studies present basic, chronological accounts of the founding and development of their organizations without any real contextualization or any kind of scholarly overlay. See, for example, Estelle Riddle Dodge, *Sixty Years in Kappa Alpha Theta* (Menasha, WI: George Banta, 1930); Florence A. Armstrong, *History of Alpha Chi Omega Fraternity, 1885–1921,* copyright Alpha Chi Omega Fraternity, 1922; Florence Burton-Roth and May Cynthia Whiting-Westermann, *The History of Kappa Kappa Gamma Fraternity, 1870–1930,* copyright Kappa Kappa Gamma Fraternity, 1932; Elizabeth Allen Clarke-Helmick, *The History of Pi Beta Phi Fraternity,* copyright Pi Beta Phi Fraternity, 1915; Mabel Harriet Siller, *The History of Alpha Chi Omega,* copyright Alpha Chi Omega, 1911; Ida Shaw Martin, *The Sorority Handbook,* copyright Ida Shaw Martin, Boston, 1923; Bessie Leach Priddy, *A Detailed Record of Delta Delta Delta, 1888–1907* (Galesburg, IL: Mail Printing Company, 1907).

Marianne Sanua's *"Here's to Our Fraternity": One Hundred Years of Zeta Beta Tau, 1898–1998,* to a certain extent parallels my own study in that it provides a historical study of the first Jewish male fraternity. Founded as a means to keep Jewish men from shirking their religions in favor of secular, mainstream pursuits, ZBT served initially as a bastion of Zionism but by the 1920s took on the characteristics of the other, non-Jewish social fraternities. Because Sanua focused entirely on Jewish males and did not address the Jewish women's Greek organizations, her conclusions bear only slightly on my own. The reasonable approach she employed, however, and her fairness toward the organization she studied merit mention. See Marianne Sanua, *"Here's to Our Fraternity": One Hundred Years of Zeta Beta Tau, 1898–1998* (Hanover and London: Zeta Beta Tau Foundation, in conjunction with Brandeis University Press and University Press of New England, 1998).

29. This point served as the topic of a panel discussion held at the CUNY Women's History Conference, "Reproducing Women's History," March 12, 1999. I am grateful to Hasia R. Diner for her keen insight into this trend and her encouragement that I pursue what some have considered, not entirely correctly, a nonfeminist or even antifeminist study.

30. Organizations, by their very nature, are products not only of their own particular cultures but of those to which their members belong, and the women of Kappa Alpha Theta, like those in the other oldest and most prominent women's fraternities, did not knowingly pledge any nonwhite members during the time period encompassed in this study, nor, most likely, did many of its colle-

giate members have any more than occasional social interaction (if even that) with African American, Latina, or Asian women students. Prior to the mid-1920s, so few nonwhite students attended college, and such a slight percentage of this number was female or enrolled in the historically white schools where Theta had chapters, that many of the sisters would have had little opportunity to meet nonwhite students on campus. See Giddings, *In Search of Sisterhood*, 7; Solomon, *Company of Educated Women*, 143–145. For a discussion of African American students' enrollment in colleges, see Raymond Wolters, *The New Negro: Black College Rebellions of the 1920s* (Princeton, NJ, and London: Princeton University Press, 1975), 313–314. See also the related discussion in chapter 3.

Defining class is a difficult feat that few scholars have attempted, most assuming, probably correctly, that we all know what we are talking about when we refer to it. Indeed, attempts to define class veer into problematic areas. Do we use income as its measure? Does it refer to the possession of certain values? Do conceptions of class differ when race or ethnicity or even geography enter into the equation? The more one tries to pin the concept down, the more questions one invariably provokes. Given the difficulty of fixing this illusive but highly important entity, for the purposes of this study I will use the term "class" to refer to the possession of certain belief systems, experiences, and values centered around respectability, propriety, and etiquette. Often, this accompanies a level of material comfort and relative wealth that allow such values to become a focus rather than mere survival, but at times income and class do not coincide, such that possessors of great wealth will still be denied "upper-class status" while those with little money may still lay claim to such a ranking. For a discussion of two historians' attempts to define class as well as a useful working definition, see Anne Firor Scott, *Natural Allies: Women's Associations in American History* (Urbana and Chicago: University of Illinois Press, 1991), 82–83, 191–192n.

31. See Carnes, *Secret Ritual*, 7, and Giddings, *In Search of Sisterhood*, for discussions concerning the difficulties inherent in studying secret societies.

32. Recorded minutes provide an important source of information concerning the activities that transpired during meetings and the ideas discussed and debated by members during these gatherings. At the same time, minutes by definition are inherently partial accounts of events and discussions, containing summaries rather than complete transcriptions of what happened. Still, they potentially deepen our understanding of the Greek system's past because they were written by members, for their eyes only, rather than having been created for publication or for disclosure. Thus, they serve as indicators of what activities and issues the sisters considered important enough to document, and also how much attention the sisters granted to the various topics they covered in their meetings.

1. Kappa Alpha Theta is considered the first Greek letter women's fraternity. I. C. Sorosis, established three years before Theta in 1867, was called a "society—not a "women's fraternity"—and it sponsored chapters in towns where no colleges were located. It was not until 1884 that I. C. Sorosis changed its name to Pi Beta Phi and limited its membership solely to college women. Thus, Kappa Alpha Theta, which from the start labeled itself a women's fraternity, calls itself the first women's Greek letter fraternity. This claim is supported by both *Baird's Manual of American College Fraternities* and *Banta's Greek Exchange*. Although two other organizations were also founded prior to Theta, at the Wesleyan Female College of Macon, Georgia, neither of these societies adopted a Greek name and thus, while older than Theta, do not contest Theta's claim to have been the first Greek letter fraternity for women. See *Handbook of Kappa Alpha Theta*, 1911, 9–10, and Sgro, 5. For a representation of Pi Beta Phi's claim to "first" status, see Mary C. Ward's "The Sorority Movement at Monmouth college," *Western Illinois Regional Studies* 4 (1981).

2. Historians Mary Ryan, Linda Kerber, and Karen Blair all addressed the elasticity of the ideal of "true womanhood" in their respective studies of women's groups. See Mary P. Ryan, *Womanhood in America: From Colonial Times to the Present*, 3rd ed. (New York and London: Franklin Watts, 1983); Mary P. Ryan, *Cradle of the Middle Class: The Family in Oneida County, New York, 1790–1865* (Cambridge, UK: Cambridge University Press, 1981), 236–242; Karen Blair, *The Clubwoman as Feminist: True Womanhood Redefined, 1868–1914* (New York and London: Holmes and Meier, 1980; and Linda K. Kerber, "Separate Spheres, Female Worlds, Women's Place: The Rhetoric of Women's History," *Journal of American History* 75 (June 1988): 9–39. See Kerber's essay especially for a detailed account of how successive historians of women have approached the concept of "separate spheres" and the ideal of "true womanhood."

3. Newcomer, *Century of Higher Education*, 46. Data taken from both *The Reports of the Commissioner of Education* and *Biennial Statistics of Education*, Office of Education. See also Gordon, "Coeducation," 171; Gordon, *Gender and Higher Education*; Solomon, *Company of Educated Women*, 63.

4. In 1868, when an average American family lived on an annual income of $680, the average annual income of families of a college graduate was $2,042. See Solomon, *Company of Educated Women*, 65–66, the findings of which are based on an Association of Collegiate Alumnae study of women college graduates between 1869 and 1898.

5. Newcomer, *Century of Higher Education*, 36; Gordon, *Gender and Higher Education*, 23.

6. Solomon, *Company of Educated Women*, 44.

7. Ibid., 52–53; Newcomer, *Century of Higher Education,* 12–13.

8. Rudolph, *The Curriculum,* 152; Newcomer, *Century of Higher Education,* 46.

9. Solomon, *Company of Educated Women,* 77.

10. Patricia Palmieri, "From Republican Motherhood to Race Suicide: Arguments on the Higher Education of Women in the United States, 1820–1920," in *Educating Men and Women Together: Coeducation in a Changing World,* ed. Carol Lasser (Urbana and Chicago: University of Illinois Press in conjunction with Oberlin College, 1987), 56.

11. Rudolph, *The Curriculum,* 156; Newcomer, *Century of Higher Education,* 46; Solomon, *Company of Educated Women,* 63.

12. Gordon, "Coeducation," 172.

13. See especially, Palmieri, "Republican Motherhood," 55; Edward Clarke, *Sex in Education: Or, A Fair Chance for the Girls* (Boston: J. R. Osgood, 1874).

14. Solomon, *Company of Educated Women,* 56–57.

15. Gordon, "Coeducation," 172; Solomon, *Company of Educated Women,* 57.

16. Gordon, "Coeducation," 173.

17. Rosalind Rosenberg, "The Limits of Access: The History of Coeducation in America," in John Mack Faragher and Florence Howe, eds., *Women and Higher Education: Essays from the Mount Holyoke College Sesquicentennial Symposia* (New York: W. W. Norton, 1988), 112.

18. Lilian Hughes Neiswanger, "The First Coeds" (unpublished manuscript, DePauw University Archives, Greencastle, IN, 1935), 5; faculty meeting minutes, July 2, 1866, DePauw University Archives.

19. Faculty meeting minutes, July 12, 1866; Neiswanger, "The First Coeds," 6.

20. Neiswanger, "The First Coeds," 11.

21. John Clark Ridpath, "Beginnings of Kappa Alpha Theta" (unpublished manuscript, DePauw University Archives, Greencastle, IN, 1890), 1; Neiswanger, "The First Coeds," 11.

22. *Asbury Review,* October 2, 1867; emphasis in the original.

23. *Asbury Review,* December 17, 1867; emphases in the original.

24. *Asbury Review,* December 17, 1867.

25. *Asbury Review,* December 17, 1867; emphases in the original.

26. Faculty meeting minutes, February 5, 1868, DePauw University Archives. *Asbury Review,* February 21, 1868; emphasis in the original.

27. Manhart, *DePauw,* 82.

28. Neiswanger, "The First Coeds," 13.

29. Bettie Locke Hamilton, quoted in *Indianapolis Star,* September 10, 1967.

30. For a discussion of the continued opposition facing the early women at Asbury, see Dodge, *Sixty Years,* 17; Manhart, *DePauw,* 83–85. According to

Manhart, just prior to the graduation ceremonies of the first female students, in 1871, the women found that their male classmates had planned a class-day program that excluded them because of their sex. In protest, the women resigned from their class, so, although four of the original five female students graduated, they did not do so as members of the senior class.

31. In the late 1860s and early 1870s, Greek fraternities claimed over 75 percent of the Asbury student body in their ranks, according to Dodge, *Sixty Years,* 17; Neiswanger, "The First Coeds," 31; and Manhart, *DePauw,* 134–135, 137.

32. Some have argued that Dr. Locke's suggestion to Bettie that she form a fraternity was "not altogether serious." See Dodge, *Sixty Years,* 20–21. As Carol Green Wilson wrote in her history of the fraternity, so unheard of was the notion of women forming a fraternity that Newman the jeweler initially addressed Bettie Locke as "Mr." in his letters. See Carol Green Wilson, *We Who Wear Kites: The Story of Kappa Alpha Theta, 1870–1956* (Menasha, WI: George Banta, 1956), 5. Letters from Newman to Locke are on file in the Kappa Alpha Theta Archives.

33. Wilson, *We Who Wear Kites,* 5.

34. In 1870, seven Greek societies for men existed on the Asbury campus, the oldest of which, Beta Theta Pi, had been founded in 1835. Manhart, *DePauw,* 134.

35. Dodge, *Sixty Years,* 28; Ridpath, "Beginnings of KAΘ," 1.

36. Ridpath, "Beginnings of KAΘ," 1.

37. Thomson, *History of Alpha Phi,* 11; Clarke-Helmick, *History of Pi Beta Phi,* 71.

38. For the founding stories of specific women's fraternities and sororities, see Thomson, *History of Alpha Phi,* 3–5, 11, 13; Roedel, *History of Alpha Phi,* 3; Clarke-Helmick, *History of Pi Beta Phi,* 20–22, 26–27; Perkins, *Sigma Kappa History,* 3. As discussed in the introduction, members of Greek-letter fraternities argued at this time and continue to argue today that the true meaning of fraternal bonds is increased in weight and importance if kept for members only. Most likely, the secrecy of the women's Greek organizations comes from the fact that they copied many facets of the men's organizations, and the men were decidedly in favor of secrecy.

39. Constitution of Kappa Alpha Theta Fraternity, January 27, 1870.

40. Constitution of Kappa Alpha Theta Fraternity, January 27, 1870; Dodge, *Sixty Years,* 55; Ridpath, "Beginnings of KAΘ"; Alpha and Beta minutes, 1870–1875.

41. Alpha and Beta minutes, 1870–1883. See, for example, Alpha minutes, December 12, 1870, and March 1, 1873; and Beta minutes, March 10, 1882 and November 5, 1881.

42. Constitution of Kappa Alpha Theta, 1870; Dodge, *Sixty Years,* 55.

43. Alpha minutes, April 22, 1870; Alpha minutes, December 10, 1880.

44. This assertion is based on close analysis of the minutes of every meeting of the Alpha chapter of Kappa Alpha Theta from 1870 through the early 1890s, as well as all available minutes from the Beta, Gamma, Sigma, Phi, Epsilon, Tau, and Alpha Beta chapters of Kappa Alpha Theta from their foundings through the early 1890s. As new chapters were founded on college campuses across the United States, the sisters of those groups followed the same practices as the older chapters' members did. See existing minutes and related documents of Alpha (Asbury College, later DePauw University, founded 1870), Beta (Indiana University, 1870), Epsilon (Wooster, 1875), Delta (University of Illinois, 1875), Sigma (University of Toronto, 1887), Tau (Northwestern, 1887), and Alpha Beta (Swarthmore, 1891). I have been unable to locate minutes from the Gamma (Butler 1874), Mu (Allegheny, 1876), Zeta (Ohio University, 1876), Eta (University of Michigan, 1879), Theta (Simpson College, 1880), Iota (Cornell University, 1881), Kappa (University of Kansas, 1881), Lambda (University of Vermont, 1881), Gamma deuteron (Ohio Wesleyan, 1881), Nu (Hanover, 1882), or Xi (Wesleyan, CT, 1883) chapters of Kappa Alpha Theta, either because the chapter returned its charter early on and so never was a real part of the fraternity or because the minutes have been lost or housed in private collections outside of the fraternity archives. That the sisters of these chapters occupied themselves in the same manner and according to the same concerns as their fellow Thetas of chapters for which I have minutes is clear from the formers' letters and chapter reports sent to the *Kappa Alpha Theta* journal and from the minutes of conventions, which contained reports on the activities of all chapters.

45. Alpha minutes, April 22, 1870.

46. Alpha minutes, June 15, 1872; November 22, 1872.

47. Alpha minutes, March 22, 1878; October 24, 1879; December 10, 1880. See also Beta minutes, October 15, 1881; December 1, 1881; January 27, 1882; emphases in the original.

48. See, for example, Alpha minutes, May 10, 1889, and May 15, 1890.

49. Alpha minutes, May 10, 1889, and June 7, 1889. See also Alpha minutes for March 9, 1877, and May 15, 1890; and Beta minutes December 1, 1881, and February 9, 1883, for further examples of the fraternity sisters hearing and criticizing one another's speeches.

50. See Alpha minutes, February 29, 1884; February 14, 1886; and October 8, 1886; Beta minutes, February 17, 1882; and Tau minutes, October 24, 1897.

51. Burton-Roth and Whiting-Westermann, *History of KKG*, 58, 108, 118, 146, 162.

52. Mary Low Carver, speech entitled, "Reminiscence," 3, 9; no definitive date—probably 1913, Sigma Kappa Sorority Archives. Untitled history of Sigma Kappa Sorority, no recorded author, no definitive date—probably 1905, Kappa Sigma. Special thanks to Mary Edith Arnold for helping to locate these documents.

53. Constitution of Sigma Kappa, Colby College Archives, 73, S63, C6, 1874; Mary Low Carver, "Reminiscence," 3.

54. Perkins, *Sigma Kappa History,* 21, 9; see also "First Woman in Alumnae is Dead," *Colby Echo,* March 10, 1926.

55. Thomson, *History of Alpha Phi,* 29–30, 39.

56. See Nancy Brown Woollett, *An Historical Sketch of the Delta Gamma Fraternity, 1874–1934* (Delta Gamma Fraternity), 1934: 5–6. This book traced the history of Delta Gamma Fraternity, founded in 1874 at the Oxford Female Institute, the female complement to the all-male State University of Oxford, Mississippi. The sisters of Kappa Alpha Theta recognized that at an all-women's college, the idea of a fraternity—at least one whose mission was largely based on academic solidarity for women—lost its purpose. On January 22, 1872, they noted, "We have found that Secret Societies in female colleges do not work for several reasons" and subsequently chose not spread to "sex-restricted" campuses. In later years, the sisters made exceptions for Wellesley, Smith, and Rockford Colleges, but no chapters ever panned out in these institutions. Kappa Alpha Theta did not form a chapter at an all-women's college until 1896, when it established a branch at Baltimore Women's College, later renamed Goucher College, in Maryland. See Alpha minutes, January 22, 1872; Minutes of the 4th Convention of Kappa Alpha Theta, 1879, 2–3; Dodge, *Sixty Years,* 84; Editorial, *Kappa Alpha Theta* 4 (November 1890): 113.

57. Alpha minutes, November 27, 1872, and December 10, 1880.

58. Constitution of Kappa Alpha Theta, 1870.

59. Constitution of Kappa Alpha Theta, 1870; Alpha minutes, October 5, 1871. According to the catalog of Asbury student grades for the years 1868–1871, the four founders of Kappa Alpha Theta were all exceptional students. Bettie Locke earned marks mainly between 95 and 100, with only four below a 90; Alice Allen earned a 65 one quarter in mathematics and an 85 in natural sciences, but in all other terms and for all other courses, she received no grade lower than a 90; Virginia (Jennie) Fitch received no mark lower than a 97 in any subject, and Bettie Tipton earned only one mark below a 90; DePauw University Archives, student ledger. It is interesting to note that immediately after the commencement exercises of this first group of female students, the trustees of Asbury passed a resolution in which they gave their "unqualified approval" to coeducation at Asbury College, thereby removing the qualifications they had placed on their decision in 1867. See Manhart, *DePauw,* 84–85.

60. At the 1885 convention, the sisters of Kappa Alpha Theta changed this rule restricting membership to college students, to allow chapters to "take into full membership, ladies who are Professors in the institution in which the chapter is located" and also to enable them to confer honorary membership upon "distinguished women." In 1893, provisions for honorary membership were stricken from the constitution and "active membership" restricted to "young women

who are at the time enrolled students of the college or university." See Constitution of Kappa Alpha Theta, 1885 and 1893.

61. Constitution of Kappa Alpha Theta, 1870.

62. The first constitution included the stipulation that "No one shall be admitted to this society without the free consent of all its members," and this requirement remained in place throughout the period encompassed by this study. See section regarding "College Chapter Membership" in Constitution of Kappa Alpha Theta, 1870 and 1924.

63. Alpha minutes, September 14, 1876; September 21, 1882; November 30, 1878; also November 16, 1888.

64. Clarke-Helmick, *History of Pi Beta Phi*, 71–74, 81–82.

65. Burton-Roth and Whiting-Westermann, *History of KKG*, xii–xiii, 3–4, 20. Piecing together Kappa Kappa Gamma's history is a somewhat challenging enterprise, as few of Kappa's early records exist. According to Kappa Kappa Gamma historians Florence Burton-Roth and May Cynthia Whiting-Westermann, "None of the original records [of the fraternity] have come down . . . and therefore the story of those early days must ever consist of a piecing together of recollections of those who participated in the events." As one of the early members put it, "We kept no record and in our uneventful and as yet unshaped fraternity life there seemed little to record and it is only the high lights that shine out through the mists of years." Another Kappa sister noted that the member who served as secretary in the early years took with her when she left college the book in which fraternity minutes were recorded, and upon her death, it disappeared. See ibid., 3, 11–12, 14, 19.

66. Alpha minutes, October 5, 1871; Dodge, *Sixty Years*, 56; Alpha minutes, undated, following May 9, 1870, meeting. See also letter from Laura Henley to Alpha chapter, November 1873.

67. For discussions of expansion, see Alpha and Beta minutes, late 1878–1881. See also discussion of letter written to registrar at Cornell University, 1881, in Dodge, *Sixty Years*, 133–134.

68. Letter from Laura Henley, Beta, to Alpha chapter, dated November, 1873, Kappa Alpha Theta Fraternity Archives; also discussed in Dodge, *Sixty Years*, 75–76.

69. Roedel, *History of Alpha Phi*, 24.

70. Documents concerning founding of Lambda (University of Vermont) and Iota (Cornell University) chapters, in "Expansion Files," Kappa Alpha Theta Archives. Also Alpha minutes, December 28, 1880, and November 12, 1880; Wilson, *We Who Wear Kites*, 12; Dodge, *Sixty Years*, 133–134. For descriptions of Kappa Kappa Gamma's early expansion, see Burton-Roth and Whiting-Westermann, *History of KKG*, 23–27.

71. Alpha minutes, December 18, 1878; April 11, 1884.

72. Alpha chapter By-Laws to Constitution of Kappa Alpha Theta, 1876.

73. See especially Beta, Delta, Epsilon, and Nu chapter reports from 1885, included in *Kappa Alpha Theta* 1 (June 1885): 20–27.

74. *Kappa Alpha Theta* 31 (November 1916): 20–22; Membership Chart, *Kappa Alpha Theta* 19 (November 1904): 26. Lida Mason and Ellen E. Hamilton, the first two female inductees into Phi Beta Kappa, later became members of Kappa Alpha Theta's Lambda chapter at the University of Vermont.

75. *Kappa Alpha Theta* 31 (November 1916): 20–22; *Kappa Alpha Theta* 1 (June 1885): 22; Catharine Planck Kircher, chart comparing data of members pre- and post-1900, March 1917, Kappa Alpha Theta Archives. In the "Alumnae Notes" section of the first issue of the journal, eleven out of eighteen alumnae respondents reported that they worked as teachers, professors, or instructors. Of the remaining seven, five were engaged in some form of study, be it of law or French, while only two listed married life or travel as their primary occupations. See "Alumnae Notes," *Kappa Alpha Theta* 1 (June 1885): 30. More than half of the alumnae sisters (14 out of 26) who wrote to the journal the following year were also engaged in teaching or training-related professions, and this number remained consistent of those who reported their activities to the November 1896 journal. "Alumnae Notes," *Kappa Alpha Theta* 1 (January 1886): 103–104; "Alumnae Notes," *Kappa Alpha Theta* 11 (November 1896): 51–57.

Theta alumnae bent on the professoriate who hailed from the Midwest chapters may have benefited from the fact that Midwestern colleges and universities hired greater numbers of female professors than did institutions in other parts of the country in the nineteenth century. For example, in 1880, of the sixty-one institutions nationwide that employed women, thirty-two were located in Ohio, Iowa, Illinois, Indiana, Michigan, Wisconsin, and Kansas. See Lucille Addison Pollard, *Women on College and University Faculties: A Historical Survey and a Study of Their Present Academic Status* (New York: Arno Press, 1997), 150–151.

76. *Quid?* Yearbook of Hanover College, 1898, 87.

77. Perkins, *Sigma Kappa History,* 21, 9; see also "First Woman in Alumnae Is Dead," *Colby Echo,* March 10, 1926.

78. Perkins, *Sigma Kappa History,* 10–17; Ruth Henderson and Florence Daly, "Mary Caffrey Low Carter [sic] Was Colby's First Woman Graduate," *Morning Sentinel,* March 27, 1985; *Colby Alumnus,* 15, no. 1, (1925–1926): 183.

79. Burton-Roth and Whiting-Westermann, *History of KKG,* 34, 41, 71.

80. As Barbara Welter correctly pointed out in a footnote to her seminal article, "The Cult of True Womanhood: 1820–1860," many scholars of nineteenth century women's history have invoked the phrase "true womanhood" without putting forth any effort to define it. Welter attributed this lack of assigned meaning to the fact that these scholars have "simply assumed—with some justification—that readers would understand intuitively exactly what they

meant." While I agree with Welter's analysis regarding the dearth of definitions of "true womanhood," I think it is important to point out that in many instances, the women and men of the nineteenth century who so frequently invoked this notion remained remarkably silent themselves on what they meant by this phrase. Especially for the mid- and late-nineteenth-century white American women who came from fairly well-to-do families such as those who belonged to Kappa Alpha Theta and other women's fraternities, the meaning of "true womanhood" and the associations it invoked must have seemed obvious, given, and unchanging, and therefore, without need of explication or definition.

When the women of Kappa Alpha Theta, Kappa Kappa Gamma, Pi Beta Phi, and other fraternities invoked the phrase "true womanhood," they did so with reference to piety, purity, and, to a certain extent, domesticity, but in marked rejection of the trait of submissiveness, by virtue of their identity as pioneers of women's higher education. From their own uses of the phrase, I take "true womanhood" when used by the sisters to encompass manners and social grace, as well as interest and skill in the arts of music, poetry, and literature. See Welter, "Cult of True Womanhood," 224–250; also Solomon, *Company of Educated Women*, 95; Kerber, "Separate Spheres," 9–39.

81. Constitution of Kappa Alpha Theta, 1870; Fraternity Ritual; see also discussions in Thomson, *History of Alpha Phi*; Roedel, *History of Alpha Phi*; Clarke-Helmick, *History of Pi Beta Phi*; Perkins, *Sigma Kappa History*; Burton-Roth and Whiting-Westermann, *History of KKG*.

82. For an example of how male students perceived their new female colleagues, see *Asbury Review*, January 9, 1868, and Ridpath, "Beginnings of KAΘ," 2. For examples of popular perceptions of collegiate women, see Clarke, *Sex in Education*.

83. *Indianapolis Star*, September 10, 1967; Dodge, *Sixty Years*, 13; and Neiswanger, "First Coeds," 28.

84. Constitution of Kappa Alpha Theta, 1870.

85. The sisters of Kappa Alpha Theta did not define what they meant by "evince a social disposition" or "sustain a good moral character," and these concepts changed over time, as later sisters interpreted their meanings differently than did the first generation of sisters. It is important to read these notions within the context of late nineteenth century Victorian concerns with "true womanhood." See Welter, "Culture of True Womanhood," 224 250; Solomon, *Company of Educated Women*, 95; and Kerber, "Separate Spheres," 9–39.

86. Alpha minutes, January 22, 1874; January 10, 1879.

87. Alpha minutes, September 14, 1876.

88. Alpha minutes, November 25, 1874.

89. Clarke-Helmick, *History of Pi Beta Phi*, 20–22, 26–27, 71. Also Alpha minutes, January 10, 1871; April 12, 1872. The first generation of fraternity sisters did not detail, as did their successors, those traits they considered faulty or

those behaviors that would have likely drawn reproach. In fact, it is unclear even within which arena—academic or social—the sisters most closely monitored each other's behavior. On rare occasions, certain unspecified decorum on the part of members proved too objectionable for mere correction or critique. In those few instances, the sisters voted to expel the errant sister from their fraternity. See, for example, Beta minutes, December 1, 1881.

90. According to historian Lawrence Levine, literature entered the U.S. college curriculum only "as a result of a long acrimonious struggle during which the protectors of the status quo spoke with religious fervor in defense of a canon they insisted had been in place through the ages; a canon without which higher education—and much else—was doomed." See Levine, *The Opening of the American Mind: Canons, Culture, and History* (Boston: Beacon Press, 1996), 38–39, 78, 80; Merle Curti and Vernon Carstensen, *The University of Wisconsin: A History, 1848–1925*, vol. 1 (Madison: University of Wisconsin Press, 1949), 429.

91. Many of the male fraternities of the time period operated as literary or debating societies, and the Theta sisters' practice of performing literary work in front of one another certainly stemmed from this tradition. The language the fraternity women used to explain and ground their performances, however, contained references to societal gender-based expectations and needs. In fact, the sisters explicitly denied that their organization bore any tendencies toward being a literary society. See Editorial, *Kappa Alpha Theta* 9 (January 1895): 21–22. For a discussion of male literary and debating societies in the nineteenth century, see Horowitz, *Campus Life*, 26–29, 31, 37. While most of the Thetas' performances "were for the purpose of practice and criticism, in order that the performers might more credibly acquit themselves before the larger college audience," at times it is difficult to tell from the meeting minutes if a sister was performing her own work for criticism or whether she was reading a literary essay strictly for the enlightenment or entertainment of her sisters, or both. See, for example, the entry for February 24, 1882, in the Beta minutes, in which the recording secretary wrote that the "chapter was favored with two very good declamations, [and] two were excused from performing." In this case, it is unclear for what purpose—practice or enlightenment—the sisters were performing. What is always apparent, however, is that the sisters considered literary performances important and strove to make them a regular part of their fraternity work. The same held for the other women's fraternities. See Dodge, *Sixty Years*, 55; Burton-Roth and Whiting-Westermann, *History of KKG*, 39.

92. Beta minutes, February 24, 1882; March 3, 1882; and March 10, 1882.

93. *Kappa Alpha Theta* 1 (April 1886): 139.

94. Tau minutes, April 16, 1894.

95. Alpha minutes, November 19, 1885; December 12, 1890. In many chapters of Kappa Alpha Theta, the members passed motions requiring each sister to

respond to roll call with a quote from some author decided upon at a previous meeting. At Tau chapter meetings at Northwestern University, for example, Kappa Alpha Theta members gave quotes from Shakespeare or Longfellow when responding to the roll. In the Epsilon chapter at the College of Wooster, the Theta sisters chose Tennyson along with Longfellow as the authors from which they most frequently drew quotes. The Asbury sisters also adhered to this practice. In 1886 they voted "to answer roll call henceforth with a quotation and [to impose] a fine of $.05 on non-performance of said quotation." See Tau minutes from 1887 to 1894, especially May 4, 1891, and October 30, 1894; see also Epsilon minutes from 1895; Alpha minutes, February 14, 1886.

96. See Burton-Roth and Whiting-Westermann, *History of KKG*, 39, 70–71.

97. See, for example, Alpha minutes, January 27, 1888. According to a survey conducted in 1893 by the Grand Council of the fraternity on work conducted in chapter meetings, nearly all branches of Kappa Alpha Theta addressed literary work in their weekly or biweekly meetings. See Grand Council Report, 1893–94.

98. Most entries in each chapter's minutes contain references along the lines of "correspondence received from Alpha chapter" or "a letter was read from the Michigan chapter." Many of these letters contained discussions of what literary work the chapter was addressing. See, for example, Alpha minutes, January 27, 1888. In addition, the letters each chapter sent to the *Kappa Alpha Theta* journal prior to the mid-1890s all dealt with literary work. See, for example, entries from Lambda and Epsilon, *Kappa Alpha Theta* 7 (January 1893): 134, 138.

99. In the spring of 1882, for example, the *Atlantic Monthly* alone featured selections by Holland, Whittier, Hawthorne, Longfellow, Holmes, and Shakespeare in their book reviews, "Books of the Month" selections, or poetry features. See *Atlantic Monthly* 49 (January 1882): 140; *Atlantic Monthly* 49 (March 1882): 49; *Atlantic Monthly* 49 (April 1882): 575; *Atlantic Monthly* 49 (May 1882). Volume 50 of the journal, encompassing the summer of 1882, contained excerpts from all of the authors the sisters addressed, with the single exception of Dickens. See *Atlantic Monthly* 50 (Summer 1882): 848.

100. See especially Tau minutes, October 7, 1889; October 14, 1889; October 21, 1889; February 17, 1890; March 3, 1890.

101. In the winter and spring of 1882, for example, the Beta sisters selected for their literary studies the exact same group of authors the *Atlantic Monthly* editors featured in their winter and spring issues of the magazine. See *Atlantic Monthly* 49 (Spring 1882); *Atlantic Monthly* 50 (Summer 1882): 848.

102. *Kappa Alpha Theta* 3 (May 1889): 95; *Kappa Alpha Theta* 7 (January 1893): 138.

103. L. Levine, *Opening of the American Mind*, 81; Thomas Harding, "College Literary Societies: Their Contribution to Higher Education in the United

States, 1815–1876 (New York: Pageant Press International Corp., 1971); see especially 262–321; Curti and Carstensen, *University of Wisconsin,* vol. 1, 423.

104. Rudolph, *College and University,* 138. A University of Wisconsin yearbook entry for a literary society, the Hyperion Club, showed the serious purpose with which its members approached their enterprise. The members wrote that this club exists "for the purpose of furnishing opportunities for a higher degree of literary and social attainment. . . . Up to the present time (1885) its efforts have been directed to the discussion of the works of Scott, Longfellow, Lowell and Tennyson, four nights being consumed with each author"; see *Badger,* University of Wisconsin Yearbook 1885, 91.

105. Curti and Carstensen, *University of Wisconsin,* vol. 1, 423.

106. L. Levine, *Opening of the American Mind,* 79.

107. Eva A. Corell, "A Word to Our Girls," *Kappa Alpha Theta* 5 (March 1891): 42.

108. Ibid., 41–42.

109. This sentiment was summed up by one sister who begged her fellow Thetas in a letter to the *Kappa Alpha Theta,* "Sisters, we must be dead to selfishness, so it is our duty to give the golden thoughts we find in literature to others. Then let us have literary work in our fraternity"; *Kappa Alpha Theta* 12 (November 1897): 19.

110. Nearly all of the women's fraternities used the term "true" or "ideal," as in the "true Theta" or "ideal Kappa," to symbolize the model of their fraternity. See, for example, Clarke-Helmick's discussion of Pi Beta Phi, *History of Pi Beta Phi,* 20–22, 26–27, 71; see also letter from May Agness Hopkins, Zeta Tau Alpha, to 18th National Panhellenic Congress, 1923. See also Welter, "Cult of True Womanhood," 224–250; Solomon, *Company of Educated Women,* 95; Kerber, "Separate Spheres," 9–39.

111. Kappa Alpha Theta Fraternity Ritual, adopted at first initiation on January 27, 1870, and codified in 1897. See also discussion of Zeta Tau Alpha's mission, "to upbuild [sic] a purer and nobler womanhood," in letter from May Agness Hopkins, Zeta Tau Alpha, to 18th National Panhellenic Congress 1923, 19–20, National Panhellenic Conference Archives, 26/20/30, Center of Student Life and Culture, University of Illinois at Urbana-Champaign.

The National Panhellenic Congress, the umbrella organization for many of the women's fraternities, was initially called the Intersorority Conference, and in 1908 changed its name to the National Panhellenic Congress. Since 1945, it has been called the National Panhellenic Conference, to signify that, unlike a congress, it does not pass legislation but rather issues recommendations and serves as a final court of appeal for college panhellenic organizations.

112. Alpha minutes, undated, but positioned between a meeting dated November 2, 1875, and one dated November 28, 1875; emphases in the original.

113. Ida Shaw Martin, *The Sorority Handbook* (Boston, 1907). See also 10th ed., 1928, 30.

114. "History of Alpha Chapter, 1870s," by daughter of Agnes Fisher, who was initiated into Kappa Alpha Theta in 1873; contained in "Theta Histories" folder, Kappa Alpha Theta Archives. See also Dodge's description of the early Theta members' family lives, *Sixty Years,* 31–54; Registrar's Report, 1878–1884, DePauw University Archives.

115. Manhart, *DePauw,* 137. See discussions in chapters 2 and 5 of Theta's push to buy a house for every chapter.

116. Dodge, *Sixty Years,* 61.

117. Ibid.; Perkins, *Sigma Kappa History,* 21; "Pioneer of Colby Women Students," *Colby Echo,* February 10, 1927; Thomson, *History of Alpha Phi,* 3–5, 11, 13; Roedel, *History of Alpha Phi.*

118. Alpha minutes, December 8, 1876; April 12, 1878; March 21, 1879; April 4, 1879.

119. Alpha minutes, December 18, 1878.

120. Neiswanger, "First Coeds," 34–36.

121. Beta minutes, October 15, 1881; Alpha minutes, January 31, 1883; October 12, 1883; October 24, 1884; December 3, 1884.

122. For a discussion of restrictions facing students of the 1870s and 1880s, see Solomon, *Company of Educated Women,* 95–96 and 100–101.

123. See discussions of Philomathean Society in Alpha minutes, 1870–1880, for example, Alpha minutes, December 15, 1870; March 3, 1877; and March 8, 1878.

124. Gordon, "Coeducation," 173; *Blue and Gold,* U.C. Berkeley Yearbook, 1883, University of California Archives; *Syllabus,* Northwestern University Yearbook, 1888, Northwestern University Archives; *University of Wisconsin Yearbook* (later renamed *The Badger*), 1885, University of Wisconsin Archives. For further discussion of the marginalization of women students, see Introduction. See also Gordon, "Coeducation," 173–175.

125. *Blue and Gold,* U.C. Berkeley Yearbook, 1883, University of California Archives. For further discussion of the marginalization of women students at Berkeley, see Gordon, "Coeducation," 173–175.

126. *Syllabus,* Northwestern University Yearbook, 1888, 1910, Northwestern University Archives.

127. *University of Wisconsin Yearbook* (later renamed *The Badger*), 1885; *The Badger,* 1910, University of Wisconsin Archives; Solomon, *Company of Educated Women,* 63.

128. Jane Eyre Smoot, "The Higher Education of Women," *Kappa Alpha Theta* 4 (January 1890): 3–5.

129. "The Ideal Theta," *Kappa Alpha Theta,* 5 (July 1891): 3.

NOTES TO CHAPTER 2

1. Newcomer, *Century of Higher Education*, 49, citing G. Stanley Hall, *Adolescence* (New York: 1904), 584, 667; also "A Kappa Alumna," *Kappa Alpha Theta* 1 (October 1885), 47–48; Gordon, *Gender and Higher Education*; Gordon, "The Gibson Girl Goes to College," *American Quarterly* 39 (Summer 1987), 214; Solomon, *Company of Educated Women*, 63; and Rosenberg, *Separate Spheres*, 110–111.

2. Gordon, *Gender and Higher Education*, 5; Gordon, "Gibson Girl," 214, 217.

3. See Horowitz, *Campus Life*, 197 and, especially, 201, for a discussion of the increasing emphasis many female collegians placed on heterosexual socializing in the 1890s.

4. William Raimond Baird, *Baird's Manual of American College Fraternities*, 7th ed. (New York: By the editor, 1912), 718–724; also, 10th ed., 1923, 756–758; Grand Council Report, 1893–1894.

5. Gordon, "Gibson Girl," 214.

6. Rosenberg, *Separate Spheres*, 115.

7. Solomon, *Company of Educated Women*, 97–101, 103; Gordon, "Coeducation," 174–175; Gordon, *Gender and Higher Education*, 108, 112–120; Bishop, *History of Cornell*, 419; Curti and Carstensen, *University of Wisconsin*, vol. 1, 664–665; vol. 2, 499, 508.

8. Gordon, "Coeducation," 176–177; Gordon, "Gibson Girl," 214–215; Bishop, *History of Cornell*, 420, 447–449.

9. Historian Lawrence Levine largely credited turn-of-the-century Harvard president Charles William Eliot with strengthening the emphasis on electives rather than a core curriculum at Harvard. L. Levine, *Opening of the American Mind*, 40–42, 46; see also Curti and Carstensen, *University of Wisconsin*, vol. 1, 429, 440.

10. Newcomer, *Century of Higher Education*, 91.

11. Gordon, *Gender and Higher Education*, 112–120; Linda Eisenmann, "'Freedom to Be Womanly': The Separate Culture of the Woman's College," in *The Search for Equality: Women at Brown University, 1891–1991*, ed. Polly Welts Kaufman (Hanover, NH, and London: Brown University Press, 1991). See also Horowitz, *Campus Life*, 202; Rosenberg, *Separate Spheres*, 112; Newcomer, *Century of Higher Education*, 91.

12. According to Solomon, these loosened restrictions resulted from administrators' reactions to "demands of young Americans for more social freedom" in the years preceding World War I. See Solomon, *Company of Educated Women*, 101–102. See also Charlotte Williams Conable, *Women at Cornell: The Myth of Equal Education* (Ithaca, NY: Cornell University Press, 1977); Roberta Frankfort, *Collegiate Women: Domesticity and Career in Turn-of-the-Century Amer-*

ica (New York: New York University Press, 1977); Taziana Rota, "Between 'True Women' and 'New Women': Mount Holyoke Students, 1837–1908" (Ph.D. diss., Department of History, University of Massachusetts, 1983); Rosenberg, *Separate Spheres*; Eisenmann, "Freedom to Be Womanly."

13. Solomon, *Company of Educated Women,* 97–101, 103; Gordon, *Gender and Higher Education,* 6; and Gordon, "Coeducation," 175–177, 183. For a discussion of female isolation on the Cornell University campus, see Bishop, *History of Cornell,* 42, 208–209.

14. Preamble, Constitution of Kappa Alpha Theta, 1893. Many other fraternities took on similar statements. See discussion of Zeta Tau Alpha's mission statement, in letter from May Agness Hopkins, Zeta Tau Alpha, to Eighteenth National Panhellenic Congress, NPC 1923, 19–20. Female collegians outside the Greek system also adopted "true" and "noble womanhood" as an important ideal. See Gordon, *Gender and Higher Education,* 3, Gordon, "Coeducation," 189; see also Newcomer, *Century of Higher Education,* 26–28; A.L.W., "The Higher Education of Women," *Kappa Alpha Theta* 3 (February 1889): 41–45.

15. See, for example, Sigma minutes, January 6, 1905, which contain a "reading from the life of Shelley" and note that "two of his beautiful poems were also read." Nearly all of the minutes of biweekly meetings of Alpha, Beta, Epsilon, Sigma, Phi, Tau, and Alpha Beta chapters, from the early 1890s through the mid-1910s, contain discussions of parties, of the planning social events, and of the organization of "at-homes" and "cozies," terms that referred to social gatherings.

16. Mu entry, *Kappa Alpha Theta* 1 (October 1885): 61. See also Kappa entry, *Kappa Alpha Theta* 2 (October 1886): 26. The term "spread" referred to gatherings at which attendees shared food and conversation.

17. Phi minutes, 1892–1901; see especially November 18, 1892; September 14, 1894; and February 26, 1897.

18. Beta minutes, May 14, 1892, and April 3, 1898; Tau minutes, December 15, 1894; February 10, 1895; November 23, 1896; December 20, 1897; and November 3, 1902.

19. Beta minutes, September 28, 1895; January 6, 1900; and October 12, 1904.

20. See, for example, Alpha minutes, December 18, 1878.

21. Phi minutes, October 30, 1896.

22. Upsilon chapter letter, *Kappa Alpha Theta* 3 (May 1889): 104.

23. Tau minutes, April 23, 1888.

24. Kappa entry, *Kappa Alpha Theta* 1 (April 1886): 140.

25. Tau minutes, June 8, 1888.

26. Beta minutes, October 12, 1904; October 31, 1904; and January 11, 1908.

27. NPC 1907, 2–3.

28. The histories of many of the major women's fraternities are striking in the changes they demonstrate over the years in terms of chapter focus. See, for example, Burton-Roth and Whiting-Westermann's history of Kappa Kappa Gamma, which described a focus in chapter meetings on literary works and other intellectual pursuits prior to the mid-1880s but showed much greater concern with social events among Kappa sisters after that time period. See also Thomson, *History of Alpha Phi*; Roedel, *History of Alpha Phi*; NPC 1902, 1904, 1907.

29. Curti and Carstensen, *University of Wisconsin*, vol. 1, 693–695, 698–699; Rudolph, *The American College and University*, 373–393; Solomon, *Company of Educated Women*, 103–104.

30. Solomon, *Company of Educated Women*, 105–107; Curti and Carstensen, *University of Wisconsin*, vol. 1, 418–421; Horowitz, *Campus Life*, 111; *Badger*, University of Wisconsin yearbook, 1910.

31. Solomon, *Company of Educated Women*, 106–111; Gordon, "Coeducation," 352; Dodge, *Sixty Years*, 312, 416.

32. Horowitz, *Campus Life*, 201; Solomon, *Company of Educated Women*, 71; see also Gordon, *Gender and Higher Education*; Palmieri, "Republican Motherhood," 56–58; Barbara Sicherman, "College and Careers: Historical Perspectives on the Lives and Work Patterns of Women College Graduates," in John Mack Faragher and Florence Howe, eds., *Women and Higher Education in American History* (New York and London: W. W. Norton, 1988), 137. For a discussion of the relative wealth of the second generation of female collegians in comparison the first, see Gordon, "Gibson Girl," 217. For a discussion of the continued deemphasis of scholarship and increased importance placed on social and extracurricular activities by students in the 1920s, see Fass, *Damned and the Beautiful*, 172–182.

33. *Baird's Manual of American College Fraternities*, 1912. In addition to the twenty-six historically white men's fraternities that were active in 1910, historically black Alpha Phi Alpha also existed and was joined by historically black Kappa Alpha Psi and Omega Psi Phi in 1911, and Phi Beta Sigma in 1914.

34. Kent Christopher Owen, "Reflections on the College Fraternity and Its Changing Nature," in *Baird's Manual of American College Fraternities*, 1991, 1–2.

35. For a discussion of the ways fraternities differed from and were similar to literary societies in the nineteenth century, see Rudolph, *The American College and University*, 145–147; also, Horowitz, *Campus Life*, 36–39.

36. Horowitz, *Campus Life*, 131–132; see also 134.

37. Ibid., 128.

38. Ibid., 201.

39. L. Levine, *Opening of the American Mind*, 79–81.

40. See Charles Franklin Emerick, "College Women and Race Suicide," *Political Science Quarterly* 24 (1909): 269–283, especially 276–279.

41. Horowitz, *Campus Life*, 201, 203–208.

42. Amy O. Parmalee, Margarethe Sheppard, and L. Pearle Green, "Extracts from Report of the Committee on Social Customs," *Kappa Alpha Theta* 25 (November 1910): 16. See also NPC 1907, 2–3; Burton-Roth and Whiting-Westermann, *History of KKG*, 40, 148–149.

43. Parmalee et al., "Extracts from Report," 21.

44. Alpha minutes, February 2, 1882; Tau minutes, May 25, 1908; chapter reports sent to Beta, 1907; Alpha minutes, February 7, 1879; Tau minutes, October 8, 1894.

45. Tau minutes, April 27, 1903; May 25, 1908; see also Tau minutes, 1907–1908, especially October 21, 1907. Also, NPC 1904, 2; NPC 1907, 3.

46. Beta minutes, April 16, 1892; see also Beta minutes, 1895–1908, and Tau minutes, October 3, 1906; March 18, 1907; and January 22, 1912.

47. Chapter reports sent to Beta, 1907.

48. Alpha minutes, May 14, 1880.

49. No discussion regarding curbing costs was recorded in any of the meeting minutes of Alpha, Epsilon, Sigma, Phi, Alpha Beta, or Tau chapters of Kappa Alpha Theta. Beta chapter held one recorded discussion on this topic, Beta minutes, October 12, 1904.

The discussions that took place at the Inter-Sorority Conferences of 1904 and 1907 regarding "extravagant expenditures" and "over-elaborateness of entertainment" among all the women's organizations indicate just how widespread the practice was. See NPC 1904, 2; NPC 1907, 2–3.

50. Editorial, *Kappa Alpha Theta* 12 (January 1898): 114.

51. "Social Side of College Life," *Kappa Alpha Theta* 15 (March 1901): 124.

52. Palmieri, "Republican Motherhood," 57.

53. See Robert J. Sprague, "Education and Race Suicide," *Journal of Heredity* 6 (1915), 158–161; Mary Cookingham, "Combining Marriage, Motherhood, and Jobs Before World War II: Women College Graduates, Classes of 1905–1935," *Journal of Family History* 9 (Summer 1984): 178–182.

54. Emerick, "College Women," especially 274; Cookingham, "Combining Marriage," 179–182.

55. As discussed in chapter 1, the first generation of Kappa Alpha Theta members also used a system of informal criticisms and instructional corrections designed to point out and eliminate in one another any traits or mannerisms considered "unbefitting a true Theta." As well as critiquing one another's scholarly performances in a manner consistent with their high standards for intellectual achievement, the early Thetas also adopted a practice whereby each member of the fraternity was charged "to correct and advise the 'sisters' in regard to

anything respecting manners, morals, or conversation and everything that is at all objectionable." See Alpha minutes, January 10, 1871; April 12, 1872.

56. Nearly all the chapters of Kappa Alpha Theta adopted this system. See especially weekly entries in Alpha minutes between October 10, 1884, when the sisters "decided to have informal criticism in the frat.," through the close of the 1890s and sporadically thereafter. See also Beta minutes, 1888–1909; Epsilon minutes, 1890–1900; Sigma minutes, 1907–1910; and Tau minutes, 1888–1910. See especially Alpha minutes, May 24, 1889; and Beta minutes, September 28, 1895, and January 3, 1889.

57. Alpha minutes, October 12, 1891, and April 2, 1892.

58. Mrs. Perley H. Markham, speech presented on unspecified date, prior to 1940 and assumed by the fraternity to be mid-1930s, on Chi chapter in the 1890s, Syracuse, NY; contained in "Theta Histories" folder, Kappa Alpha Theta Archives.

59. Beta minutes, April 4, 1896, and December 5, 1896.

60. Beta minutes, October 18, 1909; Alpha minutes, November 3, 1894.

61. Editorial, "Fraternity Criticism," *Kappa Alpha Theta* 8 (July 1894): 8–9.

62. Theodora McCoy, "Fraternity Education in Its Altruistic Aspect," *Kappa Alpha Theta* 14 (January 1900): 73–76.

63. "Fraternity Loyalty," *Kappa Alpha Theta* 10 (February 1896): 15–17.

64. Ibid.

65. Whereas Kappa Alpha Theta's constitutions of 1870 through 1901 stipulated that "no one can become a member of this society unless she has . . . received a high standing in her studies," in 1903 the Theta sisters amended this regulation to read, "To be eligible for membership . . . a student must [have] shown a desire to be an earnest student." See constitutions of Kappa Alpha Theta, 1870–1901 and 1903.

66. Minutes of the 5th Convention of Kappa Alpha Theta, 1881. See Constitution of Kappa Alpha Theta, 1881.

67. See, for example, Alpha minutes, September 29, 1876, and February 24, 1879.

68. Baird, *American College Fraternities*, 718; see also Josephine Barnaby and M. Grace Vance, "Fraternity Extension," *Kappa Alpha Theta* 22 (March 1908): 183–186.

69. In 1900, Kappa Alpha Theta met Kappa Kappa Gamma in direct competition on seventeen campuses, Pi Beta Phi on twelve campuses, Delta Gamma and Delta Delta Delta on ten campuses, Alpha Phi on nine campuses, Gamma Phi Beta on six campuses, and Alpha Chi Omega on five. *Kappa Alpha Theta* 14 (May 1900): 237. All women's fraternities experienced massive influxes in the 1890s in terms of the total number of members. Between 1890 and 1898, Kappa Alpha Theta grew from 1,180 to 2,339 members; Kappa Kappa Gamma from 1,523 to 2,937; Pi Beta Phi from 1,344 to 3,119; and Delta Gamma from 632 to

1,205, to name the four largest societies. Baird, *American College Fraternities,* 756.

70. Editorial, *Kappa Alpha Theta* 2 (October 1886): 12–13.

71. Ibid.

72. Tau minutes, September 24, 1888.

73. *Kappa Alpha Theta* 14 (May 1900): 237; *Kappa Alpha Theta Bi-Monthly* 5 (February 1914); and chapter records submitted to Beta chapter, 1883–1916. For accounts of the rivalry between the Thetas and the Kappas, see Dodge, *Sixty Years,* 76–77, and Burton-Roth and Whiting-Westermann, *History of KKG,* 106. See also Alpha's list of "Spiking Rules from 1890," which detail the agreement between Kappa Alpha Theta and Kappa Kappa Gamma to limit "rushing" and thus "ensure to both new girls and fraternities the advantage of longer acquaintance and considerate action"; Kappa Alpha Theta Archives.

74. Sabra Reece, "Kappa Alpha Theta: The First Thirty Years of Delta Chapter at Illinois 1895–1925, an Informal History," 1966, 6C, Stewart S. Howe Collection, Student Life and Culture Archives, University of Illinois at Urbana-Champaign, 14.

75. Kappa entry, *Kappa Alpha Theta* 3 (May 1889): 101–102.

76. Alpha Xi entry, *Kappa Alpha Theta* 3 (May 1889): 126–127.

77. Rho Chapter Centennial, "Rho Chapter 100th Year Celebration, 1887–1987," 5–7.

78. Tau minutes, November 14, 1898; December 5, 1898; and March 2, 1903. See also discussion of rushing in Kappa Kappa Gamma, contained in Burton-Roth and Whiting-Westermann's chapter histories.

79. Chapter reports sent to Beta, 1907 and 1909.

80. "Rushing Suggestions," *Kappa Alpha Theta* 26 (May 1912): 327–331.

81. Chapter reports sent to Beta, 1907 and 1909.

82. This point is captured especially in the Tau chapter Thetas' decision that "no college non-fraternity girls be invited to spreads unless they are to be initiated into Theta." Tau minutes, March 20, 1905.

83. For discussions of rush events, see Alpha minutes, September 22, 1894, and October 3, 1894; Beta minutes, May 30, 1904; September 24, 1904, and June 1, 1908; Tau minutes, May 17, 1909; March 5, 1912; February 10, 1913; October 19, 1914. For comment on the high cost of rush functions—"unwarranted expenditures"—throughout the women's Greek world in the early 1900s, see NPC 1907, 3.

84. See, for example, Tau minutes, November 1, 1909, and October 7, 1918. The extent to which all of the women's fraternities adhered to Theta's practice of downgrading academics while upgrading the importance of social demeanor is best displayed in the minutes of the Inter-Sorority Conference of 1907, which discuss the "evils of rushing"—simultaneous "over-elaborateness of entertainment [and] neglect of regular college work." See NPC 1907, 3.

85. See Alpha Iota entry, *Kappa Alpha Theta* 27 (November 1912): 93. Many Theta chapters reported their rushing successes in their meeting minutes. See especially Epsilon minutes, October 2, 1903.

86. Kappa Alpha Theta Bi-Monthly 5 (February 1914).

87. Parmalee et al., "Extracts from Report," 16–21; Kappa Alpha Theta Bi-Monthly 7 (September 1916).

88. Gordon, "Gibson Girl," especially 213, 216, 217.

89. Carolyn Halsted, "What a Girl Does at College: A Picture Story," *Ladies Home Journal,* part 1: 18 (December 1901): 26–27; part 2: "The Athletic Side," 18 (January 1902): 24–25; part 3: "The College Girl in Music and Drama," 19 (February 1902): 24–25; part 4: "The College Girl at Her Fun and in Her Room," 19 (March 1902): 26–27; part 5: "The College Girl at Her Studies," 19 (April 1902): 26–27; part 6: "The Close of the College Girl's Term," 19 (May 1902): 26–27; part 7: "College Girls in Shakespeare's Plays," 19 (September 1902): 26–27; "Some Secret Society College Girls," *Ladies Home Journal* 20 (June 1903): 26–27; "Fetes of College Girls," *Ladies Home Journal* 16 (June 1899): 3; "Christmas Pranks of College Girls," *Ladies Home Journal* 24 (December 1906): 17; "Some New Games for College Girls," *Ladies Home Journal* 22 (October 1905): 22–25; "Madcap Frolics of College Girls," *Ladies Home Journal* 22 (October 1905): 17, 62–63; A Graduate, "The College Scrapes We Got Into," *Ladies Home Journal* 18 (September 1901): 13–14, 34; "College Larks and Pranks," *Ladies Home Journal* 17 (August 1900): 1–2; "When College Girls Have Their Fun," *Ladies Home Journal* 20 (March 1903): 4; "College Girls' Larks and Pranks," *Ladies Home Journal* 17 (April 1900): 16–17; "College Girls' Larks and Pranks," *Ladies Home Journal* 17 (March 1900): 16–17; A Mother, "Some College Girl Follies," *Good Housekeeping* 49 (September 1909): 238–241.

90. Marchalonis, *College Girls,* 117–121.

91. Ibid., 122.

92. "Some Secret Society College Girls," *Ladies Home Journal* 20 (June 1903): 26–27.

93. P. F. Piper, "Secret Societies in Women's Colleges," *Harper's Bazar* [sic] 35 (1901): 580–584.

94. "Confessions of a Coed," *The Independent* 65 (October 1907): 871–874.

95. Survey conducted by the author of Greek-letter membership at twenty of the twenty-two colleges and universities at which Theta had a chapter during the school year of 1896–1897. According to most accounts, the Greek system also claimed roughly 30 percent of the male students, though on some campuses, as with the women, the percentage of affiliated men exceeded 70. See Horowitz, *Campus Life,* 132; Manhart, *DePauw,* 253–255.

96. Letter by Myrtle Miola Witney to her family, September 23, 1890, and

December 14, 1890, in Lisa Joan Brandt, "A Survey of Sorority Life at Northwestern University, 1881–1950," MS, 1978, 7, Northwestern University Archives.

97. Omega chapter centennial, 1890–1990.

98. Letter from Grace M. Bosworth to "Ida," September 17, 1895, Alpha Epsilon file.

99. See especially letter from C. H. Plummer to Eva R. Hall, June 15, 1911, Nu file. Letter from George Morey Miller to the Sorority of Kappa Alpha Theta, June 16, 1913, Alpha Tau file. Grand Council Report on Phi Sorority, Randolph-Macon Woman's College, 3, Beta Beta file. See also *Kappa Alpha Theta Bi-Monthly* 5 (February 1914).

100. Lucy Lilian Notestein, *Wooster of the Middle West,* vol. 1, *1866–1910* (Kent, OH: Kent State University Press, 1971).

101. To prevent such occurrences, the fraternity designated an official jeweler and required the approval of an officer before the jeweler could fill any order placed for a Theta badge. For a discussion of two of these occasions, see *Kappa Alpha Theta Bi-Monthly* 8 (April 1917). See also *Kappa Alpha Theta Bi-Monthly* 15 (February 1924).

Other women's organizations shared the same concern. At the National Panhellenic Congress meeting of 1906, the representatives authorized an investigation into "the making and wearing of badges by unauthorized persons"; NPC 1906. See also discussion the following year of desire to pass a law that would ensure that no outsiders could legally copy the design of their badges. NPC 1907, 1.

102. Neiswanger, "First Coeds," 18.

103. Letter from Myrtle Miola Witney to her family, September 23, 1890 and December 14, 1890, in Brandt, "Survey of Sorority Life," 7–8.

104. In compiling this information, I used the University of Illinois student ledger cards, which students filed upon enrollment. Choosing at random twelve Thetas from the period between 1896 and 1902 (the four years following Theta's installation at the university), fourteen women from the years between 1908 and 1911, and eleven women from the years 1916–1918, I charted and compared their responses to the request for father's occupation. See record series 25/3/4, University Archives, University of Illinois at Urbana Champaign. Of course, farmers, grain merchants, and nurserymen could have been relatively wealthy individuals for their time period, but certainly they fall into a different category than do company executives, bankers, doctors, and lawyers.

105. Minutes of the 16th Biennial Convention of Kappa Alpha Theta, 1905.

106. Horowitz, *Alma Mater: Design and Experience in the Women's Colleges from their Nineteenth-Century Beginnings to the 1930s,* 2nd ed. (Amherst: University of Massachusetts Press, 1993), 150–153. See also Horowitz, *Campus Life,* 197.

107. For a fuller discussion of nineteenth-century fears of the threats supposedly posed to polite society by confidence men and painted women, see Karen Halttunen's *Confidence Men and Painted Women: A Study of Middle-Class Culture in America, 1830–1870* (New Haven and London: Yale University Press, 1982); see especially xv, xvi.

108. Addie Lane Priest, "Fraternity Life: Spiking," *Kappa Alpha Theta* 4 (May 1890): 61.

109. Editorial, *Kappa Alpha Theta* 2 (October 1886): 12–14.

110. *Kappa Alpha Theta* 8 (January 1894): 21.

111. For a classic treatment of the insurgence of both the "petit bourgeoisie" and the new rich on the old established middle class and the threat both posed around the turn of the twentieth century in terms of status and power, see Richard Hofstadter, *The Age of Reform: From Bryan to F.D.R.* (New York: Vintage Books, a Division of Random House, 1955), especially 135–173.

112. Mary Roberts Smith, "Chapter Finance," *Kappa Alpha Theta* 8 (April 1894): 7–8.

113. Editorial, *Kappa Alpha Theta* 24 (March 1910): 243.

114. NPC 1902.

115. Ibid. The organizations invited by Alpha Phi to the first meeting of the Inter-Sorority Conference were Kappa Alpha Theta, Kappa Kappa Gamma, Delta Gamma, Gamma Phi Beta, Pi Beta Phi, Delta Delta Delta, Chi Omega, and Alpha Chi Omega. All but the last two attended the first gathering.

116. NPC 1902, 1; NPC 1903, 3; NPC 1908, 5. The representatives to the NPC from its earliest days, either by decree or by custom, all hailed from the alumnae segment of the different fraternities. In Kappa Alpha Theta, this designation was assured by an amendment to the constitution voted in by the sisters in 1914. See Constitution of Kappa Alpha Theta, 1914.

117. NPC 1902, 1; NPC 1903, 3; NPC 1904, 2; Reece, "Kappa Alpha Teta," 56.

118. NPC 1904, 2–6; NPC 1909, 3.

119. NPC 1904, 2; NPC 1911; NPC 1914, 11–12.

120. Report submitted by Kappa Kappa Gamma representative to the National Panhellenic Congress; NPC 1904, 3–6.

121. So little attention did the collegians of the early 1900s pay to their elders' recommendations for making rush a less hasty and costly procedure, that in 1917 the NPC delegates still spent a good part of their meeting discussing the same issue. See NPC 1917, 34–39.

122. Mary W. Lippincott, "Chapter Policy," *Kappa Alpha Theta* 20 (May 1906): 261.

123. Minutes of the 16th Biennial Convention, 1905; emphases in the original.

NOTES TO CHAPTER 3

1. Several women's fraternities had chapters in Canada at this time. Indeed, with the establishment of its Sigma chapter at the University of Toronto in 1887, Kappa Alpha Theta actually extended its reach internationally. Still, the sisters across the board used the term "national" to describe their fraternities.

2. See chapter 5 for a discussion of the influence Greek letter organizations brought to bear on behalf of their members in vocational arenas.

3. Of course the notion of diversity in Kappa Alpha Theta and other women's fraternities was a relative one in the 1910s. As will be discussed in this chapter, none of the historically white fraternities knowingly admitted black members, and many had firm restrictions against Jews, Catholics, and children of recent immigrants.

4. Raymond Baird, "Statistical Summary," in *American College Fraternities: A Descriptive Analysis of the Society System in the Colleges of the United States* (Philadelphia: J. B. Lippincott, 1879); ibid., "Statistical Table, General Fraternities – Women, 1883, 1890," 769, 771, 773; ibid., 10th ed., "Statistical Tables: Women's Fraternities, Membership," 756; Kappa Alpha Theta First Annual Report, 1909; Kappa Alpha Theta Bi-Monthly 8 (1916); Eighth Annual Report; Baird, "Statistical Table, General Fraternities –Women, 1920," 786; Kappa Alpha Theta Bi-Monthly 11 (February–April 1920); *Kappa Alpha Theta* 14 (May 1900): 237; Minutes of 23rd Biennial Convention of Kappa Alpha Theta, 1920, 45; Kappa Alpha Theta Bi-Monthly 11 (February–April 1920).

5. Minutes of 23rd Biennial Convention of Kappa Alpha Theta Convention, 1920; Kappa Alpha Theta Bi-Monthly 11 (February–April 1920).

6. Most entries in each chapter's minutes contain references along the lines of "correspondence received from Alpha chapter" or "a letter was read from the Michigan chapter." See, for example, Alpha minutes, January 3, 1882, and November 16, 1883; Beta minutes, October 1, 1880, and November 5, 1881, and Tau minutes, November 21, 1887, and February 16, 1888.

7. Alpha Epsilon entry, *Kappa Alpha Theta* 13 (November 1899): 25–26; letter from Grace M. Bosworth to Ida [Unknown], September 17, 1895, Alpha Epsilon file.

8. *Kappa Alpha Theta* 1 (June 1885): 4.

9. *Kappa Alpha Theta* 2 (October 1886): 11.

10. Alpha minutes, February 17, 1881, March 28, 1884, and February, 1887; Beta minutes, February 28, 1891; December 9, 1893; and October 30, 1897; Alpha Epsilon entry, *Kappa Alpha Theta* 12 (November 1897): 28–29; Tau entry, *Kappa Alpha Theta* 28 (November 1913): 103–104; Iota entry, *Kappa Alpha Theta* 20 (November 1905): 42 43; Omega entry, *Kappa Alpha Theta* 20 (November 1905): 68; Chi entry, *Kappa Alpha Theta* 19 (November 1904): 45–46.

11. Omicron chapter entry, *Kappa Alpha Theta* 2 (June 1887): 119.

12. Anna L. Guthrie, "Open Letter," *Kappa Alpha Theta* 4 (November 1890): 89–91; Alpha Epsilon entry, *Kappa Alpha Theta* 12 (November 1897): 28–29; Tau entry, *Kappa Alpha Theta* 28 (November 1913): 103–104; Dodge, *Sixty Years*, 463–477.

13. See Beta minutes, October 30, 1897; Tau minutes, November 2, 1896; November 7, 1894; and October 11, 1915; *Tau K.A.T* 2 (April 1916); Chi chapter entry, *Kappa Alpha Theta* 23 (January 1909): 303; Delta chapter entry, *Kappa Alpha Theta* 23 (January 1909): 317; Phi entry, *Kappa Alpha Theta* 23 (January 1909): 323–324. For a detailed description of the rise of football and its impact on American college campuses, see Rudolph, "The Rise of Football," in *The American College and University*, 373–393.

14. "A Summer Theta Club," *Kappa Alpha Theta* 25 (January 1911): 152–153; Eta chapter entry, *Kappa Alpha Theta* 29 (November 1914): 41.

15. Iota entry, *Kappa Alpha Theta* 20 (November 1905): 42–43. See also Omega entry, *Kappa Alpha Theta* 20 (November 1905): 67–68.

16. "A Summer Theta Club," *Kappa Alpha Theta* 25 (January 1911): 152–153. See also Alpha Epsilon entry, *Kappa Alpha Theta* 12 (November 1897): 28–29; Tau entry, *Kappa Alpha Theta* 28 (November 1913): 103–104.

17. See especially Alpha Epsilon entry, *Kappa Alpha Theta* 12 (November 1897): 28–29; and Alpha Zeta entry, *Kappa Alpha Theta* 26 (November 1911): 80–81.

18. Tau minutes, March 29, 1909; letter from L. Pearle Green to Grand Council, October 14, 1915, Omicron file.

19. See convention minutes as well as Grand Council Reports listing convention programs, all contained in Convention Files, Kappa Alpha Theta Archives. For examples, see Grand Council Report, 1909, and Minutes of 18th Biennial Convention, 1909. For a discussion of the vocational concerns of the fraternity women, see chapter 5. See introduction for discussion of debates over secrecy.

20. Grand Council Report, May 1909.

21. Letter from L. Pearle Green to Kappa Alpha Theta Fraternity, reprinted in "Editorial," *Kappa Alpha Theta* 23 (May 1909): 304.

22. "Lambda and Kappa," *Kappa Alpha Theta* 1 (April 1886): 120–121; Nellie Randell, "Fraternity Unity," *Kappa Alpha Theta* 12 (November 1897): 14–15; Alice H. Miller, "Via the Theta Special," *Kappa Alpha Theta* 26 (November 1911): 27; Bi-Monthly Report of the Grand Council 2 (December 1911), Third Annual Report; Bi-Monthly Report of the Grand Council 6 (April 1915).

23. Clarke-Helmick, *History of Pi Beta Phi*, 118–119.

24. Omega entry, *Kappa Alpha Theta* 18 (November 1903): 37.

25. Alice H. Miller, "Via the Theta Special," *Kappa Alpha Theta* 26 (November 1911): 27–28.

26. Nellie Randell, "Fraternity Unity," *Kappa Alpha Theta* 12 (November 1897): 14–15.

27. Upsilon entry, *Kappa Alpha Theta* 18 (November 1903): 44–45. See also Alpha Zeta entry, *Kappa Alpha Theta* 20 (November 1905): 48–49.

28. Minutes of 18th Biennial Convention, 1909.

29. Ibid.

30. Letter from L. Pearle Green to Ruth Hyndman, September 2, 1913, Alpha Tau chapter file, Kappa Alpha Theta Archives.

31. Grand Council Bulletin, September 1910.

32. Grand Council Bulletin, June–July 1907; Grand Council Bulletin, November 1907–March 1908; Tau minutes, March 2, 1908; Wilson, *We Who Wear Kites,* 242.

33. Letter from Aurelie Reynaud to the Grand Council of Kappa Alpha Theta, June 14, 1904, Lambda chapter file, Kappa Alpha Theta Archives.

34. For a discussion of the Pi alumnae position, see Grand Council Bulletin, June–July 1907 and Grand Council Bulletin, November 1907–March 1908.

35. Letter from Committee for Lambda Alumnae to Eva E. Capron, July 6, 1908, Lambda chapter file.

36. Minutes of First Meeting of the Executive Committee of the Grand Council, August 1908.

37. Minutes of First Meeting of the Executive Committee of the Grand Council, August 1908.

38. Letter from Aurelie Reynaud to the Grand Council of Kappa Alpha Theta, June 14, 1904, Lambda chapter file.

39. Beta minutes, October 12, 1893; Tau minutes, January 27, 1896, and November 4, 1907; Caroline M. Sutphin, "Affiliation," *Kappa Alpha Theta* 25 (November 1910): 28–29; By-Laws of Kappa Alpha Theta, 1914.

40. Iota entry, *Kappa Alpha Theta* 9 (January 1895): 26–27; Tau entry, *Kappa Alpha Theta* 9 (January 1895): 33–35; Iota entry, *Kappa Alpha Theta* 6 (January 1892): 95–96; Minutes of 21st Biennial Convention, 1915; Kappa Alpha Theta Bi-Monthly 7 (February 1916); Kappa Alpha Theta Bi-Monthly 9 (February 1918); Kappa Alpha Theta Bi-Monthly 11 (September 1920).

41. Iota entry, *Kappa Alpha Theta* 9 (January 1895): 26–27; Tau entry, *Kappa Alpha Theta* 9 (January 1895): 33–35; Iota entry, *Kappa Alpha Theta* 6 (January 1892). As discussed in chapter 1 and again in chapter 5, a significant number of fraternity women pursued graduate training. See *Kappa Alpha Theta* 31 (November 1916): 20–22; *Kappa Alpha Theta* 1 (June 1885): 22; Catharine Planck Kircher, chart comparing data of members pre- and post-1900, March 1917, Kappa Alpha Theta Archives.

42. Pi entry, *Kappa Alpha Theta* 9 (January 1895): 37.

43. Alpha Gamma entry, *Kappa Alpha Theta* 19 (November 1904): 46–47; Chi entry, *Kappa Alpha Theta* 23 (January 1909): 303–304.

44. Kappa Alpha Theta Bi-Monthly 11 (September 1920); Marie Pritchard, "Affiliation," *Kappa Alpha Theta* 27 (May 1913): 360–362; Cora E. Wells, "The Transfer," *Kappa Alpha Theta* 17 (January 1903): 134–135; Tau member, "The Transfer: By One Who Knows," *Kappa Alpha Theta* 18 (March 1904): 192–193; Caroline M. Sutphin, "Affiliation," *Kappa Alpha Theta* 25 (November 1910): 28–29.

45. Marie Pritchard, "Affiliation," *Kappa Alpha Theta* 27 (May 1913): 360–362; Cora E. Wells, "The Transfer," *Kappa Alpha Theta* 17 (January 1903): 134–135.

46. Kappa member, "Affiliation," *Kappa Alpha Theta* 19 (March 1905): 170–171.

47. Caroline M. Sutphin, "Affiliation," *Kappa Alpha Theta* 25 (November 1910): 28–29.

48. See especially Marie Pritchard, "Affiliation," *Kappa Alpha Theta* 27 (May 1913): 360–362; Cora E. Wells, "The Transfer," *Kappa Alpha Theta* 17 (January 1903): 134–135; Tau member, "The Transfer: By One Who Knows," *Kappa Alpha Theta* 18 (March 1904): 192–193; Caroline M. Sutphin, "Affiliation," *Kappa Alpha Theta* 25 (November 1910): 28–29.

49. Cora E. Wells, "The Transfer," *Kappa Alpha Theta* 17 (January 1903): 134–135.

50. Caroline M. Sutphin, "Affiliation," *Kappa Alpha Theta* 25 (November 1910): 28–29.

51. Marie Pritchard, "Affiliation," *Kappa Alpha Theta* 27 (May 1913): 360–362.

52. Amendments to Constitution of 1914, adopted in 1915 and ratified in 1917. In the years following the passage of this rule, the number of affiliates jumped from 12 to 41, and by 1920 all college chapters except for two affiliated all of the sisters who transferred to their campuses. See By-Laws of Kappa Alpha Theta, 1914, with amendments adopted 1915. See also Constitution and By-Laws of Kappa Alpha Theta, 1924; Minutes of 21st Biennial Convention, 1915; Kappa Alpha Theta Bi-Monthly 11 (September 1920); Kappa Alpha Theta Bi-Monthly 7 (February 1916); Kappa Alpha Theta Bi-Monthly 9 (February 1918).

53. See Alpha minutes, March 18, 1881, and April 8, 1881; also, Dodge, *Sixty Years,* 89, 94, 183–184; Alpha chapter minutes, January 23, 1880, and December 17, 1880. For statistics on extension, see document entitled "NPC Rate of Extension," in prep notes for Dodge's *Sixty Years in Kappa Alpha Theta,* Kappa Alpha Theta Archives. For a discussion of the elite status of the University of Michigan, see Howard H. Peckham, *The Making of the University of Michigan, 1817–1967* (Ann Arbor: University of Michigan Press, 1967), 82–83, 85–87.

54. Dodge, *Sixty Years,* 94; Alpha minutes, March 3, 1882; letter from Laura C. Hills to Kate Hammond, May 10, 1882, Lambda file. Correspondence be-

tween Alpha chapter and Iota chapter, May 9, 1882, contained in Dodge, *Sixty Years*, 96; circular letter from Jessie M. Boulton to Iota chapter, 1883, Iota file.

55. Letter from Kappa chapter to Miss Hall, November 24, 1885, Eta file; Iota minutes, June 2, 1885; September 19, 1885; October 31, 1885; January 9, 1886; and January 23, 1886. See also letter from Iota chapter corresponding secretary to Alpha sisters, December 9, 1885, Eta file; letter from Kappa chapter to Miss Hall, November 24, 1885, Eta file; letter from Juliet Holland to Miss Ridpath, October 28, 1885, Eta file.

According to one sister representing the Kappa chapter at Kansas, "Our chapters are in favor of compromising with [the Cornell and Michigan chapters] on any reasonable terms, even for the time being to limit the number of chapters and if need be to withdraw one or two, and to save Ann Arbor and Cornell. It would take us a long time to recover from such actions on the part of those two, they being among our very best." Letter from Kappa chapter to Miss Hall, November 24, 1885, Eta file. See also letter from Iota chapter corresponding secretary to Alpha chapter, December 9, 1885, Eta file.

56. Letter from Lizzie McVay Gillilan to the Grand Council, January 25, 1902, Zeta file. Letter from Jean Christie Chandler, Lambda delegate to 1886 special meeting, contained in Dodge, *Sixty Years*, 107. Zeta minutes, February 27, 1886, Zeta file.

Upon the removal of their Kappa Alpha Theta charter, most of the women who had comprised the active undergraduate Eta chapter at Michigan reorganized themselves into a society they named the University of Michigan Sorosis. Twenty-two of their initiated sisters, mostly alumnae, remained loyal to Kappa Alpha Theta. Later, two of the fifteen Sorosis members withdrew from their new organization and rejoined their sisters of Kappa Alpha Theta. Those who remained part of the fraternity later created an informal "Theta club" at the University of Michigan, which petitioned for and received a charter from Kappa Alpha Theta in 1893. See Dodge, *Sixty Years*, 107.

57. Ibid.

58. Burton-Roth and Whiting-Westermann, *History of KKG*, 35–37.

59. See Constitution of Kappa Alpha Theta, 1893; also, Minutes of 13th Biennial Convention of Kappa Alpha Theta, 1895; Minutes of 10th Biennial Convention of Kappa Alpha Theta, October 1889; Report of the Grand Council of Kappa Alpha Theta, February, 1901; NPC 1914, 20–23.

60. NPC 1914, 20–23; see also NPC 1917, 8.

61. See Kappa Alpha Theta Bi-Monthly, 1 (February 1910), for discussion of the rapid expansion of the major women's fraternities.

62. Minutes of 19th Biennial Convention, 1911.

63. Letter from Evelyn Polk Norton to the Grand Council, November 23, 1915, Beta Beta file. Letter from Amy Baker, District President, to Hazel Allison Forde, Vice President, April 5, 1917, Beta Eta file. Letter from Amy Baker,

District President, to Hazel Allison Forde, Vice President, May 9, 1917, Beta Eta file. See also discussion over establishment of chapter at Purdue University, in letter from Hope Davis to Indiana Chapters of Kappa Alpha Theta, April 6, 1914, Alpha Chi file. Also, opposition by nearby chapters to a potential reestablishment of Pi chapter at Albion College, in letter from Hazel Allison Forde to Grand Council, January 5, 1918, Pi file. Letter from Hazel Allison Forde to Mrs. Kimball, January 11, 1918, Pi file. In addition, see debate between members of the Berkeley and Stanford chapters of Kappa Alpha Theta regarding who should and should not be allowed into the fraternity. Letter from L. Pearle Green to Grand Council, October 14, 1915, Omicron file.

64. According to Dodge, one of the founders of the group stated that the three Ks stood for Karacter, Kulture, and Knowledge. There is no indication that the Tri Kappa name had anything to do with the Ku Klux Klan. See Alpha Epsilon file; also Dodge, *Sixty Years*, 161.

65. Grand Council Report, November, 1896.

66. Ibid.; Dodge, *Sixty Years*, 162.

67. See chapter 2 for a discussion of the high costs of fraternity membership in the years after 1890.

68. Grand Secretary's Report on Phi Sorority of Randolph Macon Women's College, May 16, 1915, Beta Beta file.

69. Private Report to Grand Council, attached to L. Pearle Green's Grand Secretary's Report on Phi Sorority of Randolph-Macon Women's College, May 16, 1915, Beta Beta file.

70. Ibid.

71. Letter from Marion Conover to L. Pearle Green, November 22, 1915; letters entitled, "Correspondence of Psi and Grand Council," October–November 1915; letter from L. Pearle Green to Alpha Eta and Psi chapters, January 24, 1915; letter from Alpha Eta chapter to Grand Council, November 23, 1915, all in Beta Beta file.

72. Minutes of 20th Biennial Convention of Kappa Alpha Theta, 1913. See also letter from Hope Davis to Indiana Chapters of Kappa Alpha Theta, April 6, 1914, Alpha Chi file. Letter from Estelle Riddle Dodge to Hazel Allison Forde, March 5, 1917, Beta Epsilon file.

73. Survey entitled "Admission of Limited-Membership Groups to N.P.C.: Summary of Questionnaires," conducted by Committee on Eligibility and Nationalization of Social Groups of the National Panhellenic Congress, June 11, 1925, NPC 1926, 45–51.

74. See Constitution of Kappa Alpha Theta, 1893. For a discussion of the adoption of the Moral Code by Kappa Alpha Theta, see Dodge, *Sixty Years*, 285–287.

75. "Admission of Limited-Membership Groups to N.P.C.: Summary of Questionnaires," NPC 1923, 45–51.

76. Solomon, *Company of Educated Women,* 143.

77. Winton Solberg, "Early Years of the Jewish Presence at the University of Illinois," *Religion and American Culture: A Journal of Interpretation* (Summer 1992): 215.

78. Ibid., 215, 223.

79. Nitza Rosovsky, *The Jewish Experience at Harvard and Radcliffe* (Cambridge, MA: Harvard Semitic Museum, 1986), 35; Solberg, "Early Years," 216, 223; Solomon, *Company of Educated Women,* 109.

80. Turk, "College Students," 259–260; Solberg, "Early Years," 219.

81. Ruth Sapinsky, "The Jewish Girl at College," in Jacob R. Marcus, ed., *The American Jewish Woman: A Documentary History* (New York: KTAV Publishing House, 1981), 702–703.

82. L. Levine, *Opening of the American Mind,* 126–129; Marcia Graham Synnott, *The Half-Opened Door: Discrimination and Admissions at Harvard, Yale, and Princeton, 1900–1970* (Westport, CT, and London: Greenwood Press, 1979), especially 26–57.

83. L. Levine, *Opening of the American Mind,* 58–59, 127–129; see also Solberg, "Early Years," 219.

84. Solomon, *Company of Educated Women,* 107, 143; Solberg, "Early Years," 219–221; Harold Wechsler, *The Qualified Student: A History of Selective College Admissions in America* (New York and London: John Wiley and Sons, 1977), especially 135–138, 149, 155–156; Synnott, *Half-Opened Door,* especially 33, 38–47, 61–62.

85. Solomon, *Company of Educated Women,* 143.

86. Rosovsky, *Jewish Experience,* 38; Solomon, *Company of Educated Women,* 141–145; Turk, "College Students," 259–260.

87. NPC 1917, 8. While perhaps speaking on behalf of her fraternity, which did have an explicit exclusionary clause, this representative to NPC certainly did not speak on behalf of all of the NPC representatives, though it would take an additional five decades for the organization to formally eradicate any overt prejudice regarding race and skin color. See conclusion for a discussion of the struggle to eradicate exclusionary clauses in those fraternities that had them.

88. NPC 1923, 69–70.

89. "Admission of Limited-Membership Groups to N.P.C.: Summary of Questionnaires," NPC 1926, 45–51. See also responses filed by Kappa Kappa Gamma, Pi Beta Phi, and Alpha Phi, especially. Whereas, like Theta, neither Kappa Kappa Gamma nor Pi Beta Phi used exclusionary causes, both allowed chapters to create bylaws excluding Jews and had chapters that did so. Alpha Phi fraternity, while having no exclusionary clause, followed a "national unwritten rule" barring "other races." Importantly, the composer of Kappa Alpha Theta's responses, Grand Secretary L. Pearle Green, consistently supported the petition

of Jewish fraternities to join the National Panhellenic Congress. See NPC 1917, 1923.

90. Turk, "College Students," 262; Sanua, "Jewish College Fraternities and Sororities," MS, 2–3, 9; Solberg, "Early Years," 228. Of course, prejudice toward members of their own religion was not unique to the Jewish sororities. Accounts abound of the harsh ways many "assimilated Jews" treated their newly arrived kin in the early decades of the twentieth century. Indeed, Pulitzer Prize winner Karl Shapiro was so stung by the poor treatment he endured as an eastern European Jew at the hands of German Jewish students of the University of Virginia that he opened his poem "University" with the lines, "To hurt the Negro and avoid the Jew / Is the curriculum." For a discussion of Shapiro's biography, see http://www.departments.bucknell.edu/stadler_center/shapiro/bio.htm. See also Ronald Steel's depiction of Walter Lippmann's biases against recently arrived Jews and the nouveaux riches as well as his acceptance of the quota system at Harvard, "A Conspicuous Race," in *Walter Lippmann and the American Century* (Boston: Little, Brown, 1980), 186–196.

91. For a discussion of same-race prejudice in African American sororities, see Kathy Russell, Midge Wilson, and Ronald Hall, *The Color Complex: The Politics of Skin Color among African Americans* (New York: Anchor Books/Doubleday, 1992), 30; Jennifer Otto, "Making the Best out of Bad Situations," News Website of the College of Communication and Information Sciences, University of Alabama, September 10, 2001; Connie Ogle, "Talcott Explores Racial Strife and the Death of the Judge," *Miami Herald,* June 9, 2002.

92. The following organizations, all the oldest and most prominent of the women's fraternities, were members of the National Panhellenic Congress: Alpha Chi Omega, Alpha Delta Pi, Alpha Gamma Delta, Alpha Omicron Pi, Alpha Phi, Alpha Xi Delta, Beta Phi Alpha, Chi Omega, Delta Gamma, Delta Delta Delta, Delta Zeta, Gamma Phi Beta, Kappa Alpha Theta, Kappa Delta, Kappa Kappa Gamma, Phi Mu, Pi Beta Phi, Sigma Kappa, and Zeta Tau Alpha. With the exceptions of Delta Delta Delta and Kappa Delta, all took part in this study. This study did not include Jewish, Catholic, or African American secret societies. See "Admission of Limited-Membership Groups to N.P.C.: Summary of Questionnaires," NPC 1926, 45–51.

The men's fraternities, too, followed similar practices. As historian Anthony James showed, most of the historically white organizations for men also adopted some form of exclusionary practice. "By the early twentieth century, many social fraternities adopted written clauses that specifically required whiteness and Christian affiliation for membership. Fraternities that lacked these clauses followed gentlemen's agreements to maintain identical restrictions." See Anthony James, "The College Social Fraternity Antidiscrimination Debate, 1945–1949," *The Historian: A Journal of History* 62 (Winter 2000), 304.

93. NPC 1926, 47.

94. G.L.E., "Report on Alpha Phi Local Petitioning for Kappa Alpha Theta at Sophie Newcomb College," October 5, 1913, Alpha Phi file.

95. Letter from President Davis to Hester A. Roberts, March 27, 1914; memo from Hester A. Roberts, April 7, 1914; notes on memo by May A. Johnson; letter from May A. Johnson, recipient unknown, June 1914. Hunter College file; letter from Frances D. Lyon to Hope Davis, April 27, 1915. Teacher's College at Albany file. Subsequent investigations of Hunter in the early 1920s provoked similar opposition from alumnae and officers alike. See letter from Mrs. Earl Gafford to Mrs. Haviland, January 31, 1922; letter from L. Pearle Green to Elizabeth Brownell Collier, August 23, 1924; and letter from unknown to Mary Titus, February 12, 1926, all in Hunter College file. See also discussion in the National Panhellenic Congress regarding whether to admit a fraternity that had a branch at Hunter: "As far as I can see they have the required number of chapters and they claim that they are non-sectarian," one representative noted of a petitioning organization, "But it seems to me they are essentially Jewish, and I think it should be brought to the attention of this conference. What the situation at other places is I don't know, but my feeling is that it must be Jewish at Hunter, because there is so much Jewish element at Hunter, and the same thing might be true of New York University. I think the delegates ought to know this, although they have claimed they are non-sectarian." The group was denied entry as a result of its "restricted membership." See NPC 1917, 7–8; NPC 1926, 40.

96. Apparently, the Catholic religion of some of the members wasn't the main issue; their Irish ethnicity combined with Catholicism was. See letter from Frances D. Lyon to Hope Davis, April 27, 1915, Teacher's College at Albany file.

97. Letter from L. Pearle Green to Grand Council, January 13, 1914, Alpha Omega file.

98. Letter from Ruth Townley to Hope Davis, January 29, 1914, Alpha Omega file.

99. Letter from L. Pearle Green to Grand Council, January 13, 1914, Alpha Omega file. The Theta sisters' attraction to schools with what they labeled "American" as opposed to ethnically diverse student bodies also played an important factor in their chartering of the Beta Gamma chapter at Colorado State University (previously called Colorado Agricultural College). In a letter recommending a petitioning group at the school for a Theta charter, Grand Vice President Hazel Allison Forde listed the institution's "native American population" (referring to white individuals who had lived in the United States for several generations) as her foremost reason for supporting the petitioning group's cause. See Hazel Allison Forde, "Report on Colorado Agricultural College," 1917, Beta Gamma file.

100. Letter from Amy Baker to Hazel Allison Forde, April 5, 1917, Beta Eta file. Because the collegiate Theta sisters never recorded why they chose certain women as rushees, nor did they indicate why they failed to pledge certain

women whom they had rushed, it is impossible to uncover who, if anyone, was excluded by individual chapters because of religious affiliation.

101. See Horowitz, *Campus Life,* for a discussion of the psychic challenge that the "outsiders" posed to campus "insiders," especially members of the white, Anglo-Saxon Protestant establishment, especially 104–105.

102. L. Levine, *Opening of the American Mind,* 127, 128.

103. Madison Grant, *The Passing of the Great Race* (New York: C. Scribner, 1916), 80–81, 228, and passim, quoted in L. Levine, *Opening of the American Mind,* 129. See also ibid., 126–129.

104. Letter from L. Pearle Green to Alpha Beta chapter, October 1, 1929, Alpha Beta file. While this letter deals with a specific instance that occurred outside the time boundaries of my study, I have chosen to address it because, better than any other piece of evidence I could find, it explains and clarifies a possible reason why the fraternity resisted pledging Jewish women and illuminates the history of the issue within Kappa Alpha Theta.

105. Letter from L. Pearle Green to Alpha Beta chapter, October 1, 1929, Alpha Beta file; Kappa Alpha Theta Bi-Monthly 17 (December 1926). According to a memo in the Panhellenic file housed in Northwestern University's archives, it was a "definite policy" of the Theta chapter that "no Jewish, or part Jewish girl [could] be pledged to the sorority or initiated as a member." Memo dated 11/19/36, Panhellenic File, Northwestern University Archives; cited in Brandt, "A Survey of Sorority Life at Northwestern University, 1881–1950," unpublished paper, 1978.

106. At the 1915 convention of Kappa Alpha Theta, members passed a rule barring the collegiate chapters from initiating any woman who had transferred from an institution where there was a Theta chapter without prior consultation regarding the girl's character with the said chapter or the dean of women. See Amendments to the Kappa Alpha Theta Constitution and Statutes, 1915. Later, this rule was expanded by the sisters to mandate, "No chapter shall invite to membership a girl from the normal territory of another chapter without first consulting that chapter and securing its approval of the girl." See Constitution of Kappa Alpha Theta, 1927. See also letter from L. Pearle Green to Alpha Beta chapter, October 1, 1929, Alpha Beta file.

107. Of course the Greek organizations were not the only ones whose whiteness and relative homogeneity in terms of class and religion fostered conservatism. In her study of the formation of the New Right in Orange County, California, in the 1960s, Lisa McGirr showed that monocultural settings tend to augment and reinforce conservatism. See Lisa McGirr, *Suburban Warriors: The Origins of the New American Right* (Princeton, NJ: Princeton University Press, 2001).

108. See, for example, NPC 1923, especially 69–70.

109. "Kappa Alpha Theta Fraternity Notable Members—Initiated between

1870 and 1920," internal document created by Mary Edith Arnold, Fraternity Archivist, March 2003.

110. Editorial, *Kappa Alpha Theta* 9 (January 1895): 21–22; see also Alpha Zeta entry, *Kappa Alpha Theta* 26 (November 1911): 80–81; Solomon, *Company of Educated Women,* 125–126. In her study of Delta Sigma Theta Sorority, Paula Giddings addressed this notion in relation to change. Change cannot come too quickly in an organization such as a fraternity or a sorority, she wrote, because "its viability is dependent on the growth of its membership, which in turn is largely determined by the number of its members who feel that the sorority's goals are in harmony with their own." See Giddings, *In Search of Sisterhood,* 6–7.

111. Katherine Stoughton Hart, "Theta Service," *Kappa Alpha Theta* 27 (May 1913): 326–329.

112. "Kappa Alpha Theta Fraternity Notable Members—Initiated between 1870 and 1920," Internal Document, Kappa Alpha Theta.

113. For a discussion of the involvement of clubwomen in the suffrage movement, see Blair, *Clubwoman as Feminist,* especially 44–45, 111–114.

114. The historically Protestant groups were not the only organizations reluctant to take potentially controversial positions on social issues. The historically Jewish fraternities and sororities also demonstrated an unwillingness to associate with groups whose actions their members supported but whose affiliation might taint the reputation of the organizations. In the 1930s and 1940s, for example, the issue of what Jewish sisters and brothers should do in response to Nazism and the increase in anti-Semitism across the country prompted a great deal of discussion in the Jewish Greek system. Stung personally by the backlash against them but wary of affiliating themselves too strongly with any cause that might be deemed radical, Jewish Greek leaders warned their sisters and brothers that all Jews would be judged by the members' behavior. As Alpha Epsilon Phi National President Reba B. Cohen reminded her sisters in 1939, "We can, as college women, best serve our people by creating better understanding between Jews and non-Jews, by paying special attention to our dress, manners, and speech, and by cooperating amongst ourselves." The best action was to avoid messy political struggles, the leaders determined. Instead of taking a strong and united stance against those who spouted anti-Semitic beliefs, the Jewish Greek organizations chose instead to aid the Jewish cause by serving as "model representatives" of their faith. See Sanua, "Jewish College Fraternities and Sororities," MS, 17, 33.

NOTES TO CHAPTER 4

1. Baird, "Statistical Table: Women's Fraternities, Membership," in *Baird's Manual of American College Fraternities,* 10th ed., 1923, 756.

2. Rudolph, *American College and University,* 147–149.

3. Curti and Carstensen, *University of Wisconsin,* vol. 1, 665–666. For discussions of anti-Greek efforts, see Rudolph, *American College and University,* 147–149; Horowitz, *Campus Life,* 29–30; George Banta, "The Sorority Situation at Wisconsin," *Banta's Greek Exchange* 6 (July 1918): 294–295; "As Our Sisters See It," *Banta's Greek Exchange* 8 (December 1919): 38–51; Editorial, *Kappa Alpha Theta* 27 (May 1913): 366–367; Minutes of 19th Biennial Convention of Kappa Alpha Theta, 1911; John L. Kind, "The Fraternity Situation at Wisconsin," *Western Intercollegiate Magazine* (January 1911): 3–12. For other discussions of antifraternity agitation, see articles collected together in the section entitled, "As Our Sisters See It," in the December 1919 issue of *Banta's Greek Exchange* 8 (December 1919): 38–51; Barnard College, *Report of the Dean,* 1913, 5; Lucy Lilian Notestein, "Hurricane Alpha," in *Wooster of the Middle West*; Solomon, *Company of Educated Women,* 108.

4. "A Poisoned Spring," 1901, in "Fraternity Histories," Settlemyer folder, F9029, U58, PO, University of Wisconsin Archives; emphases in the original. For further discussion of opposition to fraternities at the University of Wisconsin, see Curti and Carstensen, *University of Wisconsin,* vol. 1, 664–667; vol. 2, 174, 183, 190, 502; George Banta, "The Sorority Situation at Wisconsin," *Banta's Greek Exchange* 6 (July 1918): 294–295; "As Our Sisters See It," *Banta's Greek Exchange* 8 (December 1919): 38–51; Editorial, *Kappa Alpha Theta* 27 (May 1913): 366–367; Minutes of 19th Biennial Convention of Kappa Alpha Theta, 1911.

5. Report of the Faculty Committee, Faculty File Book, July 1, 1910, contained in Curti and Carstensen, *University of Wisconsin,* vol. 2, 501; also, "Regent's Report on Fraternities," *Wisconsin Alumni Magazine* (June 1911). See also Carrie E. Morgan, "The Sorority Situation at Wisconsin," *Banta's Greek Exchange* 2 (March 1914), 188, 190.

6. "Regents' Report on Fraternities," *Wisconsin Alumni Magazine* 12 (June 1911): 405. "Fraternities/Clippings" file, University of Wisconsin Archives.

7. Michael Jahn, "Greeks on the Peak: Fraternity Power at the University of Wisconsin from the Teens through the Thirties," unpublished paper, 1998, "Fraternities/Clippings" file, University of Wisconsin Archives. See also "Bills Affecting the University," *Wisconsin Alumni Magazine* 14 (March 1913): 273–274; Curti and Carstensen, *University of Wisconsin,* vol. 2, 502; Minutes of 19th Biennial Convention of Kappa Alpha Theta, 1911.

8. Editorial, *Kappa Alpha Theta* 27 (May 1913): 366–367; letter from L. Pearle Green to Charlotte Walker Stone, January 9, 1913, Epsilon file; Kappa Alpha Theta Bi-Monthly 4 (February 1913), Fourth Annual Report; Kappa Alpha Theta Bi-Monthly 8 (February 1916), Eighth Annual Report; Walter B. Palmer, "Antagonism to Fraternities: A Review," *Banta's Greek Exchange* 8 (December 1919), 9.

9. Palmer, "Antagonism to Fraternities," 8.

10. Ibid., 8–9.

11. H. T. Parlin, "A Brief History of the Regulation of Fraternities in the University of Texas," *University of Texas Bulletin* (July 1917): 34–39.

12. *Daily Cardinal* of the University of Wisconsin, April 26, 1901, in Curti and Carstensen, *University of Wisconsin*, vol. 1, 666–667; Minutes of 19th Biennial Convention of Kappa Alpha Theta, 1911; Editorial, *Kappa Alpha Theta* 27 (May 1913): 366–367; letter from L. Pearle Green to Charlotte Walker Stone, January 9, 1913, Epsilon file; Kappa Alpha Theta Bi-Monthly 4 (February 1913), Fourth Annual Report; Kappa Alpha Theta Bi-Monthly 8 (February 1916), Eighth Annual Report.

13. W. H. P. Faunce, "Opinion of the Executive Committee," paper read in chapel at Brown University, November 14, 1911; letter from W. H. P. Faunce, R. H. I. Goddard, Stephen O. Metcalf, Henry M. King, and Lidia Shaw King to the fraternities at Brown, December 5, 1991. Both included in article written by Kappa Alpha Theta Grand Council, "Fraternity Situation at Brown University," *Kappa Alpha Theta* 26 (January 1912): 150–154; Hazel M. Fowler, "The Passing of Alpha Epsilon," *Kappa Alpha Theta* 26 (May 1912): 346–347; Grand Council of Kappa Alpha Theta, "The Fraternity's Loss," *Kappa Alpha Theta* 26 (May 1912): 347–348; letter from Mabel Hale to Mrs. Moulton, February 26, 1912; letter from L. Pearle Green to Mrs. Moulton, February 23, 1912. All correspondences on the Brown University matter contained in Alpha Epsilon file. See also Eisenmann, "Freedom to Be Womanly," 73–74.

14. See Notestein, *Wooster of the Middle West,* 54–64, 68–69; letter from Louis E. Holden to Mabel Hale, January 31, 1913, Epsilon file; letter from Louis E. Holden to Charles R. Compton, financial secretary, November 14, 1912, in Notestein, *Wooster of the Middle West,* 61–62; letter from L. Pearle Green to Charlotte Walker Stone, January 9, 1913; letter from L. Pearle Green to Miss Fulton and Girls of Epsilon, December 31, 1912. Letters from Amy Parmalee, Delta Delta Delta; May L. Kellar, Pi Beta Phi; Mary McEachin Rodes, Kappa Kappa Gamma; and Mabel Hale, Kappa Alpha Theta, to the Trustees of Wooster University, January 15, 1913. Letter from Louis E. Holden to Mabel Hale, January 31, 1913; Winona Hughes, "Statement Concerning the Surrender of Charters by the Local Chapters of the Pi Beta Phi, Kappa Kappa Gamma, Kappa Alpha Theta Sororities in the University of Wooster," February 15, 1913, Epsilon file.

15. See NPC 1914, 9–10; John L. Kind, "The Fraternity Situation at Wisconsin," *Western Intercollegiate* Magazine (January 1911): 3. For a discussion of Greek system closures on certain campuses, see Kappa Alpha Theta Bi-Monthly 3 (December 1912), Fourth Annual Report; see also Eva Reed Hall, "Directory of Kappa Alpha Theta, 1870–1924," "Directories" folder, Kappa Alpha Theta

Archives; "Extracts from Brief Submitted to Committee of the Board," August 18, 1919, Alpha Phi file.

16. Louise Monning, "Impressions of the Twelfth National Pan-Hellenic Congress," *Banta's Greek Exchange* 2 (December 1913): 8. Stewart S. Howe Collection; NPC 1914, 9.

17. Sabra Reece, "Kappa Alpha Theta: The First Thirty Years of Delta Chapter at Illinois 1895–1925, an Informal History," 1966, 6C, Stewart S. Howe Collection, Student Life and Culture Archives, University of Illinois at Urbana-Champaign, 122.

18. Leulah J. Hawley, "A Symposium," *Banta's Greek Exchange* 8 (December 1919): 38–40.

19. Ethelyn M. Hartwich, "A Loose Rivet in Our Sorority Panhellenism," *Banta's Greek Exchange* 4 (March 1916), 193–200; NPC 1914.

20. NPC 1915, 25.

21. NPC 1917, 39.

22. NPC 1917, 34; NPC 1926, 60, 72–73. The NPC passed several pieces of legislation designed to impel all Greek-letter women to conduct themselves in manners befitting their organizations' ideals in order to raise the image of women's Greek organizations in the eyes of campus administrators and social critics. For evidence of Thetas' role in bringing together the NPC organizations to combat opposition en masse, see letter from L. Pearle Green to Amy Parmalee, Delta Delta Delta; May L. Kellar, Pi Beta Phi; and Mary McEachin Rodes, Kappa Kappa Gamma, December 31, 1912, all in Epsilon file. Also the letter from May L. Kellar to L. Pearle Green, January 2, 1913, Epsilon file. For further discussions of the role played by the NPC in responding to opposition, see Martha Louise Railsback, "Impressions of the Fourteenth National Panhellenic Congress," *Banta's Greek Exchange* 3 (September 1915): 449–450; Carrie E. Morgan, "The Sorority Situation at Wisconsin," *Banta's Greek Exchange* 2 (March 1914): 187–192; L. Pearle Green, "As Our Sisters See It," *Banta's Greek Exchange* 8 (December 1919): 41–43; Ruth Haynes Carpenter, "The Future of Women's Greek Letter Fraternities," *Banta's Greek Exchange* 3 (July 1915): 291–294; and especially Leulah Hawley, "As Our Sisters See It," *Banta's Greek Exchange* 8 (December 1919): 39–40. For discussions of the Fraternity Reference Bureau, founded in 1913 to serve as a clearinghouse for information on fraternities and antifraternity agitation, see "Position of Fraternities Today: Chicago Conference of Fraternities," 20th Biennial Convention, 1913; "Conference of Fraternities, May 1913," *Kappa Alpha Theta* 28 (November 1913): 54–58; "Report of the Official Committee on Anti-Fraternity Legislation," *Kappa Alpha Theta* 28 (March 1914): 291–303.

23. Parlin, "Brief History," especially 9–32.

24. "Report of the Official Committee on Anti-Fraternity Legislation," *Kappa Alpha Theta* 28 (March 1914): 291–303.

25. Ibid.; Kind, *The Fraternity Situation at Wisconsin*, 11.

26. NPC 1914, 16.

27. NPC 1914, 23–24.

28. While most chapters of Kappa Alpha Theta had maintained from their earliest days the practice of reading aloud or posting members' grades and numbers of "cuts," or missed classes, in any given week, academic concerns took little of the active sisters' time or efforts in the 1890s and early 1900s, and intellectual achievements earned no mention in their quarterly reports to the fraternity journal. See, for example, Beta minutes, June 9, 1906, and March 2, 1907; Tau minutes, December 12, 1910, and April 6, 1914; Epsilon minutes, February 2, 1912; Edith D. Cockins, "Scholarship," *Kappa Alpha Theta* 26 (March 1912): 263.

29. "Scholarship Honors to Kappa Alpha Theta Members, College Year 1909–10," *Kappa Alpha Theta* 25 (January 1911): 139. See second number of subsequent volumes of *Kappa Alpha Theta* for additional examples of scholarship lists.

30. Constitution of Kappa Alpha Theta, 1914. See also references to scholarship committees in minutes. For example, see Beta minutes, March 2, 1907, and Tau minutes, November 16, 1914.

31. See, for example, "Scholarship, 1915–1917," *Kappa Alpha Theta* 31 (March 1917): 280; Kappa Alpha Theta Bi-Monthly 7 (February 1916).

32. "Scholarship Averages," *Kappa Alpha Theta* 26 (May 1912): 338; "Scholarship Averages for 1913–1914," *Kappa Alpha Theta* 29 (January 1915): 103–108; Kappa Alpha Theta Bi-Monthly 8 (1916), Eighth Annual Report; Kappa Alpha Theta Bi-Monthly 11 (December 1920).

33. Tau minutes, March 20, 1916. See also Tau minutes, November 25, 1912; December 16, 1912; November 27, 1916; December 3, 1917; and December 10, 1917; and see Constitution of Kappa Alpha Theta, 1914.

34. Kappa Alpha Theta Bi-Monthly 11 (December 1920); Kappa Alpha Theta Bi-Monthly 7 (February 1916). See also Section 7, Statute 13, Constitution of Kappa Alpha Theta, 1914.

35. Kappa Alpha Theta Bi-Monthly 7 (February 1916).

36. Kappa Alpha Theta Bi-Monthly 11 (December 1920).

37. See, for example, Tau minutes, December 3, 1917; March 11, 1918; and October 23, 1918.

38. Emma Weitz, "What Kappa Alpha Theta Can Do," *Kappa Alpha Theta* 27 (May 1913): 339–341.

39. For discussion of women's fraternities and sororities as subversive of class loyalty and campus community, see Horowitz, *Campus Life*, 38, 193–219; also, Gordon, *Gender and Higher Education*, 61, 105–107.

40. Gordon, *Gender and Higher Education*, 105–107; Gordon, "Coeducation," 357–358.

41. NPC 1907, 8, 9; Weitz, "What Kappa Alpha Theta Can Do," 339–341; L. Pearle Green, "The Fraternity and the College Today," *Kappa Alpha Theta* 28 (January 1914): 165–166.

42. Minutes of 24th Biennial Convention of Kappa Alpha Theta, 1924; NPC 1914, 10; NPC 1917, 20.

43. NPC 1914, 9. So interested were the fraternity women in working with the deans of women that in 1926 they voted to hold the National Panhellenic Congress meetings at the same time and in the same location as the national gathering of deans of women. See NPC 1926, 59.

44. Minutes of 21st Biennial Convention of Kappa Alpha Theta, 1915, 37. See also Horowitz, *Campus Life*, 111.

45. Mary Longbrake Harshman, "Some Gleanings from the Conference of Deans of Women," *Banta's Greek Exchange* (July 1925): 258–259; Kind, *The Fraternity Situation at Wisconsin*, 3; Leulah J. Hawley, "A Symposium," *Banta's Greek Exchange* 8 (December 1919): 39; Jessica Nelson North, "As Our Sisters See It," *Banta's Greek Exchange* 8 (March 1920), 186, 188. For additional arguments along the lines that the women's fraternities were being blamed for faults that would exist in any group, be it a Greek-letter organization or not, see Carrie E. Morgan, "The Sorority Situation at Wisconsin," *Banta's Greek* Exchange 2 (March 1914), 187; "Committee Report," Committee for the Investigation of Fraternities and Sororities, University of Wisconsin, 1910, Charles R. Van Hise Records, Box 22, Folder 315, University of Wisconsin Archives.

The fraternity world was quick to label its opponents "socialists," "Bolsheviks," and "peculiar individualists." In the battle to save the Greek system at Wisconsin, George Banta, publisher of the popular journal *Banta's Greek Exchange,* wrote that a "strange spirit of bolshevikism . . . threads all through the thought and life of the University people." In discussions of the antifraternity movement at Barnard, the fraternity women labeled the student leader a "violent socialist" who had turned the student body against the Greek system. As one prominent member stated before the National Panhellenic Congress, "There is no hope of change except from the student council, and that council has as its chairman the girl who has been most prominent against fraternities. None of us can hold out more than this year. . . . They resent our nationalism; the race question has entered in, and we have the student body, not the faculty to deal with." See George Banta, "The Sorority Situation at Wisconsin," *Banta's Greek Exchange* 6 (July 1918), 294–295; NPC 1914, 26.

46. NPC 1917, 43–44.

47. Kappa Alpha Theta Bi-Monthly 3 (December 1912), Fourth Annual Report (emphasis in the original); Mary Isabel Saunders, "What Can You Do?" *Kappa Alpha Theta* 30 (March 1916): 227–228. See also Editorial, *Kappa Alpha Theta* 27 (March 1913): 257–258.

48. Green, "As Our Sisters See It," 41–43; Kappa Alpha Theta Bi-Monthly 3

(December 1912), Fourth Annual Report; Kappa Alpha Theta Bi-Monthly 4 (December 1913); Editorial, *Kappa Alpha Theta* 27 (March 1913): 257–258; Ruth Haynes Carpenter, "Grand President's Address," Minutes of 21st Biennial Convention, Kappa Alpha Theta, 1915.

49. Most collegiate members eagerly welcomed chances to meet and socialize with sisters on other campuses, but they resisted efforts to conform to other chapters' mores and standards and chafed when forced by their officers to absorb into their own group a sister whom they considered different. See chapter 3 for a discussion of rifts among chapters and also for treatment of the issue of transferring students.

50. NPC 1917, 3; letter from L. Pearle Green to Catherine Bigelow, January 9, 1913, Epsilon file; Green, "As Our Sisters See It," 41–43; Kappa Alpha Theta Bi-Monthly 6 (December 1915), Seventh Annual Report.

51. See, for example, Fannie Preston, "Alpha Theta's Plea," *Kappa Alpha Theta* 26 (May 1912): 340–341; K.G.O., "Intelligent Fraternity Women," *Kappa Alpha Theta* 22 (March 1908): 203–204. See also discussions in NPC 1915, 1917, 1923.

52. Minutes of Grand Council Meeting, August 1908.

53. "The Social Side of College Life," *Kappa Alpha Theta* 15 (March 1901): 124–127.

54. Grand Council Bulletin, November 1911.

55. Alpha Gamma, "Undergraduate Department," *Kappa Alpha Theta* 12 (May 1898): 200–201; "Who Goes to College Next Fall?" *Kappa Alpha Theta* 27 (May 1913): 369.

56. See, for example, Tau minutes, April 25, 1910; November 11, 1912; November 18, 1912; October 5, 1914; and November 12, 1917. Also Kappa Alpha Theta Bi-Monthly 17 (December 1926).

57. A.M.R., "The Essential Test," *Kappa Alpha Theta* 14 (January 1900): 88; "What Qualities Should the Desirable Girl Possess," *Kappa Alpha Theta* 15 (January 1901): 59–62, letter from L. Pearle Green to Alpha Beta chapter, October 1, 1929, Alpha Beta file.

58. A.M.R., "The Essential Test," *Kappa Alpha Theta* 14 (January 1900): 88; "What Qualities Should the Desirable Girl Possess," 59–62.

59. See especially Ednah Harmon Wickson, "President's Letter," *Kappa Alpha Theta* 16 (May 1902): 259–261.

60. Kappa Alpha Theta Bi-Monthly 17 (December 1926). See also letter from L. Pearle Green to Alpha Beta chapter, October 1, 1929, Alpha Beta file.

61. See, for example, Alpha chapter entry, *Kappa Alpha Theta* 27 (November 1912): 57.

62. Kappa entry, *Kappa Alpha Theta* 27 (November 1912): 66; Alpha Lambda entry, *Kappa Alpha Theta* 29 (November 1914): 67. By the 1920s, the fraternity rolls contained so many groups of Theta relatives that an effort to

publish in one issue of the journal all the names and their relationships to one another failed due to lack of space. See "Mothers, Daughters, Sisters," *Kappa Alpha Theta* 39 (March 1925): 269–279.

Other fraternities also privileged relatives. In Pi Beta Phi, members bragged of their Pi Phi relatives. On the information sheets sent to all living alumnae of the Illinois Zeta chapter in 1995, a dedicated space was set aside for "Pi Phi Legacies." Of the five received from alumnae initiated before 1930, three listed relatives who had pledged the fraternity, two of these noting that both daughters and granddaughters were members. See Pi Beta Phi Alumnae reports, 1919–1930, Stewart S. Howe Collection, Student Life and Culture Archives, University of Illinois, Urbana-Champaign.

63. "Fraternity Daughters and Sisters," *Kappa Alpha Theta* 22 (May 1908): 275–277. See also letter from L. Pearle Green to Grand Council, October 14, 1915, Omicron file.

64. Minutes of 21st Biennial Convention, 1915, 14–15.

65. Constitution of Kappa Alpha Theta, adopted in 1915 and ratified in 1917. See "Rulings" section of Constitution of Kappa Alpha Theta, 1924, for finalized version.

66. A.M.R., "The Essential Test," 88.

67. Letter from Hazel Allison Forde to Mary Moses Glessner, November 22, 1915; letter from L. Pearle Green to Ruth Hyndman, September 2, 1913, both in Alpha Tau file.

68. See frequent references to "returning sisters" in existing Alpha and Beta minutes, 1870–1890. See also letter from Clara Colburne to *Kappa Alpha Theta* 4 (May 1890): 68; also references to active "resident Thetas" in chapter reports, contained in file, "Chapter Reports Ca. Late 1800s Early 1900s Sent to Beta Chapter." See chapter 5 for further discussion of alumnae involvement in fraternity affairs.

69. For examples of discussions of informal alumnae involvement in chapter lives, see Eta entry, *Kappa Alpha Theta* 26 (November 1911): 52; Alpha Lambda entry, *Kappa Alpha Theta* 27 (November 1912): 95; Beta minutes, April 25, 1907; and Tau minutes, November 1, 1909, and January 30, 1911.

70. Constitution of Kappa Alpha Theta, 1914; Josephine Meissner, "Alumnae Cooperation," *Kappa Alpha Theta* 24 (March 1910): 227–229.

71. See Minutes of 20th Biennial Convention, 1913, emphases in the original; Mabel P. Stilwell, "Alumnae Cooperation with College Chapter," *Kappa Alpha Theta* 33 (May 1919): 288–289; Editorial, "Things Alumnae Should be Doing," *Kappa Alpha Theta* 34 (May 1920): 350–352; Alice Towne Deweese, "Ho Alumna!" *Kappa Alpha Theta* 33 (March 1919): 163–165; Hilda Laurier Weber, "A Plea for More Intimate Relation between Active and Alumnae Members," *Kappa Alpha Theta* 20 (January 1906): 87–94; Blanche McGough, "Greater Alumnae Loyalty," *Kappa Alpha Theta* 22 (May 1908): 265–266;

Marion Whipple Garrettson, "President's Message," *Kappa Alpha Theta* 21 (May 1907): 241–243; Leola Vancil Randall, "Value of Alumnae Chapters," *Kappa Alpha Theta* 28 (March 1914): 280–281; Josephine Meissner, "Alumnae Cooperation," *Kappa Alpha Theta* 24 (March 1910): 227–229; Helen Biddle, "Alumnae and College Chapter Relations," Minutes of 24th Biennial Convention, 1922.

72. By the mid-1910s, all active chapters wrote newsletters to their alumnae members to keep them abreast of college activities and to "introduce" new members to the older sisters. See, for example, copies of the "Annual Alumnae Letter" sent by the Delta chapter sisters to their alumnae, or the *Kite* newsletters compiled by the collegiate members of the Tau chapter. While alumnae participation in active fraternity affairs hovered at 13 percent in 1910, that number nearly doubled by 1916, to a figure closer to 25 percent. See chapter files, Kappa Alpha Theta Archives; Kappa Alpha Theta First Annual Report, 1909; Bi-Monthly Report of the Grand Council 1 (December 1910), Second Annual Report; Dodge, *Sixty Years*, 456–457; Kappa Alpha Theta Eighth Annual Report, 1916 (Supplement to Kappa Alpha Theta Bi-Monthly 8 (February 1916).

73. Bi-Monthly Report of the Grand Council 6 (April 1915). In the case of the weaker chapters, such as Alpha Theta at the University of Texas, the Grand Council expedited the granting of alumnae charters to local residents in order to speed their involvement and aid to the struggling groups. See Petition for Alumnae Charter, submitted by Austin, Texas, Local Alumnae Club, November 12, 1915, Alumnae Program files.

74. For example, see Tau minutes, November, 1908; October 4, 1909; February 28, 1910; November 3, 1913; and November 16, 1914.

75. See especially Tau minutes, April 29, 1907; October 4, 1909; and January 22, 1912.

76. Mary W. Lippincott, "Chapter Policy," *Kappa Alpha Theta* 20 (May 1906): 261.

77. Both Alpha and Beta's entries contain frequent references to meeting in sisters' houses and attempts to procure rooms and halls. See, for example, Alpha minutes, January 8, 1880, and November 23, 1883; Beta minutes, September 2, 1881, and September 28, 1895. See also Dodge, *Sixty Years*, 338.

78. For a discussion of the housing crunch that plagued many campuses in the 1890s and early 1900s, see Solomon, *Company of Educated Women*, 107. By 1900, the members of nearly half of Kappa Alpha Theta's twenty collegiate branches lived together in houses the fraternity either owned or rented, and this percentage remained consistent for the next twenty years. See Dodge, *Sixty Years*, 344; *Handbook of Kappa Alpha Theta*, 1911, Tau Chapter Archives.

79. Editorial, *Kappa Alpha Theta* 2 (June 1887): 103–106.

80. Lena L. House, "The Chapter House Question," *Kappa Alpha Theta* 13 (January 1899): 79.

81. Editorial, *Kappa Alpha Theta* 26 (March 1912): 257; Kappa Alpha Theta Bi-Monthly 5 (September 1914).

82. Mary W. Lippincott, "Chapter Policy," *Kappa Alpha Theta* 20 (May 1906): 261–262; Editorial, *Kappa Alpha Theta* 16 (May 1902): 268.

83. Alice Crittenden Derby, "The Ideal Theta," *Kappa Alpha Theta* 18 (March 1904): 101.

84. "What the Fraternity Expects," *Kappa Alpha Theta* 11 (February 1897): 95–96.

85. Phi Alumnae, "Our Responsibilities," *Kappa Alpha Theta* 27 (March 1913): 243–244.

86. "The Ideal Theta," *Kappa Alpha Theta* 18 (March 1904): 101; Carolyn Elizabeth Golding, *Kappa Alpha Theta* 17 (October 1903): 308.

87. C.G.L., "After Rushing Season," *Kappa Alpha Theta* 13 (January 1899): 69.

88. See Kappa Alpha Theta Ritual, Kappa Alpha Theta Archives.

89. K.S.S., "Self-Development," *Kappa Alpha Theta* 15 (March 1901): 117–119; Kappa Alpha Theta Bi-Monthly 4 (April 1913). All references to Kappa Alpha Theta's ritual are based on historical accounts of the fraternity's ritual. They do not refer to practices followed at the time of this writing, as Kappa Alpha Theta's leadership has changed both the language and the practices associated with the fraternity's ritual in the past several decades. Interview conducted by the author with Lissa Bradford, former president, Kappa Alpha Theta Fraternity, May 21, 2003.

90. Alpha minutes, April 31 [*sic*], 1875; September 19, 1876; November 24, 1876.

91. Beta minutes, November 5, 1881; see also Alpha and Beta minutes, 1870–1895, and Tau minutes, 1888–1903. In 1877, the sisters collected each chapter's Theta songs and organized them into a songbook. They issued copies of the songbook to each existing chapter and then to new chapters upon their establishment, updating the songbook at varying intervals. According to Dodge, many chapters continued to sing from these songbooks through the 1920s. See *Songs of the Kappa Alpha Theta Fraternity, 1877*, and additional editions, 1884, 1890, 1902, and 1908, in file entitled "Songbooks," Kappa Alpha Theta Archives. See also Dodge, *Sixty Years,* 82.

92. "Initiation Song" and "Reunion Song," in *Songs of the Kappa Alpha Theta Fraternity, 1884*; "Kappa Alpha Theta," in *Songs of the Kappa Alpha Theta Fraternity, 1877.*

93. Clearly, we need to be skeptical when trying to ascertain meaning ascribed to songs, as people can and often do sing words and phrases that hold little meaning for them. But in the case of Kappa Alpha Theta, it is important not to dismiss the songs' import too quickly. Theta members and those of other women's organizations spent a great deal of time penning their songs and prac-

ticing them together. Especially in the first two to three decades of the fraternity's existence, no one pushed the sisters to write songs and sing them, and no one prescribed for them how to conduct their meetings. When they chose to perform overt acts that reaffirmed their loyalty, they did so of their own volition. And as discussed in the first chapter, it is easy to see the central place fraternity held in these first-generation sisters' lives when we look not only at their songs but at their letters, articles, and actions.

94. Grand Council Report, 1893–1894.

95. May E. Brown, "Vice President's Letter," *Kappa Alpha Theta* 8 (July 1894): 13–14; Jane V. Pollack, "Method of Pursuing Our Educational Work," *Kappa Alpha Theta* 15 (November 1900): 6; "Noblesse Oblige," *Kappa Alpha Theta* 23 (January 1909): 282; Dodge, *Sixty Years,* 244; Minutes of the 13th Biennial Convention, August, 1899. See also By-Laws of Kappa Alpha Theta, 1899, 1901.

96. Kappa Alpha Theta Bi-Monthly 1 (April 1910); Phi minutes, October 23, 1899; Kappa entry, *Kappa Alpha Theta* 16 (January 1902): 95. See also Tau minutes, October 18, 1909; October 3, 1910; and November 3, 1913; Mrs. Perley H. Markham, speech presented on unspecified date, prior to 1940 and assumed to be mid-1930s, on Chi chapter in the 1890s, Syracuse, NY. Contained in "Theta Histories" folder, Kappa Alpha Theta Archives. Also Pollack, "Method of Pursuing Our Educational Work," 6; "Report of Education Committee, 1901–03," Minutes of the 15th Biennial Convention, 1903.

97. Kappa Alpha Theta Bi-Monthly 1 (April 1910).

98. "Report of Education Committee, 1907–09," Minutes of the 18th Biennial Convention, 1909.

99. Kappa Alpha Theta Bi-Monthly 5 (September 1914); Kappa Alpha Theta Bi-Monthly 7 (September 1916).

100. "Report of Education Committee, 1901–03," Minutes of the 15th Biennial Convention, 1903; "Report of Education Committee, 1903–05," Minutes of the 16th Biennial Convention, 1905; Grand Council Report, May 1909.

101. Kappa Alpha Theta Bi-Monthly 5 (September 1914); Kappa Alpha Theta Bi-Monthly 7 (September 1916); Minutes of the 23rd Biennial Convention, 1920.

102. See especially Sarah Pomeroy Rugg, "'Rushing'—The Root of All Evil," *Banta's Greek Exchange* 8 (March 1920), 181–186; Horowitz, *Campus Life,* 132–134.

103. Horowitz, *Campus Life,* 119; "Report to the National Panhellenic Congress from the Extension Committee of the City Panhellenic Associate at Seattle, Wash.," NPC 1923.

104. Hartwich, "A Loose Rivet," 193–194.

105. The National Panhellenic Congress fraternities were so agreed that alumnae should serve as the spokespeople for the women's fraternities that as a

solution to faults of their organizations, they proposed having "a trained alumna always with every chapter as chaperon," and only when unable to secure funding for it, called for "a plan of resident alumnae interest and support of its college chapters that will supply the momentum, encouragement, wisdom that shall hold the undergraduates steadily on the plan of progress." See Green, "As Our Sisters See It," 42–43.

106. See Newcomer, *Century of Higher Education,* 29–30; Grand Council Report, 1903. As Cookingham shows, the number and proportion of college women getting married and doing so at an earlier age increased dramatically in the 1910s. Cookingham, "Combining Marriage," 178–180.

107. As Barbara Solomon noted, "In the economic prosperity of the decades preceding World War I, upper-middle-class parents found college a convenient parking place for adolescent daughters." See Solomon, *Company of Educated Women,* 71.

108. Minutes of 18th Biennial Convention, 1909; Kappa Alpha Theta Bi-Monthly 1 (December 1910); Kappa Alpha Theta Bi-Monthy 8 (1916), Eighth Annual Report; Minutes of 23rd Biennial Convention, 1920; Kappa Alpha Theta Bi-Monthly 7 (February 1916); Kappa Alpha Theta Bi-Monthly 11 (February–April 1920). *Note:* The total number of active members in 1920 appears small here for two reasons. First, as a by-product of World War I and the influenza epidemic that ravaged many campuses across the Midwest in 1917–1918, the number of women comprising the junior class fell below the other classes by nearly one hundred. Second, the fraternity had outlawed the initiation of women before a term's worth of credit had been earned, thereby removing from the count an estimated 250–300 pledges who would be initiated shortly after publication of the membership statistics.

109. Speech by Tau chapter representative, Minutes of 16th Biennial Convention, 1905.

110. Speech by President of Gamma District, Minutes of 16th Biennial Convention, 1905.

111. Minutes of 18th Biennial Convention, 1909, 13; Editorial, *Kappa Alpha Theta* 23 (May 1909): 502–503.

112. Minutes of 23rd Biennial Convention, 1920; Kappa Alpha Theta Bi-Monthly 6 (December 1915), Seventh Annual Report.

113. Kappa Alpha Theta Bi-Monthly 6 (December 1915), Seventh Annual Report. See also Minutes of Grand Council Meeting, July 1909; Kappa Alpha Theta Bi-Monthly 5 (December 1914); Minutes of 23rd Biennial Convention, 1920.

114. Deweese, "Ho Alumna!" 163–165.

NOTES TO CHAPTER 5

1. "Delta Alumnae," *Kappa Alpha Theta* 11 (February 1897): 86; see frequent references to "returning sisters" in existing Alpha and Beta minutes, 1870–1890; also references to active "resident Thetas" in chapter reports, contained in file, "Chapter Reports Ca. Late 1800s Early 1900s Sent to Beta Chapter"; letter from Clara Colburne to *Kappa Alpha Theta* 4 (May 1890): 68; Rho, "Our Alumnae," *Kappa Alpha Theta* 14 (March 1900): 130–131. See also Burton-Roth and Whiting-Westermann, *History of KKG,* chapter 16.

2. Clara Snyder, *Kappa Alpha Theta* 1 (April 1886): 143.

3. Gertrude Bell, *Kappa Alpha Theta* 4 (January 1890): 8.

4. A.M., "A True Theta," *Kappa Alpha Theta* 14 (May 1900): 189; emphasis in original.

5. Grace Louise Keiser Mayes, "Illinois Zeta Chapter of Pi Beta Phi Centennial Celebration Information Form," 1995, Stewart S. Howe Collection, Student Life and Culture Archives, University of Illinois, Urbana-Champaign. See also Ruth Olurn Dawson's response in the same collection.

6. Emma Powell, *Kappa Alpha Theta* 1 (October 1885): 65–66. See also Burton-Roth and Whiting-Westermann, *History of KKG,* 705.

7. Lena M. Hunt, "The Power of the Kite," *Kappa Alpha Theta* 17 (May 1903): 305–306.

8. While active alumnae participation in Kappa Alpha Theta's affairs hovered at 13 percent in 1910, that number soared by 1916 to a figure closer to 25 percent. Kappa Alpha Theta First Annual Report, 1909; Bi-Monthly Report of the Grand Council 1 (December 1910), Second Annual Report; Dodge, *Sixty Years,* 456–457; Kappa Alpha Theta Eighth Annual Report, 1916, Supplement to Kappa Alpha Theta Bi-Monthly 8 (February 1916). For a discussion of alumnae participation in Kappa Kappa Gamma affairs, see Burton-Roth and May Cynthia Whiting-Westermann, *History of KKG,* 720.

9. See letter from C. H. Plummer to Eva R. Hall, June 15, 1911, Nu file; letter from George Morey Miller to the Sorority of Kappa Alpha Theta, June 16, 1913, Alpha Tau file; and Grand Council Report on Phi Sorority, Randolph-Macon Woman's College, 3, Beta Beta file. See also Bi-Monthly Report of the Grand Council 5 (February 1914); Lucy Lilian Notestein, "Hurricane Alpha," in *Wooster of the Middle West* (Kent, OH: Kent State University Press, 1971).

10. Letter from L. Pearle Green to Grand Council, October 14, 1915, Omicron file; Emma Weitz, "What Kappa Alpha Theta Can Do," *Kappa Alpha Theta* 27 (May 1913): 339–341.

11. Louise Bresee Shappert-Cowger, "Illinois Zeta Chapter of Pi Beta Phi Centennial Celebration Information Form," 1995, Stewart S. Howe Collection, Student Life and Culture Archives, University of Illinois, Urbana-Champaign.

12. Burton-Roth and Whiting-Westermann, *History of KKG,* 713.

13. Mary Schofield Ash, "Theta Alumnae," *Kappa Alpha Theta* 13 (May 1899): 210–211.

14. "Kappa Alpha Theta Club of Southern California," *Kappa Alpha Theta* 13 (January 1899): 77–78; Florence Sarles Durstine, "Gamma Alumnae—New York," *Kappa Alpha Theta* 19 (November 1904): 59–60.

15. Minutes of 21st Biennial Convention of Kappa Alpha Theta, 1915; Estelle Riddle Dodge, "Something Big," *Kappa Alpha Theta* 30 (November 1915): 45–46.

16. Grace Louise Keiser Mayes, "Illinois Zeta Chapter of Pi Beta Phi Centennial Celebration Information Form."

17. For a discussion of the origins of the Kappa Alpha Theta catalogue, see Dodge, *Sixty Years,* 441–448. For a discussion of the Kappa Kappa Gamma catalog, see Burton-Roth and Whiting-Westermann, *History of KKG,* 712, 749. Additionally, see entries for individual fraternities, *Baird's Manual of American College Fraternities,* vol. 9, 1920, for references to dates of published catalogs.

18. Catalog of Kappa Alpha Theta, 1916; notations by Bernice Hall Glass. I am very grateful to Mary Edith Arnold, fraternity archivist, for calling this annotated catalog to my attention and to Noraleen Young, archivist of Kappa Alpha Theta, for locating it for me.

19. Hope Davis, "What Are Our Alumnae Chapters Doing?" *Kappa Alpha Theta* 26 (May 1912): 322–325.

20. Linda Fitz-Gerald Root, "Illinois Zeta Chapter of Pi Beta Phi Centennial Celebration Information Form," 1995, Stewart S. Howe Collection, Student Life and Culture Archives, University of Illinois, Urbana-Champaign.

21. "Lucretia Whitehead Payne's Account of the History of the Denver Alumnae Chapter, Written for the 25th Anniversary," undated, Alumnae Program files.

22. Alpha Lambda Alumna, "What Theta Meant to a Bride," *Kappa Alpha Theta* 36 (November 1921): 39; emphasis in the original.

23. Elizabeth M. Cole, "Two Thetas in Germany," *Kappa Alpha Theta* 18 (March 1904): 180–181.

24. Burton-Roth and Whiting-Westermann, *History of KKG,* 21.

25. "Study of Kappa Alpha Theta Chapters Active in 1916," March 1917, Kappa Alpha Theta Archives.

26. See chapter 2 for a discussion of societal fears of "race suicide" and the blame that collegiate women attracted from proponents of this belief.

27. Dodge, *Sixty Years,* 314, 319, 459–478.

28. Kappa Alpha Theta Bi-Monthly 4 (April 1913).

29. Kappa Alpha Theta 18th Annual Report, 1926; Burton-Roth and Whiting-Westermann, *History of KKG,* 710.

30. See Mary E. Eichrodt, "Alumnae Chapters and the Scholarship Fund," *Kappa Alpha Theta* 24 (March 1910): 232–233; Bi-Monthly Report of the

Grand Council 4 (April 1913); letter from L. Pearle Green to 18th National Panhellenic Congress, NPC 1923; Isabel Clingensmith, "What Alumnae Chapters Did in 1916," *Kappa Alpha Theta* 31 (January 1917): 159–163; Bi-Monthly Report of the Grand Council 6 (December 1915), Seventh Annual Report; Kappa Alpha Theta 8th Annual Report, Supplement to Kappa Alpha Theta Bi-Monthly 8 (February 1916); Dodge, *Sixty Years,* 396–397.

An article in the January 1904 issue of the *Kappa Alpha Theta* by the fund's founder, Josephine Lippincott, suggested that she envisioned the Scholarship Fund primarily as a means of providing "a definite, tangible, and common object to work for" to encourage alumnae members to "establish closer ties" between themselves and their fraternity. See Josephine Cook Lippincott, "The Question of a Kappa Alpha Theta Scholarship," 18 (January 1904): 102–104; "History of the Starting of Rho Alumnae Chapter," February 1909; Minutes of Rho Alumnae chapter, September 20, 1909, Alumnae Program files; Ada Edwards Laughlin, "The Scholarship and the Scholarship Fund," *Kappa Alpha Theta* 23 (January 1909): 266–268; Bi-Monthly Report of the Grand Council 4 (April 1913).

31. Pi Beta Phi entry, *Baird's Manual of American College Fraternities,* vol. 9, 1920, 477; section containing letters from fraternities to the convention, NPC 1923.

32. Section containing letters from fraternities to the convention, NPC 1923; Burton-Roth and Whiting-Westermann, *History of KKG,* 720–721.

33. NPC 1914, 4. The NPC representatives also worried about training their collegians to understand political and civic processes. As an officer of Gamma Phi Beta argued, and her fellow representatives agreed, "It seems to me the girls should be trained for civic life by teaching them to accept the rule of the majority and abide by it. Leading them to take advantage of their position as a minority is not training them for conditions as they are found in America today"; NPC 1917, 5.

34. Jessie Eastham, "Opportunities for Vocational Training in Boston," *Kappa Alpha Theta* 30 (March 1916): 198–201; E. Mabel Brownell, "Special Training Centers for Vocational Work for Women," *Kappa Alpha Theta* 27 (May 1913): 331–335; Kathryn Turney, "Life Insurance as a Business for Women," *Kappa Alpha Theta* 33 (March 1919): 211–212; Margaret Boynton Windsor, "Nature Study and Children," *Kappa Alpha Theta* 32 (January 1918): 120–121; Ethel E. Clarke, "Nursing and Its Opportunities for the College Graduate," *Kappa Alpha Theta* 35 (November 1920): 25–26. See additional articles in *Kappa Alpha Theta,* 1913–1920.

35. "Vocational Suggestions for the Trained Woman," *Kappa Alpha Theta* 28 (May 1914): 457–459; Eleanor G. Karsten, "Various Vocations for Women," *Kappa Alpha Theta* 28 (May 1914): 459–463.

36. "Want a Job?" *Kappa Alpha Theta* 24 (May 1920): 349; "Employment Committee of Service Bureau," *Kappa Alpha Theta* 32 (January 1918): 108;

"Are You Hunting a Job?" *Kappa Alpha Theta* 32 (January 1918): 122; "Vocation Notes," *Kappa Alpha Theta* 32 (January 1918): 131–134.

37. "Where, Oh Where Have the Seniors Gone," *Kappa Alpha Theta* 33 (January 1919): 118–126.

38. For one of the few examples of career-related writing in the *Kappa Alpha Theta* journal prior to 1900, see I.G.M., "Library Work for Women," *Kappa Alpha Theta* 13 (March 1899): 132–134. For a discussion of the areas in which the early Theta women pursued employment, see chapter 1. Also see "Alumnae Notes," *Kappa Alpha Theta* 1 (June 1885): 30; "Alumnae Notes," *Kappa Alpha Theta* 1 (January 1886): 103–104; "Alumnae Notes," *Kappa Alpha Theta* 11 (November 1896): 51–57. It is important to note that until 1895, the journal was edited by college students, so this may partially account for the lack of career-related writings during this time period.

39. Opportunities for women varied according to field. See chart entitled "Women in Selected Professional Occupations, 1910–82, as a Percentage of all Workers in Those Fields," in Solomon, *Company of Educated Women*, 127.

40. See Bi-Monthly Report of the Grand Council 2 (December 1911), Third Annual Report; Constitution of Kappa Alpha Theta, 1914; *Kappa Alpha Theta,* 32 (January 1918), 49–50.

41. Bi-Monthly Report of the Grand Council 5 (December 1914), Sixth Annual Report. The Vocational Committee members published this list in the January 1918 issue of the fraternity journal in an article entitled "Vocational Training." See "Vocational Training," *Kappa Alpha Theta* 32 (January 1918): 109–117.

42. Minutes of 21st Biennial Convention, 1915; Bi-Monthly Report of the Grand Council 9 (February 1918).

43. NPC 1914, 7.

44. *Kappa Alpha Theta* 32 (November 1917): 49–50; Solomon, *Company of Educated Women,* 86–87. See also letter from Hazel Allison Forde to Beta chapter, December 18, 1917, Beta Gamma file; Constitution of Kappa Alpha Theta, 1914; letter from Hazel Allison Forde to Elizabeth Andrews, November 9, 1916, Beta Gamma file.

45. NPC 1917, 64.

46. Bi-Monthly Report of the Grand Council 5 (December 1914), Sixth Annual Report.

47. Bi-Monthly Report of the Grand Council 5 (December 1914), Sixth Annual Report. See also NPC 1914, 10.

48. Membership Chart, *Kappa Alpha Theta* 19 (November 1904): 26; Catharine Planck Kircher, chart comparing data of members pre- and post-1900, March 1917; "Where, Oh Where Have the Seniors Gone," 118–126.

49. "Where, Oh Where Have the Seniors Gone," 118–126.

50. Cookingham, "Combining Marriage," 183; Mary Van Kleeck, "A Cen-

sus of College Women," *Journal of the Association of Collegiate Alumnae* 9 (May 1918): 561; Solomon, "After College, What?" 115–140.

51. Van Kleeck, "Census," 562; Mary Caroline Crawford, *The College Girl in America, and the Institutions Which Made Her What She Is* (Boston: L. C. Page, 1905), 291–308; Louese Monning, "Impressions of the Twelfth National Panhellenic Congress," *Banta's Greek Exchange* 2 (December 1913): 8–13.

52. "Kappa Alpha Theta Club of Southern California," *Kappa Alpha Theta* 13 (March 1899): 139.

53. Letter from Secretary of Seattle Alumnae Chapter of Kappa Alpha Theta to the School Board of the City of Seattle, April 15, 1919, Seattle Alumnae file.

54. See especially "Employment Committee of Service Bureau," *Kappa Alpha Theta* 32 (January 1918): 108. While a report of Kappa Alpha Theta's Vocational Committee stated that a survey of members' vocations was in the works, no findings of this study have been saved. The Kappa Alpha Theta Bi-Monthly for February 1926 indicates that such a study was in the works, but there is no evidence that it was ever completed. Given how meticulously the Theta sisters preserved all of their documents, it is fair to conclude that either not enough sisters responded to make the survey worthwhile or something else happened to prevent this study from being completed. See "Report of Vocational Committee of Kappa Alpha Theta," 1925; letter from Hope Davis Mecklin to Miss Tillett, October 5, 1925, Alumnae Program file; Kappa Alpha Theta Bi-Monthly 17 (February 1926).

55. Dodge, *Sixty Years*, 462; Burton-Roth and Whiting-Westermann, *History of KKG*, 34, 41, 71, 707; Lillian M. Perkins, *Sigma Kappa History*, Sigma Kappa Sorority, 1950; Mary L. Gilbert, "Relation of Alumnae to the World's Work," *Kappa Alpha Theta* 27 (January 1913): 133–137; articles in *Kappa Alpha Theta* 27 (January 1913). See also Dodge, "What Some Thetas Are Doing," 459–484.

56. Dodge, *Sixty Years*, 461–477; Burton-Roth and Whiting-Westermann, *History of KKG*, 707. See also Wilson's chapters, "Honored for Individual Achievement" and "Serving Communities across the Land, in *We Who Wear Kites*, 104–198. For a list of the sisters considered "notable" by the fraternity, see "Kappa Alpha Theta Fraternity Notable Members—Initiated Between 1870 and 1920," Internal Document, Kappa Alpha Theta.

57. See "Efficiency," *Kappa Alpha Theta* 29 (November 1914): 5–8; "Efficiency," *Kappa Alpha Theta* 29 (January 1915): 126–129; Bi-Monthly Report of the Grand Council 7 (December 1916). See also articles in *Kappa Alpha Theta* 29 (January 1915) and *Kappa Alpha Theta* 29 (March 1915).

58. See, for example, Lindsey Barbee, "As Our Sisters See It," *Banta's Greek Exchange* 8 (December 1919), 49–51; Arema O'Brien, "As Our Sisters See It," *Banta's Greek Exchange* 8 (March 1920), 180–181; Burton-Roth and Whiting-Westermann, *History of KKG*, 720–721, 768–780; Dodge, *Sixty Years*, chapter entitled, "Ideals in Action," 393–421; letter from Alice T. Deweese to Alumnae

Chapters, December 15, 1919, Kappa Alpha Theta Alumnae chapter folder. Discussion of all NPC organizations' charities is included in NPC 1923, 1–26. See also Dodge, *Sixty Years,* 393–421.

59. Burton-Roth and Whiting-Westermann, *History of KKG,* 721.

60. Ibid., 768–780; O'Brien, "As Our Sisters See It," 180.

61. NPC 1917, 76; letter from Margaret Archdeacon, War Fund Committee chairman, to Seattle Alumnae chapter, January 31, 1919; Kappa Alpha Theta Ninth Annual Report, 1917, Supplement to Bi-Monthly 9; Omaha Alumnae chapter minutes, April 2, 1919, Alumnae chapter folder, Kappa Alpha Theta Archives; Minutes of 23rd Biennial Convention of Kappa Alpha Theta, 1920; Wilson, *We Who Wear Kites,* 213; Burton-Roth and Whiting-Westermann, *History of KKG,* 773–780; Barbee, "As Our Sisters See It," 50. See also numerous entries in section entitled "Overseas Record," *Kappa Alpha Theta* 33 and 34 (1919–1920).

62. Barbee, "As Our Sisters See It," 50.

63. Obviously not all sisters chose to identify themselves as fraternity members throughout their lives and thus refused the offers of assistance and support from their organizations. Even those women, however, most likely benefited at some point during their lives from the social connections and accesses that their fraternity membership granted them.

64. See Joanne J. Meyerowitz, *Women Adrift: Independent Wage Earners in Chicago, 1880–1930* (Chicago and London: University of Chicago Press, 1988); also, "New York Alumnae," *Kappa Alpha Theta* 28 (May 1914): 378.

NOTES TO CHAPTER 6

1. Karen Blair, *The Clubwoman as Feminist: True Womanhood Redefined, 1868–1914* (New York and London: Holmes and Meier, 1980), quoted from pp. 4, 45, 5. For additional discussions of the enabling roles played by other women-centered organizations, see Scott, *Natural Allies,* 142–144; Theodora Penny Martin, *The Sound of Our Own Voices: Women's Study Clubs, 1860–1910* (Boston: Beacon Press, 1987); Robyn Muncy, *Creating a Female Dominion in American Reform, 1890–1935* (Oxford and New York: Oxford University Press, 1991); Faith Rogow, *Gone to Another Meeting: The National Council of Jewish Women, 1893–1993* (Tuscaloosa and London: University of Alabama Press, 1993); Marsha Wedell, *Elite Women and the Reform Impulse in Memphis, 1875–1915* (Knoxville: University of Tennessee Press, 1991).

2. Blair, *Clubwoman as Feminist,* 5; also, 4, 45, 58–61.

3. Robert Wiebe, *The Search for Order, 1877–1920* (New York: Hill and Wang, 1967), especially 11–75.

4. Ibid.; Hofstadter, *Age of Reform,* especially 131–173.

5. Carnes, *Secret Ritual,* 2.

6. National Panhellenic Conference Website, www.npcwomen.org.

7. Enclosure 5, "Statements from Fraternities and Fraternity Leaders Concerning Discrimination and Discriminatory Clauses," in Burt Hiller, "Report to the Committee on Student Life and Interests Concerning Discriminatory Clauses in Fraternity Constitutions," January 1949, especially 3 and 5. Reports on Discrimination Clauses, 19/2/6–7, Box 1, University of Wisconsin Archives.

As discussed in chapter 3, not all the women's—or men's—fraternities had formal exclusionary clauses. Some, like Kappa Alpha Theta, never adopted written policies. Most organizations adhered to unwritten rules, however, believing that the inclusion of individuals of whom some members might not approve would tax the unity they were trying to engender. See James, "College Social Fraternity," 303–324.

8. Hiller, "Report to the Committee on Student Life and Interests," 5, also 3.

9. James, "College Social Fraternity," especially 304, 306–312, 316–321; Hiller, "Report to the Committee on Student Life and Interests," 3, 5; "The Selectivity Principle," in *Michigan Daily,* October 13, 1953; Jon Sobeloff, "NY 'Time Limit' Bias Plan Gets Mild OK Here," in *Michigan Daily* (May 12, 1953); Alice Bogdonoff and Harry Lunn, "The Bias Claus [*sic*] Problem—Here and at Columbia," in *Michigan Daily,* May 19, 1953; Harry Lunn, "The Bias Clause Situation," in *Michigan Daily,* March 27, 1953; "Brotherhood, Fraternities," in *Detroit Free Press,* February 15, 1953. All documents contained in Reports on Discrimination Clauses, University of Wisconsin Archives, 19/2/6–7, Boxes 1 and 2.

10. E. David Cronon and John W. Jenkins, *The University of Wisconsin: A History, 1945–1971; Renewal to Revolution,* vol. 4 (Madison: University of Wisconsin Press, 1999), 395; *Daily Cardinal,* December 9, 1965, February 8, 1996, also, "The Selectivity Principle," in *Michigan Daily,* October 13, 1953; Jon Sobeloff, "NY 'Time Limit' Bias Plan Gets Mild OK Here," in *Michigan Daily,* May 12, 1953; Bogdonoff and Lunn, "The Bias Claus [*sic*]"; Harry Lunn, "The Bias Clause Situation," in *Michigan Daily,* March 27, 1953; Harold S. Wechsler, *The Qualified Student: A History of Selective College Admissions in America* (New York and London: John Wiley and Sons, 1977), 9. See James, "College Social Fraternity," 303–324, for an excellent discussion of the struggles waged by many chapters of men's fraternities to force their national organizations to drop their exclusionary clauses.

11. In these stances, the women's fraternities in many ways mirrored their male counterparts, which, as historian Anthony James showed, accused chapters that challenged the written and unwritten restrictive policies of their national groups of disloyalty and lack of fraternal spirit. According to James, as with the women's fraternities, alumnae by and large controlled the government of the men's Greek societies. It was they who posed the greatest blocks to efforts to make their groups more inclusive. See James, "College Social Fraternity," 303–324.

Bibliography

Allport, Gordon W. *The Nature of Prejudice.* Garden City, NY: Doubleday Anchor Books, 1958.

Alpern, Sara, Joyce Antler, Elisabeth Isreals Perry, and Ingrid Winther Scobie, eds. *The Challenge of Feminist Biography: Writing the Lives of Modern American Women.* Urbana: University of Illinois Press, 1992.

Angell, Robert Cooley. *The Campus: A Study of Contemporary Undergraduate Life in the American University.* New York and London: D. Appleton and Company, 1928.

Antler, Joyce. *Lucy Sprague Mitchell: The Making of a Modern Woman.* New Haven: Yale University Press, 1987.

Antler, Joyce, and Sari Knopp Biklen, eds. *Changing Education: Women as Radicals and Conservators.* Albany: State University of New York Press, 1990.

Armstrong, Florence A. *History of Alpha Chi Omega Fraternity, 1885-1921.* Copyright Alpha Chi Omega Fraternity, 1922.

———. "Progressive Women." *History of Education Quarterly* 24 (Spring 1984): 129-136.

Bailey, Beth L. *From Front Porch to Back Seat: Courtship in Twentieth Century America.* Baltimore and London: Johns Hopkins University Press, 1988.

Baird, William Raimond. *American College Fraternities: A Descriptive Analysis of the Society System in the Colleges of the United States.* Philadelphia: J. B. Lippincott, 1879.

Barry, Kathleen. "Biography and the Search for Women's Subjectivity." *Women's Studies International Forum* 12 (1990): 561-577.

Baum, Charlotte, Paula Hyman, and Sonya Michel. *The Jewish Woman in America.* New York: Dial Press, 1976.

Bernard, Jessie. *Academic Women.* University Park: Pennsylvania State University Press, 1964.

Birken, Lawrence. *Consuming Desire: Sexual Science and the Emergence of a Culture of Abundance, 1871-1914.* Ithaca, NY, and London: Cornell University Press, 1988.

Bishop, Morris. *A History of Cornell.* Ithaca, NY: Cornell University Press, 1962.

Blair, Karen J. *The Clubwoman as Feminist: True Womanhood Redefined, 1868–1914.* New York and London: Holmes and Meier, 1980.

———. *The History of American Women's Voluntary Associations, 1810–1960: A Guide to Sources.* Boston: G. K. Hall, 1989.

Burstyn, Joan N. *Victorian Education and the Ideal of Womanhood.* New Brunswick, NJ: Rutgers University Press, 1984.

Burton-Roth, Florence, and May Cynthia Whiting-Westermann. *The History of Kappa Kappa Gamma Fraternity, 1870–1930.* Copyright Kappa Kappa Gamma Fraternity, 1932.

Butcher, Patricia Smith. *Education for Equality: Women's Rights Periodicals and Women's Higher Education, 1849–1920.* New York, Westport, CT, London: Greenwood Press, 1989.

Canfield, James Hulme. *The College Student and His Problems.* New York and London: Macmillan, 1914.

Carnes, Mark C. *Secret Ritual and Manhood in Victorian America.* New Haven and London: Yale University Press, 1989.

Cate, Rodney M., and Sally A. Lloyd. *Courtship.* Newbury Park, CA, London, and New Delhi: Sage Publications, 1992.

Conable, Charlotte Williams. *Women at Cornell: The Myth of Equal Education.* Ithaca, NY: Cornell University Press, 1977.

Conkin, Paul K. *Gone with the Ivy: A Biography of Vanderbilt University.* Knoxville: University of Tennessee Press, 1985.

Conway, Jill K. *The Female Experience in Eighteenth- and Nineteenth-Century America: A Guide to the History of American Women.* New York: Garland, 1992.

Cookingham, Mary E. "Combining Marriage, Motherhood, and Jobs before World War II: Women College Graduates, Classes of 1905–1935." *Journal of Family History* 9 (Summer 1984): 178–194.

Cott, Nancy F. *The Bonds of Womanhood: "Women's Sphere" in New England, 1780–1835.* New Haven, CT: Yale University Press, 1977.

———. *The Grounding of Modern Feminism.* New Haven and London: Yale University Press, 1987.

Crawford, Mary Caroline. *The College Girl of America and the Institutions Which Make Her What She Is.* Boston: L. C. Page, 1905.

Cronon, E. David, and John W. Jenkins. *The University of Wisconsin: A History, 1945–1971,* vol. 4: *Renewal to Revolution.* Madison: University of Wisconsin Press, 1999.

Crow, Mary B. "The Sorority Movement at Monmouth College." *Western Illinois Regional Studies* 4:1 (1981): 37–49.

Curti, Merle, and Vernon Carstensen. *The University of Wisconsin: A History, 1848–1925.* 2 vols. Madison: University of Wisconsin Press, 1949.

Deegan, Mary Jo, and Michael Hill, eds. *Women and Symbolic Interaction.* Boston and London: Allen and Unwin, 1987.

Degler, Carl. *At Odds: Women and the Family in America from the Revolution to the Present.* Oxford and New York: Oxford University Press, 1980.

Dill, Bonnie Thornton. "Race, Class, and Gender: Prospects for an All-Inclusive Sisterhood." In *Women and Symbolic Interaction,* ed. Mary Jo Deegan and Michael Hill. Boston and London: Allen and Unwin, 1987.

Diner, Steven. *A City and Its Universities: Public Policy in Chicago, 1892–1919.* Chapel Hill: University of North Carolina Press, 1980.

Dodge, Estelle Riddle. *Sixty Years in Kappa Alpha Theta.* Menasha, WI: George Banta, 1930.

Edwards, G. Thomas. *The Triumph of Tradition: The Emergence of Whitman College, 1859–1924.* Walla Walla, WA: Whitman College, 1992.

Eisenmann, Linda. "'Freedom to Be Womanly': The Separate Culture of the Woman's College." In *The Search for Equality: Women at Brown University, 1891–1991,* ed. Polly Welts Kaufman. Hanover and London: Brown University Press, 1991.

Emerick, Charles Franklin. "College Women and Race Suicide." *Political Science Quarterly* 24:2 (1909): 269–283.

Eschbach, Elizabeth Seymour. *The Higher Education of Women in England and America, 1865–1920.* New York and London: Garland, 1993.

Faragher, John Mack, and Florence Howe, eds. *Women and Higher Education in American History: Essays from the Mount Holyoke College Sesquicentennial Symposium.* New York: W. W. Norton, 1988.

Farnham, Christie Anne. *The Education of the Southern Belle: Higher Education and Student Socialization in the Antebellum South.* New York and London: New York University Press, 1994.

Fass, Paula S. *The Damned and the Beautiful: American Youth in the 1920s.* New York: Oxford University Press, 1977.

———. *Outside In: Minorities and the Transformation of American Education.* New York and Oxford: Oxford University Press, 1989.

Fitzpatrick, Ellen. *Endless Crusade: Women Social Scientists and Progressive Reform.* New York and Oxford: Oxford University Press, 1990.

Frankfort, Roberta. *Collegiate Women: Domesticity and Career in Turn-of-the-Century America.* New York: New York University Press, 1977.

Freedman, Estelle. "Separatism as Strategy: Female Institution Building and American Feminism, 1870–1930." *Feminist Studies* 3 (Fall 1979): 512–529.

Galloway, Bonnie. "Evolving Sisterhood: An Organizational Analysis of Three Sororities, 1870–1930." Ph.D. diss., Western Michigan University, 1994.

Giddings, Paula. *In Search of Sisterhood: Delta Sigma Theta and the Challenge of the Black Sorority Movement.* New York: Murrow Press, 1988.

Gordon, Lynn D. "Coeducation on Two Campuses: Berkeley and Chicago, 1890–1912." In *Association for the Study of Higher Education Reader on the History of Higher Education* (1989). Reprinted from *Woman's Being, Woman's Place: Female Identity and Vocation in American History*, ed. Mary Kelley. Boston: G. K. Hall, 1979.

———. "Female Gothic: Writing the History of Women's Colleges." *American Quarterly* 37:2 (1985): 299–304.

———. "Annie Nathan Meyer and Barnard College: Mission and Identity in Women's Higher Education, 1889–1950." *History of Education Quarterly* 26 (Winter 1986): 503–522.

———. "The Gibson Girl Goes to College: Popular Culture and Women's Higher Education in the Progressive Era, 1890–1920." *American Quarterly* 39 (Summer 1987): 211–230.

———. *Gender and Higher Education in the Progressive Era*. New Haven and London: Yale University Press, 1990.

———. "Introduction to the Special Issue on the History of Women and Education." *History of Education Quarterly* 33 (Winter 1993): 493.

Gordon, Sarah H. "Smith College Students: The First Ten Classes, 1879–1888." *History of Education Quarterly* 3 (Summer 1975): 147–166.

Graebner, William. "Outlawing Teenage Populism: The Campaign against Secret Societies in the American High School, 1900–1960." *Journal of American History* 14:2 (1987): 411–435.

Graham, Patricia. "Expansion and Exclusion: A History of Women in American Higher Education." *Signs: Journal of Women in Culture and Society* 3 (Summer 1978): 759–773.

Greenberg, Michael, and Seymour Zenchelsky. "Private Bias and Public Responsibility: Anti-Semitism at Rutgers in the 1920s and 1930s." *History of Education Quarterly* 33 (Fall 1993): 460–319.

Gurock, Jeffrey S. *The Men and Women of Yeshiva: Higher Education, Orthodoxy, and American Judaism*. New York: Columbia University Press, 1988.

Handler, Lisa. "In the Fraternal Sisterhood: Sororities as Gender Strategy." *Gender and Society* 9 (April 1995): 236–255.

Hansen, Karen V. "Challenging Separate Spheres in Antebellum New Hampshire: The Case of Brigham Nims." *Historical New Hampshire* 43 (1988): 120–135.

Hartley, William G. "The Delta Phi Debating and Literary Society: Utah's First Fraternity, 1869–1904." *Utah Historical Quarterly* 60:4 (1992): 353–374.

Hartman, Mary S., and Lois W. Banner, eds. *Clio's Consciousness Raised: New Perspectives in the History of Women*. New York: Harper and Row, 1974.

Hartman, Moshe, and Harriet Hartman. *Gender Equality and American Jews*. Albany: State University of New York Press, 1996.

Hartson, Louis D. "Marriage Record of Alumnae for the First Century of a Co-educational College." *Journal of Heredity* 31 (1940): 403–406.

Helly, Dorothy O., and Susan M. Reverby, eds. *Gendered Domains: Rethinking Public and Private in Women's History.* Ithaca, NY: Cornell University Press, 1992.

Hewitt, Nancy A. "Beyond the Search for Sisterhood: American Women's History in the 1980s." *Social History* 10 (October 1985): 299–321.

Hiller, Burt. "Report to the Committee on Student Life and Interests Concerning Discriminatory Clauses in Fraternity Constitutions." Reports on Discrimination Clauses, 19/2/6–7, Box 1, University of Wisconsin Archives, January 1949.

Hofstadter, Richard. *The Age of Reform: From Bryan to F.D.R.* New York: Vintage Books, a Division of Random House, 1955.

Holland, Dorothy C., and Margaret Eisenhart. *Educated in Romance: Women, Achievement, and College Culture.* Chicago: University of Chicago Press, 1990.

Horowitz, Helen Lefkowitz. *Campus Life: Undergraduate Cultures from the End of the Eighteenth Century to the Present.* New York: Alfred A. Knopf, 1987.

———. *Alma Mater: Design and Experience in the Women's Colleges from Their Nineteenth-Century Beginnings to the 1930s.* 2nd ed. Amherst: University of Massachusetts Press, 1993.

James, Anthony. "The College Social Fraternity Antidiscrimination Debate, 1945–1949." *The Historian: A Journal of History* 62 (Winter 2000): 303–324.

Kay, Ernest, ed. *The World's Who's Who of Women in Education.* Cambridge, UK, and New York: International Biographical Center, 1978.

Kerber, Linda K. "Separate Spheres, Female Worlds, Women's Place: The Rhetoric of Women's History." *Journal of American History* 75 (June 1988): 9–39.

———. *Toward an Intellectual History of Women.* Chapel Hill and London: University of North Carolina Press, 1997.

Kerber, Linda K., Alice Kessler-Harris, and Kathryn Kish Sklar, eds. *U.S. History as Women's History: New Feminist Essays.* Chapel Hill: University of North Carolina Press, 1995.

Kern, Louis J. *An Ordered Love: Sex Roles and Sexuality in Victorian Utopias—the Shakers, the Mormons, and the Oneida Community.* Chapel Hill: University of North Carolina Press, 1981.

Kind, John L. "The Fraternity Situation at Wisconsin." *Western Intercollegiate Magazine* (January 1911): 3–12.

Komarovsky, Mirra. *Women in College: Shaping New Feminine Identities.* New York: Basic Books, 1985.

Kraditor, Aileen S., ed. *Up from the Pedestal: Selected Essays in the History of American Feminism.* Chicago: Quadrangle Books, 1968.

Lagemann, Elen Condliffe. *A Generation of Women: Education in the Lives of Progressive Reformers.* Cambridge, MA: Harvard University Press, 1979.

Lasser, Carol, ed. *Educating Men and Women Together: Coeducation in a Changing World.* Urbana: University of Illinois Press, 1987.

Lavender, Abraham D. "Jewish College Women: Future Leaders of the Jewish Community?" *Journal of Ethnic Studies* 5 (1977): 81–90.

Levine, Lawrence W. *The Opening of the American Mind: Canons, Culture, and History.* Boston: Beacon Press, 1996.

Levine, Susan. *Degrees of Equality: The American Association of University Women and the Challenge of Twentieth-Century Feminism.* Philadelphia: Temple University Press, 1995.

Lieberson, Stanley, and Mary C. Waters. *From Many Strands: Ethnic and Racial Groups in Contemporary America.* New York: Russell Sage Foundation, 1988.

Lystra, Karen. *Searching the Heart: Women, Men, and Romantic Love in Nineteenth-Century America.* New York and Oxford: Oxford University Press, 1989.

Manhart, George B. *DePauw through the Years.* Vols. 1 and 2. Greencastle, IN: DePauw University, 1962.

Marchalonis, Shirley. *College Girls: A Century in Fiction.* New Brunswick, NJ: Rutgers University Press, 1995.

Marcus, Jacob R. *The American Jewish Woman: A Documentary History.* New York: KTAV Publishing House, 1981.

Martin, Ida Shaw. *The Sorority Handbook.* Copyright Ida Shaw Martin, Boston, 1923.

Martin, Theodora Penny. *The Sound of Our Own Voices: Women's Study Clubs, 1860–1910.* Boston: Beacon Press, 1987.

Maynard, Mary, and Jane Purvis, eds. *Researching Women's Lives from a Feminist Perspective.* London: Taylor and Francis, 1994.

McCandless, Amy Thompson. "Preserving the Pedestal: Restrictions on Social Life at Southern Colleges for Women, 1920–1940." *History of Education Annual* 7 (1987): 45–67.

McGirr, Lisa. *Suburban Warriors: The Origins of the New American Right.* Princeton, NJ: Princeton University Press, 2001.

Meyerowitz, Joanne J. *Women Adrift: Independent Wage Earners in Chicago, 1880–1930.* Chicago and London: University of Chicago Press, 1988.

Miner, James Burt. "A Vocational Census of College Students." *Educational Review* (September 1915): 144–165.

Moffatt, Michael. *Coming of Age in New Jersey: College Life and American Culture.* New Brunswick, NJ: Rutgers University Press, 1989.

Morse, Genevieve Forbes. *A History of Kappa Delta Sorority: 1897–1972.* Vol. 1. Springfield, MO: Kappa Delta Sorority, 1973.

Muncy, Robyn. *Creating a Female Dominion in American Reform, 1890–1935.* Oxford and New York: Oxford University Press, 1991.

Murolo, Priscilla. *The Common Ground of Womanhood: Class, Gender, and Working Girls' Clubs, 1884–1928.* Urbana and Chicago: University of Illinois Press, 1997.

Neiswanger, Lilian Hughes. "The First Coeds." Unpublished manuscript, 1935. Swarthmore College Archives.

Newcomer, Mabel. *A Century of Higher Education for American Women.* New York: Harper and Brothers, 1959.

Notestein, Lucy Lilian. *Wooster of the Middle West,* vol. 1, *1866–1910.* Kent, OH: Kent State University Press, 1971.

Palmieri, Patricia A. "Here Was Fellowship: A Social Portrait of Academic Women at Wellesley College, 1895–1920." *History of Education Quarterly* (Summer 1983): 195–214.

———. "From Republican Motherhood to Race Suicide: Arguments on the Higher Education of Women in the United States, 1820–1920." In *Educating Men and Women Together: Coeducation in a Changing World,* ed. Carol Lasser. Champaign: University of Illinois Press, 1987.

———. *In Adamless Eden: The Community of Women Faculty at Wellesley.* New Haven, CT: Yale University Press, 1995.

Parlin, H. T. "A Brief History of the Regulation of Fraternities at the University of Texas." *University of Texas Bulletin* 1737 (July 1917).

Peckham, Howard H. *The Making of the University of Michigan, 1817–1967.* Ann Arbor: University of Michigan Press, 1967.

Perkins, Lillian. *Sigma Kappa History.* Sigma Kappa Sorority, 1950.

Pollard, Lucille Addison. *Women on College and University Faculties: A Historical Survey and a Study of Their Present Academic Status.* New York: Arno Press, 1977.

Pomeroy, Sarah Gertrude. "The Service of the Women's Fraternities." *The Independent* 19 (September 1914): 413–414.

Priddy, Bessie Leach. *A Detailed Record of Delta Delta Delta, 1888–1907.* Galesburg, Il.: Mail Printing Company, 1907.

Reece, Salma. "Kappa Alpha Theta: The First Thirty Years of Delta History at Illinois, 1895–1925." Unpublished manuscript, 1966. Student Life and Culture Archives, University of Illinois at Urbana-Champaign.

Risman, Barbara J. "College Women and Sororities: The Social Construction and Reaffirmation of Gender." In *Women and Symbolic Interaction,* ed. Mary Jo Deegan and Michael Hill. Boston and London: Allen and Unwin, 1987.

Roedel, Alice Morgan. *History of Alpha Phi Fraternity: From the Founding in 1872 through the Year 1951.* Stanford, CA: Stanford University Press, 1951.

Rogow, Faith. *Gone to Another Meeting: The National Council of Jewish Women, 1893–1993*. Tuscaloosa and London: University of Alabama Press, 1993.

Rosenberg, Rosalind. *Beyond Separate Spheres: Intellectual Roots of Modern Feminism*. New Haven, CT: Yale University Press, 1982.

———. "The Limits of Access: The History of Coeducation in America." In *Women and Higher Education in American History: Essays from the Mount Holyoke College Sesquicentennial Symposia*, ed. John Mack Faragher and Florence Howe. New York and London: W. W. Norton, 1988.

Rosovsky, Nitza. *The Jewish Experience at Harvard and Radcliffe*. An Introduction to an Exhibition Presented by the Harvard Semitic Museum on the Occasion of Harvard's 350th Anniversary, September 1986. Cambridge, MA: Harvard Semitic Museum; distributed by Harvard University Press, 1986.

Rota, Taziana. "Between 'True Women' and 'New Women': Mount Holyoke Students, 1837–1908." Ph.D. diss., Department of History, University of Massachusetts, 1983.

Rothman, Ellen K. *Hands and Hearts: A History of Courtship in America*. New York: Basic Books, 1984.

Rudolph, Frederick. *The American College and University: A History*. New York: Alfred A. Knopf, 1968.

———. *Curriculum: A History of the American Undergraduate Course of Study since 1636*. Prepared for the Carnegie Council on Policy Studies in Higher Education. San Francisco, Washington, London: Jossey-Bass, 1977.

Rugoff, Milton. *Prudery and Passion*. New York: G. P. Putnam's Sons, 1971.

Russell, Kathy, Midge Wilson, and Ronald Hall. *The Color Complex: The Politics of Skin Color among African Americans*. New York: Anchor Books/Doubleday, 1992.

Ryan, Mary P. *Cradle of the Middle Class: The Family in Oneida County, New York, 1790–1865*. Cambridge, UK: Cambridge University Press, 1981.

———. *Womanhood in America: From Colonial Times to the Present*. 3rd ed. New York: New Viewpoints, a Division of Franklin Watts, 1983.

Sanua, Marianne. "'We Hate New York': Negative Images of the Promised City as a Source for Jewish Fraternity and Sorority Members, 1920–1940." In *An Inventory of Promises: Essays on American Jewish History in Honor of Moses Richin*, ed. Jeffrey S. Gurock and Marc Lee Raphael. Brooklyn: Carlson, 1995.

———. *Here's to Our Fraternity: One Hundred Years of Zeta Beta Tau, 1898–1998*. Published by Zeta Beta Tau Foundation. Hanover and London: Brandeis University Press and University Press of New England, 1998.

———. "Jewish College Fraternities and Sororities in American Jewish Life, 1895–1968: An Overview." Unpublished paper with accompanying notes (the latter labeled "Sanua, Notes" in text).

Sapinsky, Ruth. "The Jewish Girl at College." In Jacob R. Marcus, ed. *The American Jewish Woman: A Documentary History.* New York: KTAV Publishing House, 1981.

Scott, Anne Firor. *Natural Allies: Women's Associations in American History.* Urbana and Chicago: University of Illinois Press, 1991.

Seidman, Steven. *Romantic Longings: Love in America, 1830–1980.* New York and London: Routledge, 1991.

Sgro, Beverly H. "The Evolution of Fraternities for Women." Unpublished paper, Virginia Polytechnic Institute and State University, 1985. Student Life and Culture Archives.

Sheldon, Henry D. *Student Life and Customs.* New York: D. Appleton, 1901.

Shosteck, Robert. "Five Thousand Women College Graduates Report: Findings of a National Survey of the Social and Economic Status of Women Graduates of Liberal Arts Colleges of 1946–1949." Washington, DC: B'Nai B'rith Vocational Service Bureau, 1953.

Sicherman, Barbara. "College and Careers: Historical Perspectives on the Lives and Work Patterns of Women College Graduates." In *Women and Higher Education in American History: Essays from the Mount Holyoke College Sesquicentennial Symposia,* ed. John Mack Faragher and Florence Howe. New York and London: W. W. Norton, 1988.

Siller, Mabel Harriet. *The History of Alpha Chi Omega.* Copyright Alpha Chi Omega, 1911.

Simmons, Adele. "Education and Ideology in Nineteenth-Century America: The Response of Educational Institutions to the Changing Role of Women." In *Liberating Women's History: Theoretical and Critical Essays,* ed. Berenice A. Carroll. Urbana: University of Illinois Press, 1976.

Sklar, Kathryn Kish. *Catharine Beecher: A Study in American Domesticity.* New Haven, CT: Yale University Press, 1973.

Smith-Rosenberg, Carroll. *Disorderly Conduct: Visions of Gender in Victorian America.* New York and Oxford: Oxford University Press, 1986

Solberg, Winton. "Early Years of the Jewish Presence at the University of Illinois." *Religion and American Culture: A Journal of Interpretation* (Summer 1992): 215–245.

Solomon, Barbara Miller. *In the Company of Educated Women: A History of Women and Higher Education in America.* New Haven and London: Yale University Press, 1985.

Solomon, Barbara Miller, and Patricia M. Nolan. "Education, Work, Family, and Public Commitment in the Lives of Radcliffe Alumnae, 1883–1928." In *Changing Education: Women as Radicals and Conservators,* ed. Joyce Antler and Sari Knopp Biklen. Albany: State University of New York Press, 1990.

Sprague, Robert J. "Education and Race Suicide." *Journal of Heredity* 6 (1915): 158–161.

Steel, Ronald. *Walter Lippmann and the American Century.* Boston: Little, Brown, 1980.

Synnott, Marcia Graham. *The Half-Opened Door: Discrimination and Admissions at Harvard, Yale, and Princeton, 1900–1970.* Westport, CT, and London: Greenwood Press, 1979.

Thomson, Ruth Sanders. *History of Alpha Phi Fraternity: From the Founding in 1872 through the Year 1902,* vol. 1. Norwood, MA: The Alpha Phi International Fraternity, Plimpton Press, 1943.

Toll, George S. "Colleges, Fraternities, and Assimilation." *Journal of Reform Judaism* (1985): 93–103.

Treichler, Paula A. "Alma Mater's Sorority: Women and the University of Illinois, 1890–1925." In *For Alma Mater: Theory and Practice in Feminist Scholarship,* ed. Paula A. Treichler, Cheris Kramarae, and Beth Stafford. Urbana and Chicago: University of Illinois Press, 1985.

Turk, Diana. "College Students." In *Jewish Women in America: An Historical Encyclopedia,* vol. 1, ed. Paula E. Hyman and Deborah Dash Moore. New York and London: Routledge, 1998.

Van Kleek, Mary. "A Census of College Women." *Journal of the Association of Collegiate Alumnae* 9 (1918): 557–591.

Walters, Ronald G. *Primers for Prudery: Sexual Advice to Victorian America.* Englewood Cliffs, NJ: Prentice Hall, 1974.

Wechsler, Harold S. *The Qualified Student: A History of Selective College Admissions in America.* New York and London: John Wiley and Sons, 1977.

Wedell, Marsha. *Elite Women and the Reform Impulse in Memphis, 1875–1915.* Knoxville, TN: University of Tennessee Press, 1991.

Wein, Roberta. "Women's Colleges and Domesticity, 1875–1918." *History of Education Quarterly* 14 (Spring 1974): 31–47.

Welter, Barbara. "The Cult of True Womanhood, 1820–1860." *American Quarterly* 18 (Summer 1966): 151–174.

———. *Dimity Convictions: The American Woman in the Nineteenth Century.* Athens: Ohio University Press, 1976.

Wiebe, Robert. *The Search for Order, 1877–1920.* New York: Hill and Wang, 1967.

Wilson, Carol Green. *We Who Wear Kites: The Story of Kappa Alpha Theta, 1870–1956.* Menasha, WI: George Banta, 1956.

Wolters, Raymond. *The New Negro on Campus: Black College Rebellions of the 1920s.* Princeton, NJ, and London: Princeton University Press, 1975.

Woody, Thomas. *A History of Women's Education in the United States.* 2 vols. New York: Octagon Books, 1929, 1980.

Zschoche, Sue. "Dr. Clarke Revisited: Science, True Womanhood, and Female Collegiate Education." *History of Education Quarterly* 29 (Winter 1989): 545–569.

Index

Page numbers in italic refer to illustrations.

About the Author

Diana Turk is Assistant Professor in the Department of Teaching and Learning at New York University. She received her Ph.D. in American Studies from the University of Maryland at College Park.